𝕯edicated
to the
memories of

Doug Branigan
and
David Forsee

They might not
have known each other.
They died within hours
of each other, just before
this book was finished.
They both watched over
the making of this book.

First Edition
Printed by Gauvin in Gatineau, Quebec, Canada

Library and Archives Canada Cataloguing in Publication

Collier, David, 1963-, author, illustrator
Morton : a cross-country rail journey / David Collier.

ISBN 978-1-77262-012-2 (softcover)

1. Collier, David, 1963- --Travel--Comic books, strips, etc. 2. Artists--Canada--Biography--Comic books, strips, etc. 3. Railroad travel--Canada--Comic books, strips, etc. 4. Autobiographical comics-- I. Title.

PN6733.C65Z46 2017 741.5'971 C2017-900276-7

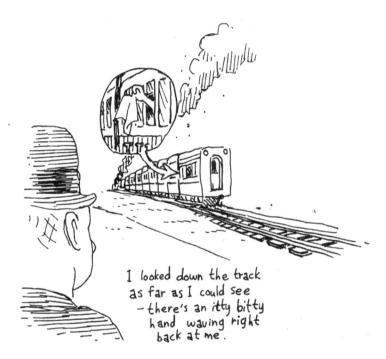

I looked down the track
as far as I could see
- there's an itty bitty
hand waving right
back at me.

Conundrum Press
Wolfville, NS
www.conundrumpress.com

Distribution in Canada: Litdistco
Distribution in UK: Turnaround
Distribution in US: Consortium

Conundrum Press acknowledges the financial support of the Canada Council for the Arts, the government of Canada through the Canada Book Fund, and the Province of Nova Scotia's Creative Industries Fund toward its publishing activities.
David Collier also acknowledges the support of the Canada Council for the Arts.

Canada Council for the Arts Conseil des Arts du Canada NOVA SCOTIA Canada

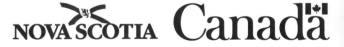

Note to the *Reader*:

Square panels are in the *present*

And then, it's finally *done!*
Well, here goes th' MS for another book.
Hope the publisher likes it.
HUSH
BEWARE
J.H.
CHIMO
D&Q
Konica 1015
RUBBER CEMENT

It turned out they were serious, **British**, **birders**.

Maybe *today* we shall spot that sage *thrasher*!
!

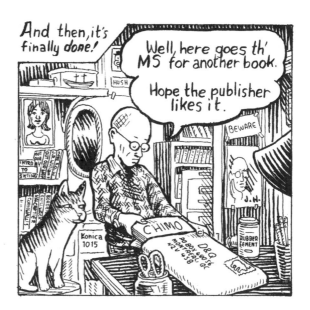

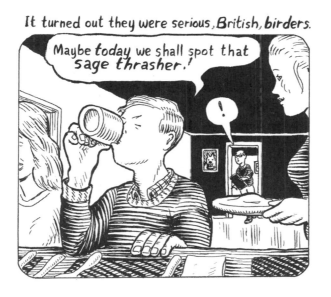

Rounded panels, in the *past*

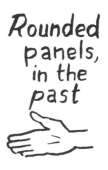

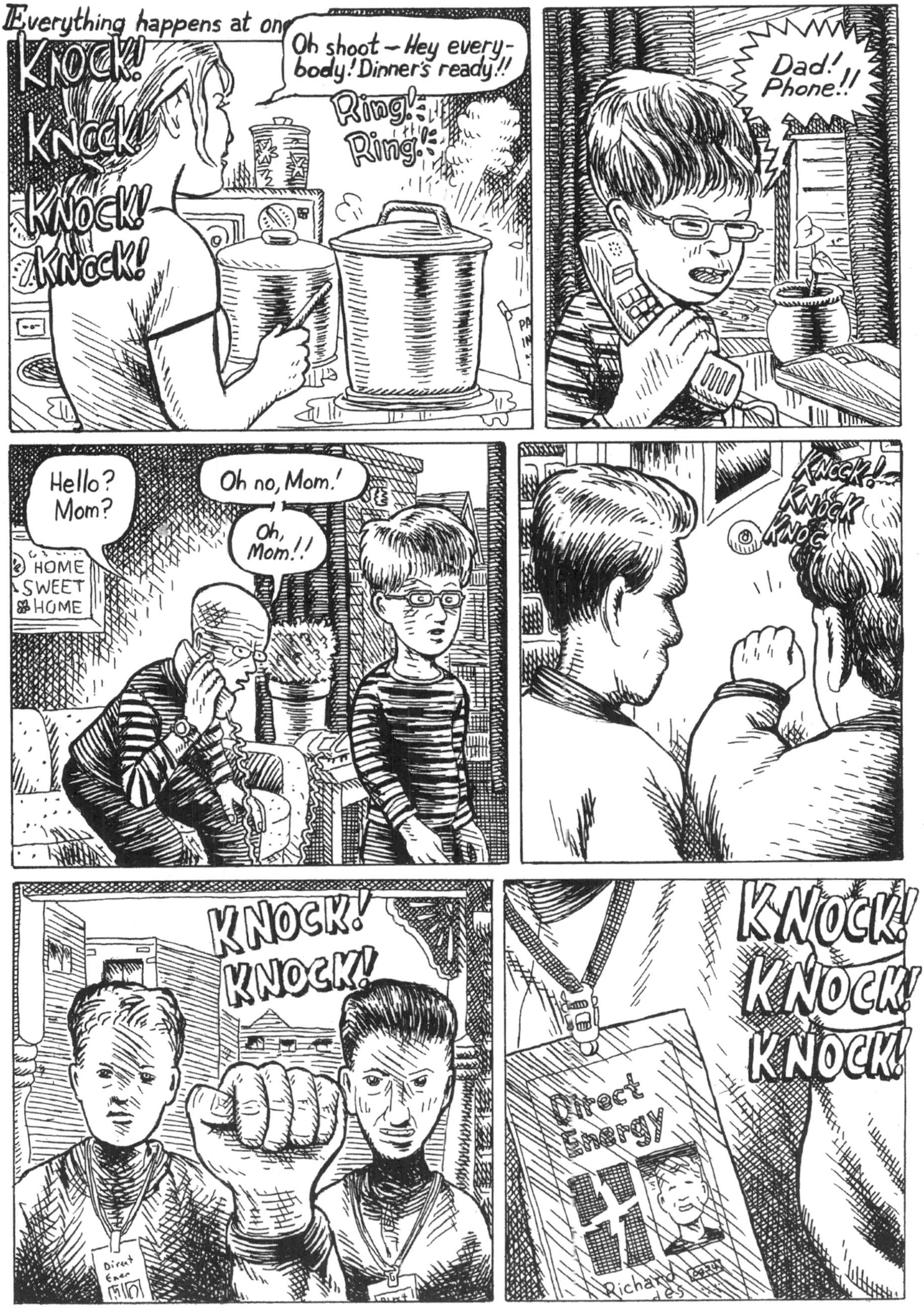
Everything happens at on
KNOCK!
KNOCK!
KNOCK!
KNOCK!
Oh shoot — Hey everybody! Dinner's ready!!
Ring!
Ring!
Dad! Phone!!
Hello? Mom?
HOME SWEET HOME
Oh no, Mom!
Oh, Mom!!
KNOCK! KNOCK KNOC
KNOCK! KNOCK!
Direct Ener
KNOCK! KNOCK! KNOCK!
Direct Energy
Richard es

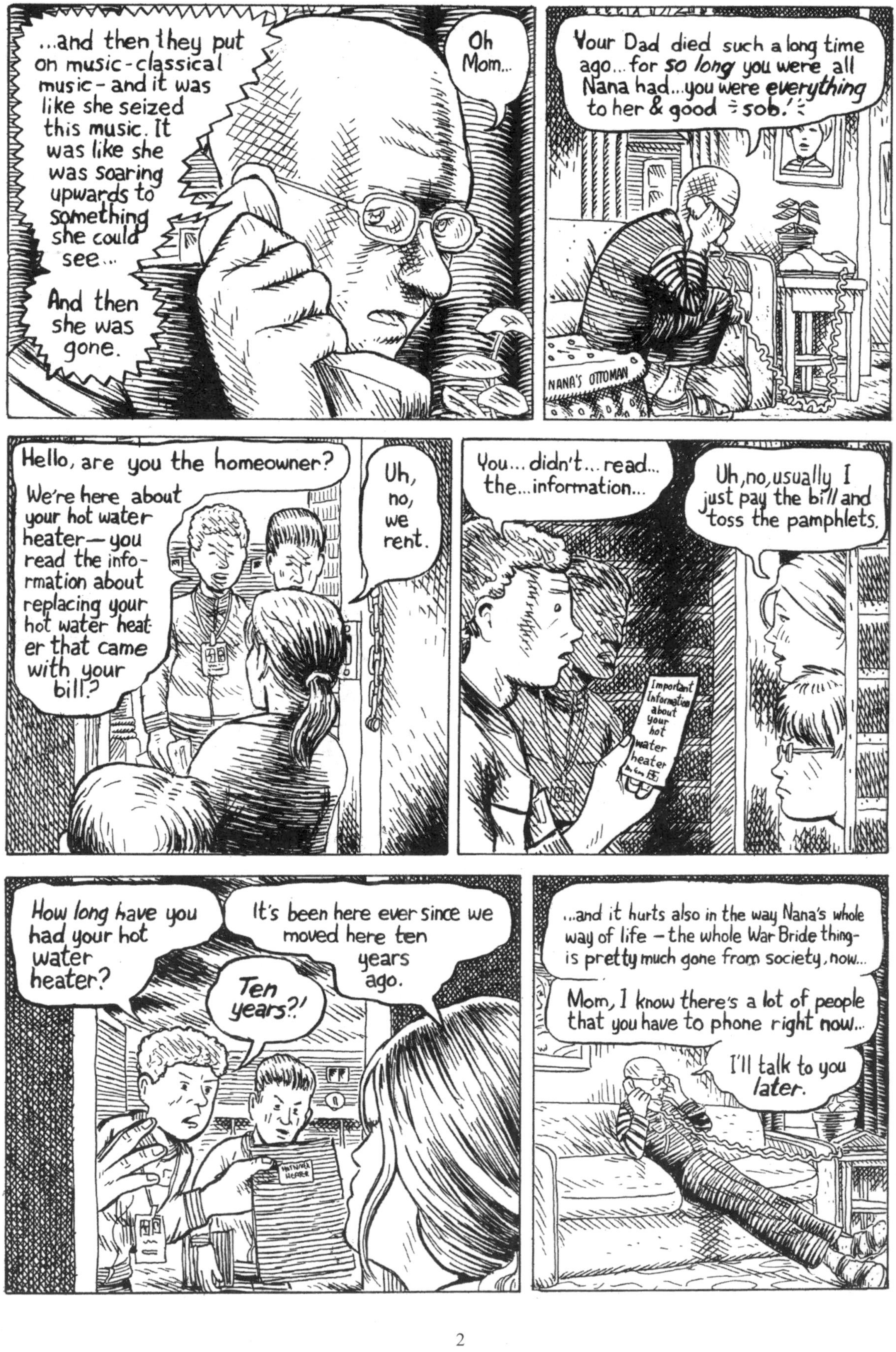

...and then they put on music-classical music - and it was like she seized this music. It was like she was soaring upwards to something she could see...
And then she was gone.
Oh Mom...
Your Dad died such a long time ago... for *so long* you were all Nana had... you were *everything* to her & good ⁼sob!⁼
NANA'S OTTOMAN
Hello, are you the homeowner?
We're here about your hot water heater— you read the information about replacing your hot water heater that came with your bill?
Uh, no, we rent.
You... didn't... read... the... information...
Uh, no, usually I just pay the bill and toss the pamphlets.
Important Information about your hot water heater
How *long* have you had your hot water heater?
It's been here ever since we moved here ten years ago.
Ten years?!
...and it hurts also in the way Nana's whole way of life — the whole War Bride thing- is pretty much gone from society, now...
Mom, I know there's a lot of people that you have to phone right now...
I'll talk to you *later*.

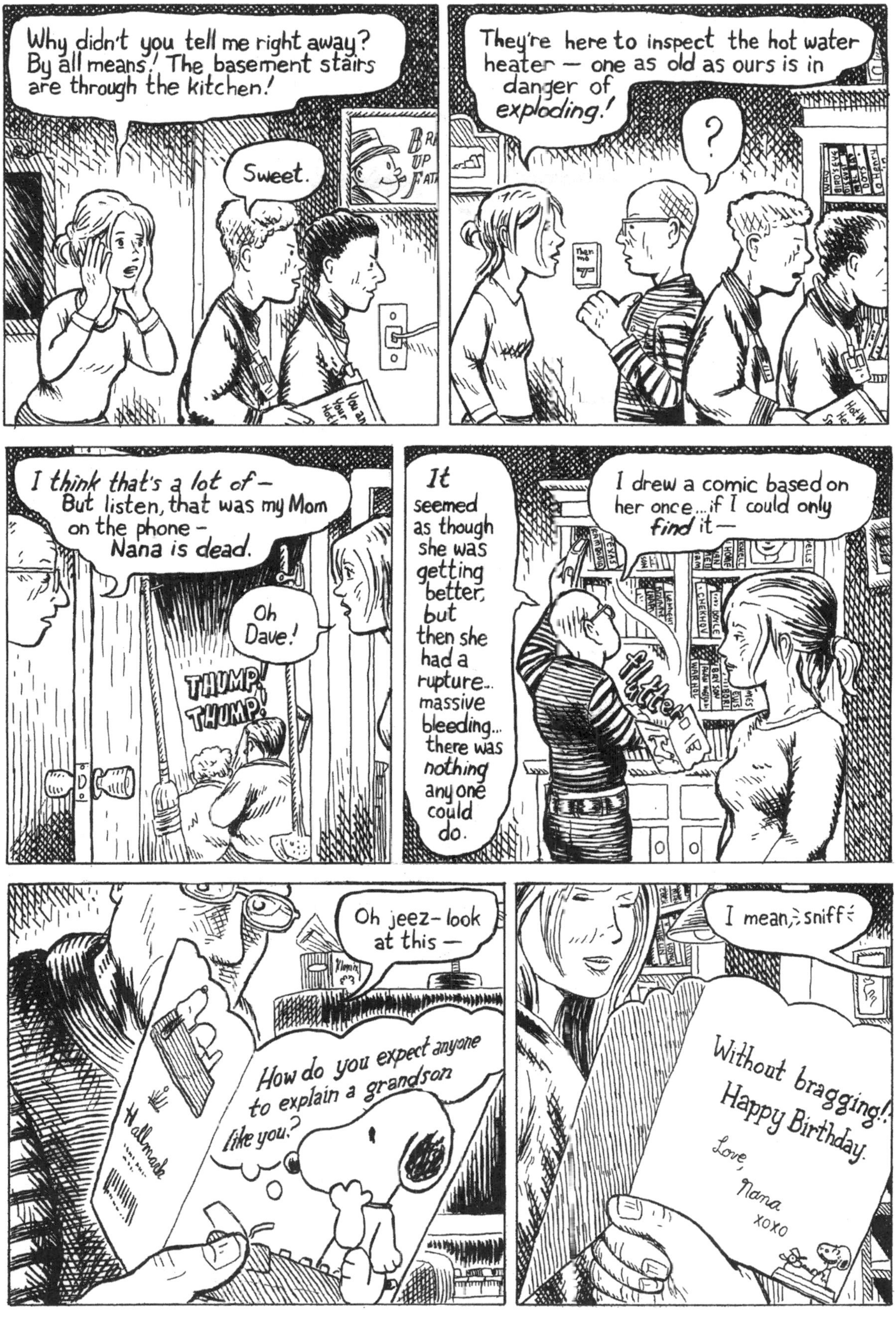
Why didn't you tell me right away? By all means! The basement stairs are through the kitchen!
Sweet.
They're here to inspect the hot water heater — one as old as ours is in danger of *exploding*!
?
I *think* that's a lot of — But listen, that was my Mom on the phone — Nana is *dead*.
Oh Dave!
THUMP! THUMP!
It seemed as though she was getting better, but then she had a rupture.. massive bleeding... there was *nothing* anyone could do.
I drew a comic based on her once... if I could only *find* it —
flutter
Oh jeez — look at this —
How do you expect anyone to explain a grandson like you?
Hallmark
I mean, sniff
Without bragging! Happy Birthday.
Love, Nana xoxo

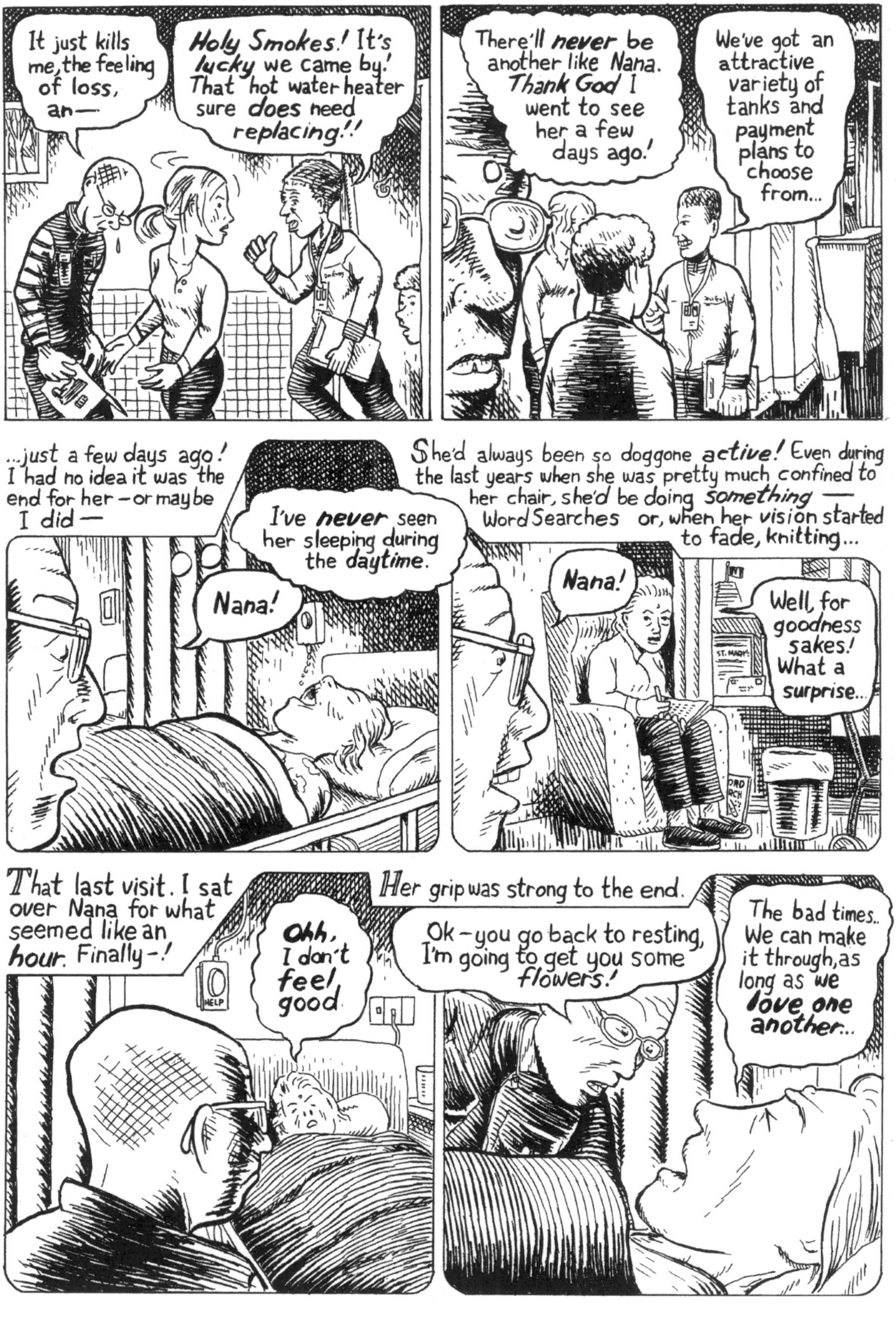

It just kills me, the feeling of loss, an—
Holy Smokes! It's lucky we came by! That hot water heater sure does need replacing!!
There'll never be another like Nana. Thank God I went to see her a few days ago!
We've got an attractive variety of tanks and payment plans to choose from...
...just a few days ago! I had no idea it was the end for her—or maybe I did—
I've never seen her sleeping during the daytime.
Nana!
She'd always been so doggone active! Even during the last years when she was pretty much confined to her chair, she'd be doing something — Word Searches or, when her vision started to fade, knitting...
Nana!
Well, for goodness sakes! What a surprise...
That last visit. I sat over Nana for what seemed like an hour. Finally—!
Ohh, I don't feel good.
HELP
Her grip was strong to the end.
Ok—you go back to resting, I'm going to get you some flowers!
The bad times.. We can make it through, as long as we love one another...

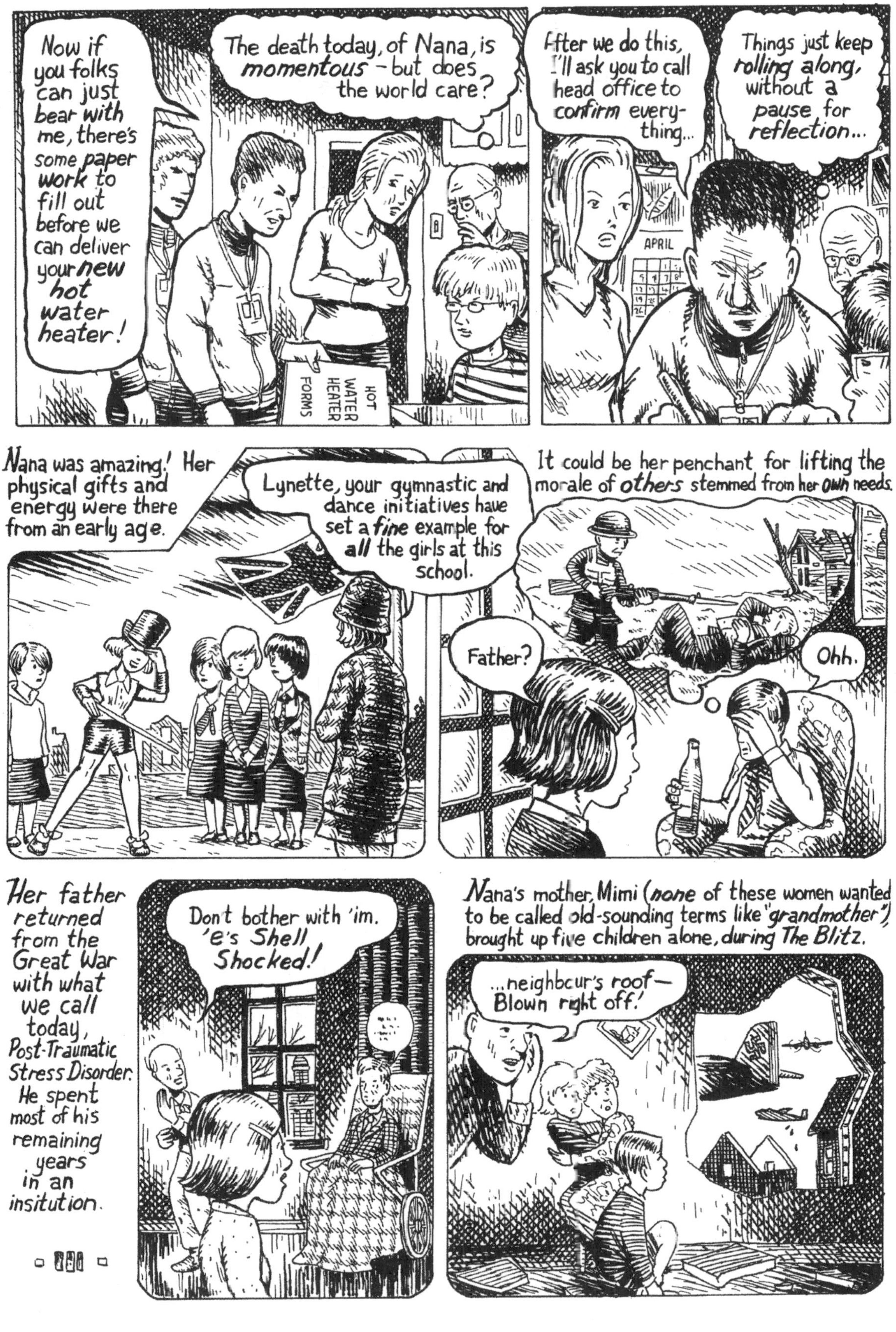
Now if you folks can just bear with me, there's some paper work to fill out before we can deliver your new hot water heater!
The death today, of Nana, is momentous - but does the world care?
HOT WATER HEATER FORMS
After we do this, I'll ask you to call head office to confirm everything...
Things just keep rolling along, without a pause for reflection...
APRIL
Nana was amazing! Her physical gifts and energy were there from an early age.
Lynette, your gymnastic and dance initiatives have set a fine example for all the girls at this school.
It could be her penchant for lifting the morale of others stemmed from her own needs.
Father?
Ohh.
Her father returned from the Great War with what we call today, Post-Traumatic Stress Disorder. He spent most of his remaining years in an insitution.
Don't bother with 'im. 'e's Shell Shocked!
Nana's mother, Mimi (none of these women wanted to be called old-sounding terms like "grandmother"), brought up five children alone, during The Blitz.
...neighbour's roof— Blown right off!

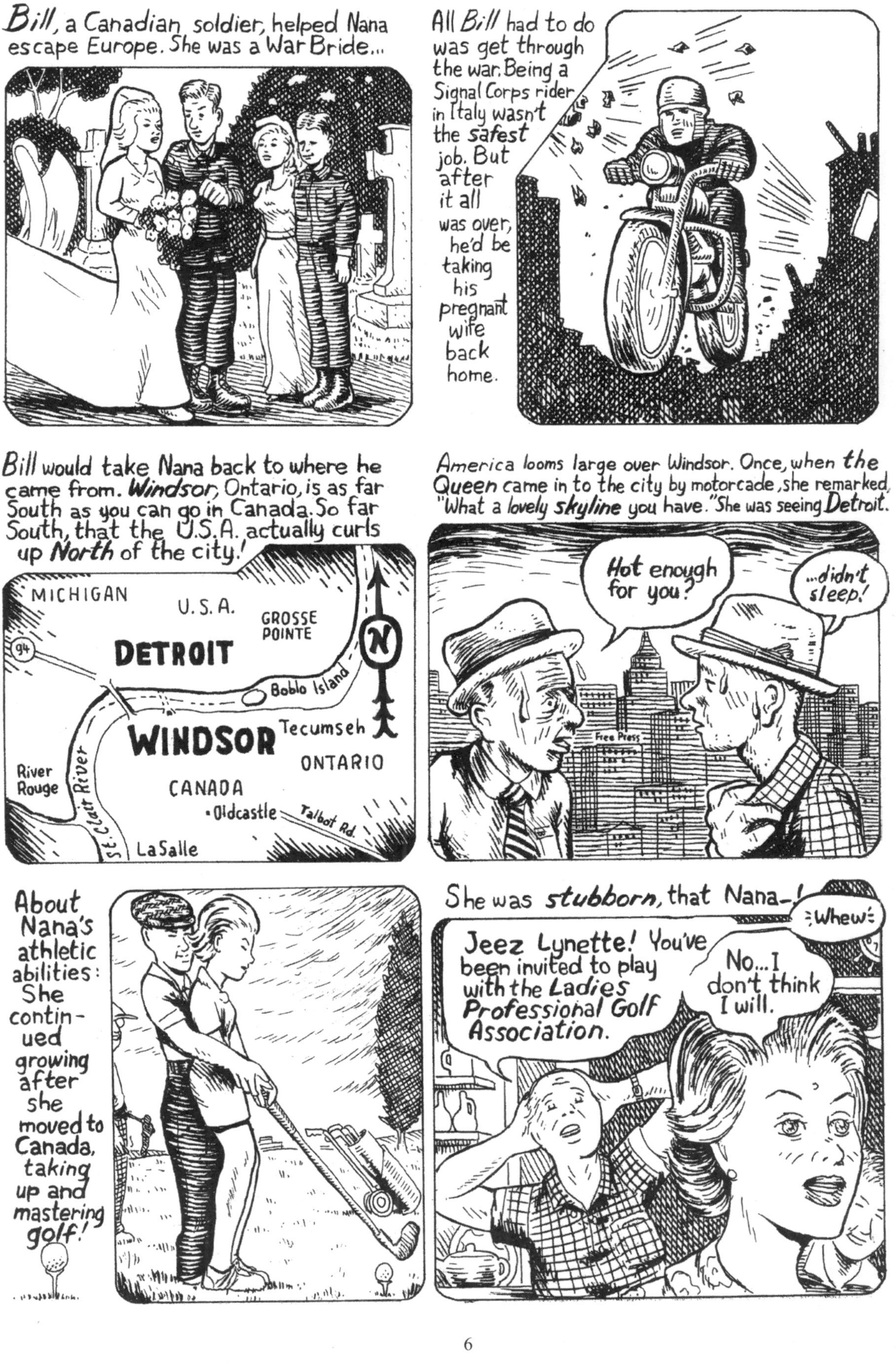
Bill, a Canadian soldier, helped Nana escape Europe. She was a War Bride...
All Bill had to do was get through the war. Being a Signal Corps rider in Italy wasn't the safest job. But after it all was over, he'd be taking his pregnant wife back home.
Bill would take Nana back to where he came from. Windsor, Ontario, is as far South as you can go in Canada. So far South, that the U.S.A. actually curls up North of the city!
MICHIGAN
U.S.A.
GROSSE POINTE
N
94
DETROIT
Boblo Island
Tecumseh
WINDSOR
ONTARIO
River Rouge
St. Clair River
CANADA
Oldcastle
Talbot Rd.
LaSalle
America looms large over Windsor. Once, when the Queen came in to the city by motorcade, she remarked, "What a lovely skyline you have." She was seeing Detroit.
Hot enough for you?
...didn't sleep!
Free Press
About Nana's athletic abilities: She contin-ued growing after she moved to Canada, taking up and mastering golf!
She was stubborn, that Nana-!
Whew
Jeez Lynette! You've been invited to play with the Ladies Professional Golf Association.
No... I don't think I will.

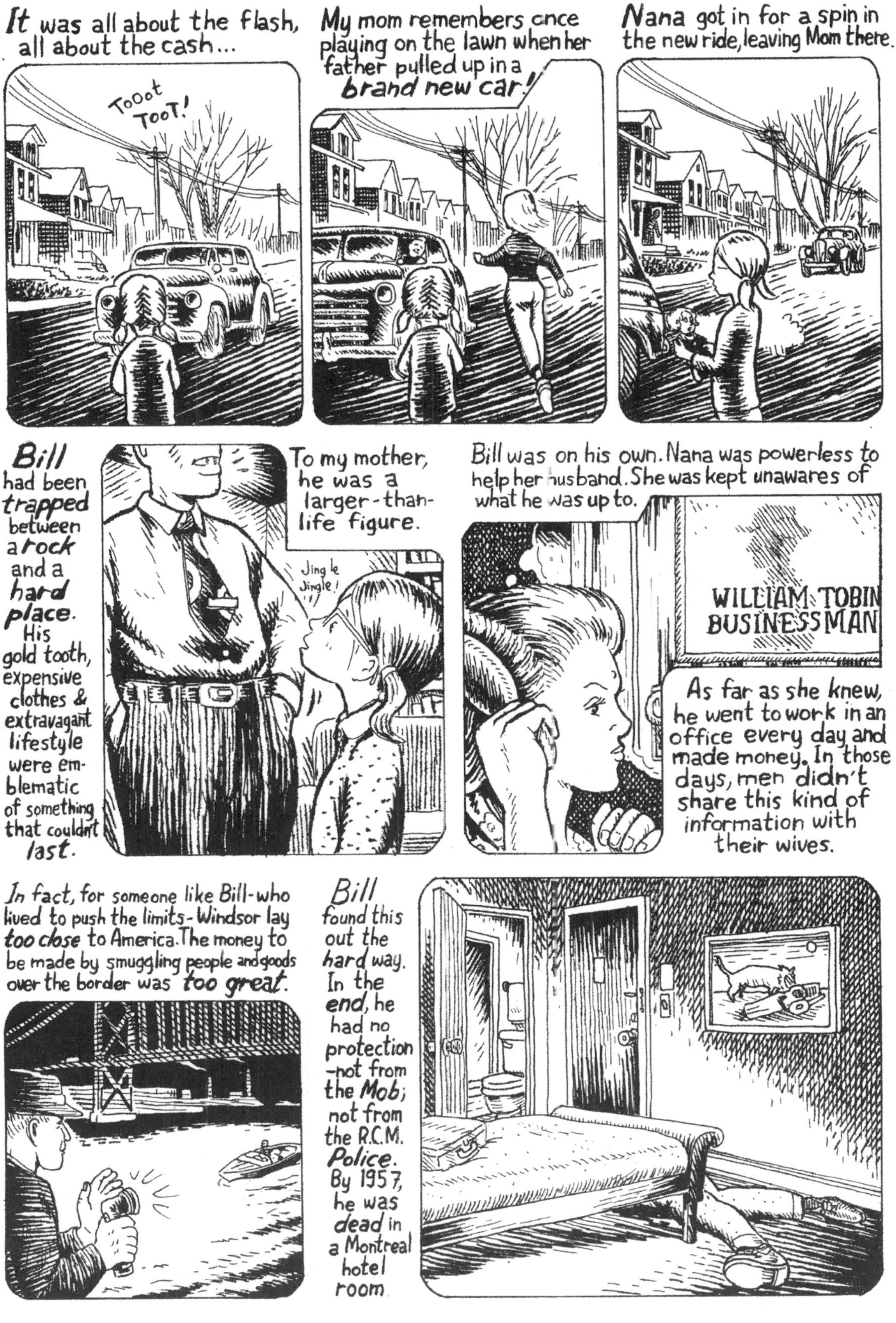
It was all about the flash, all about the cash...
TOoot TooT!
My mom remembers once playing on the lawn when her father pulled up in a brand new car!
Nana got in for a spin in the new ride, leaving Mom there.
Bill had been trapped between a rock and a hard place. His gold tooth, expensive clothes & extravagant lifestyle were emblematic of something that couldn't last.
To my mother, he was a larger-than-life figure.
Jingle Jingle!
Bill was on his own. Nana was powerless to help her husband. She was kept unawares of what he was up to.
WILLIAM TOBIN
BUSINESSMAN
As far as she knew, he went to work in an office every day and made money. In those days, men didn't share this kind of information with their wives.
In fact, for someone like Bill-who lived to push the limits-Windsor lay too close to America. The money to be made by smuggling people and goods over the border was too great.
Bill found this out the hard way. In the end, he had no protection -not from the Mob; not from the R.C.M. Police. By 1957, he was dead in a Montreal hotel room.

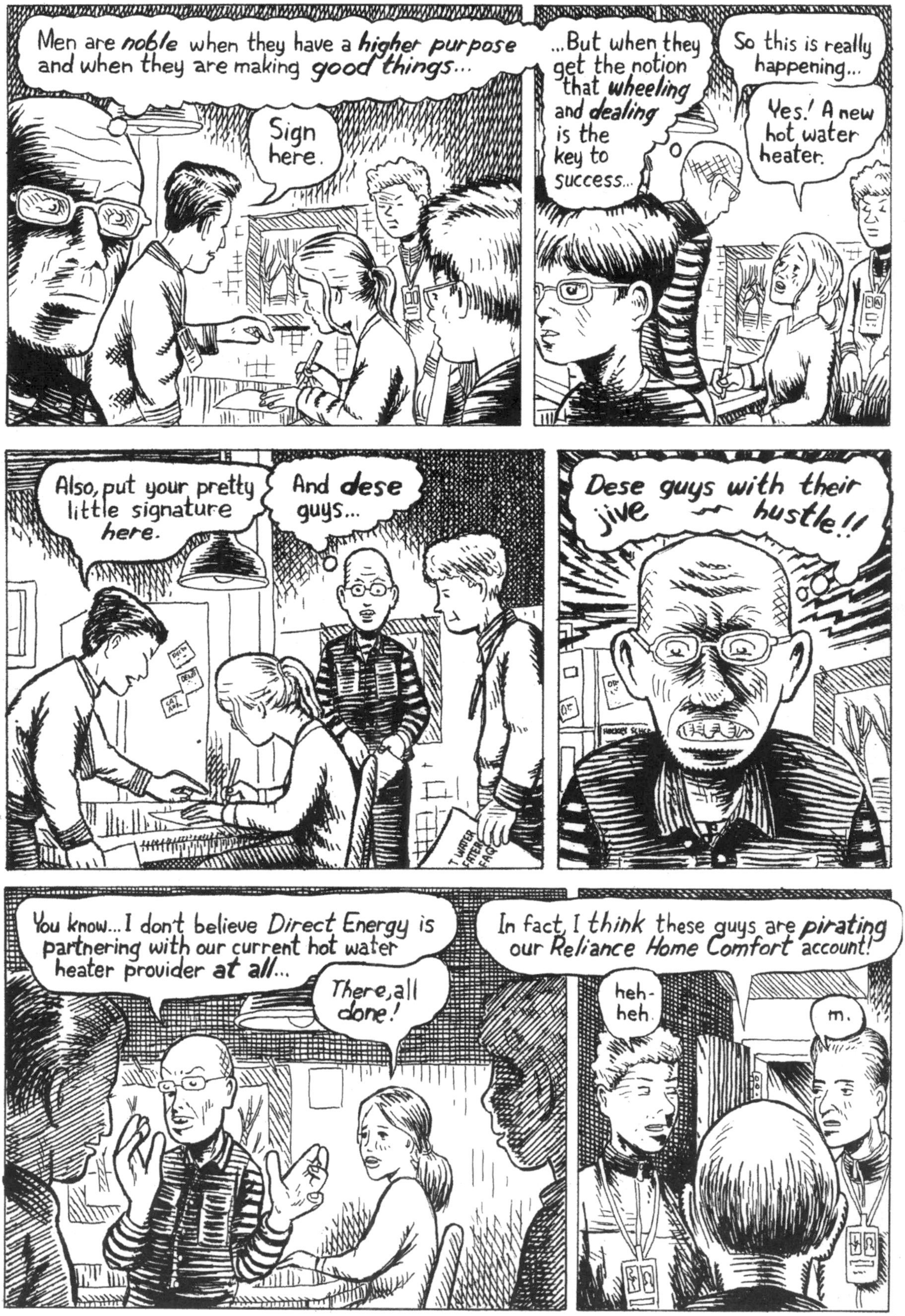
Men are noble when they have a higher purpose and when they are making good things...
Sign here.
...But when they get the notion that wheeling and dealing is the key to success...
So this is really happening...
Yes! A new hot water heater.
Also, put your pretty little signature here.
And dese guys...
T WATER EATER FAQ
Dese guys with their jive ~ hustle!!
You know...I don't believe Direct Energy is partnering with our current hot water heater provider at all...
There, all done!
In fact, I think these guys are pirating our Reliance Home Comfort account!
heh-heh.
m.

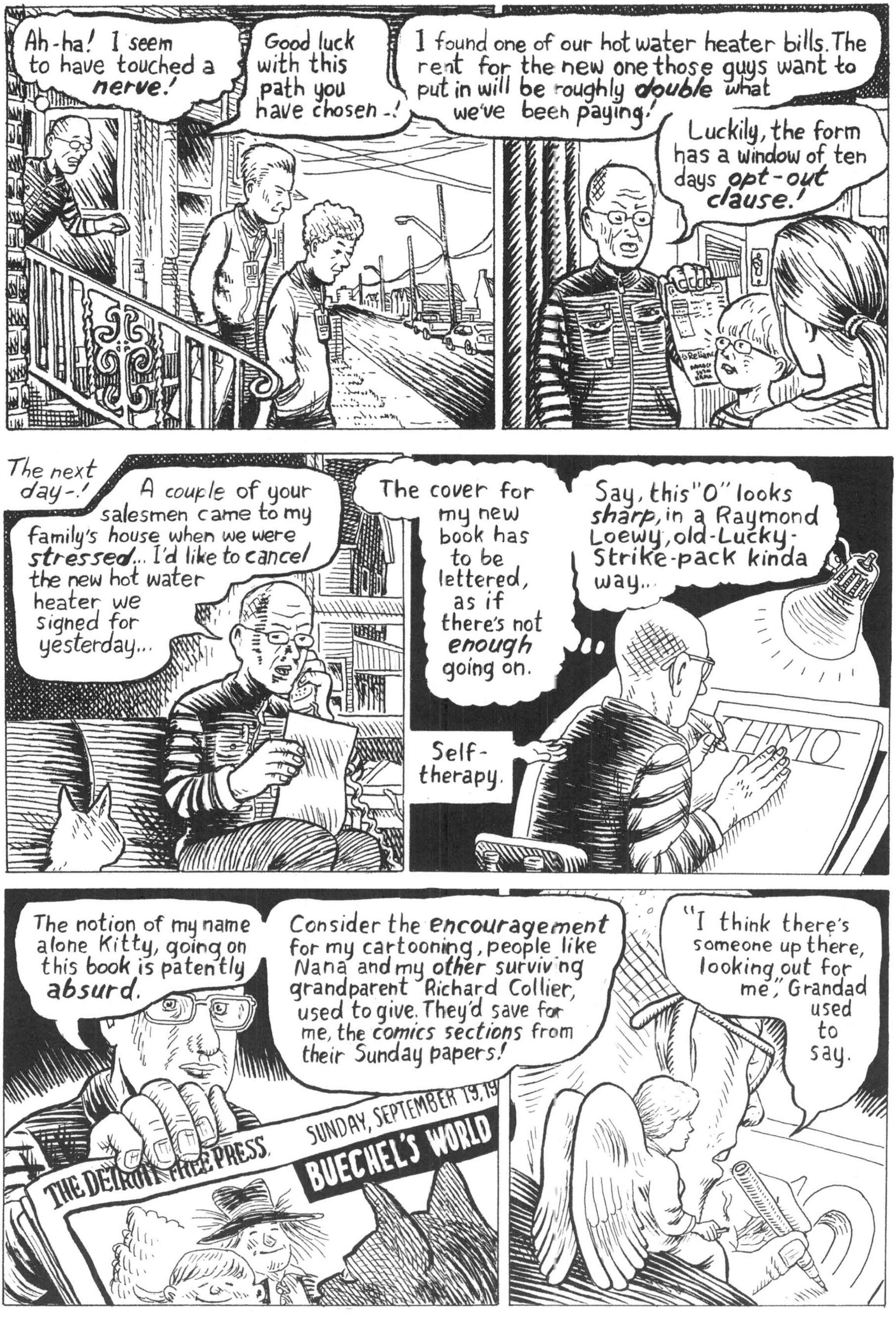

Ah-ha! I seem to have touched a *nerve!*
Good luck with this path you have chosen -!
I found one of our hot water heater bills. The rent for the new one those guys want to put in will be roughly *double* what we've been paying!
Luckily, the form has a window of ten days *opt-out clause!*
The next day-!
A couple of your salesmen came to my family's house when we were *stressed*... I'd like to cancel the new hot water heater we signed for yesterday...
The cover for my new book has to be lettered, as if there's not *enough* going on.
Say, this "O" looks *sharp*, in a Raymond Loewy, old-Lucky-Strike-pack kinda way...
CHIMO
Self-therapy.
The notion of my name alone Kitty, going on this book is patently **absurd**.
Consider the **encouragement** for my cartooning, people like Nana and my *other* surviving grandparent Richard Collier, used to give. They'd save for me, the *comics sections* from their Sunday papers!
SUNDAY, SEPTEMBER 19, 19
FREE PRESS.
BUECHEL'S WORLD
"I think there's someone up there, looking out for me," Grandad used to say.

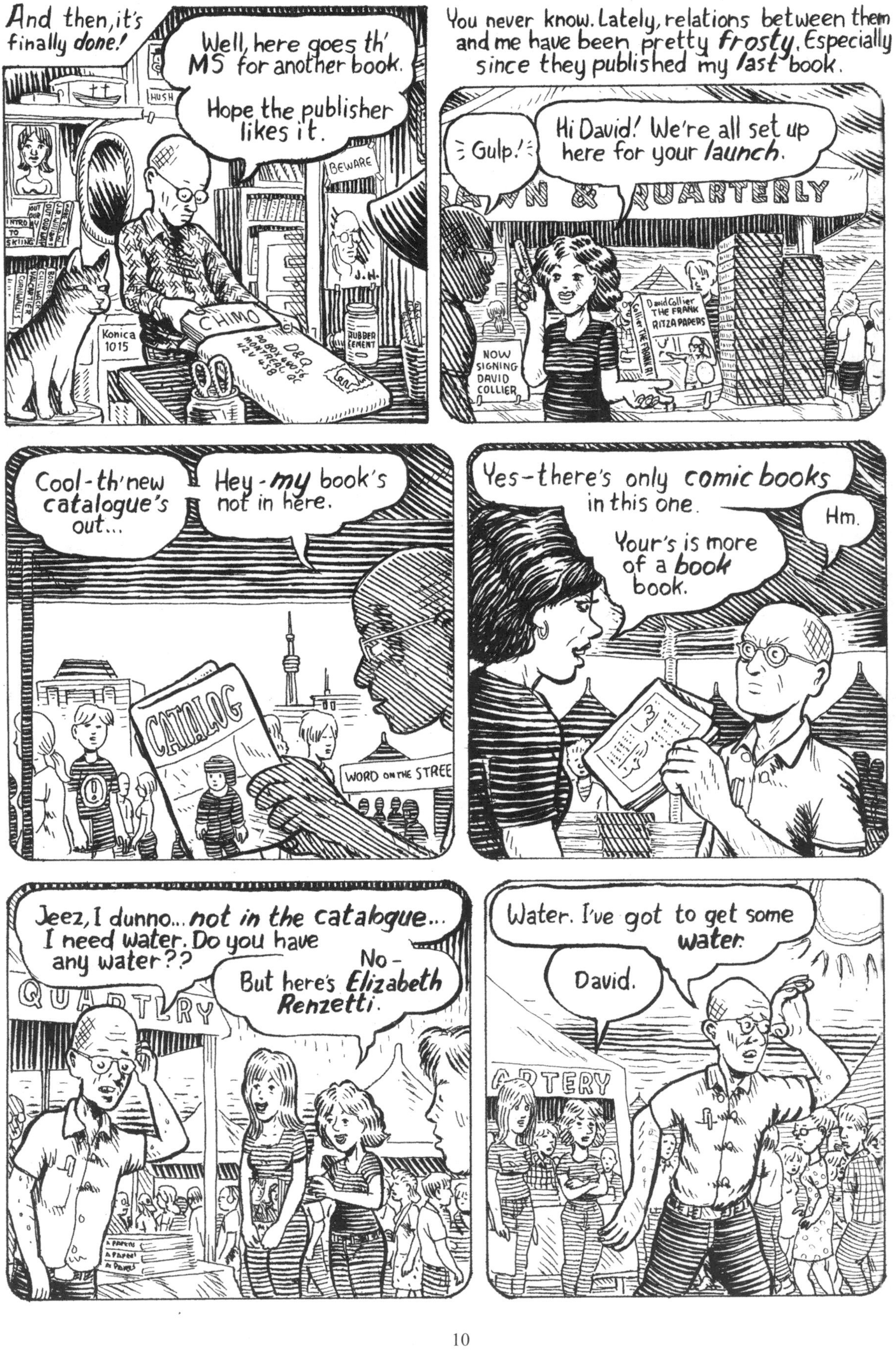
And then, it's finally done!
Well, here goes th' MS for another book.
Hope the publisher likes it.
HUSH
BEWARE
CHIMO
Konica 1015
RUBBER CEMENT
You never know. Lately, relations between them and me have been pretty frosty. Especially since they published my last book.
Gulp!
Hi David! We're all set up here for your launch.
NOW SIGNING DAVID COLLIER
David Collier THE FRANK RITZA PAPERS
Cool-th'new catalogue's out...
Hey-my book's not in here.
CATALOG
WORD ON THE STREE
Yes-there's only comic books in this one.
Your's is more of a book book.
Hm.
Jeez, I dunno... not in the catalogue... I need water. Do you have any water??
No-
But here's Elizabeth Renzetti.
Water. I've got to get some water.
David.

Okay, I was taking the catalogue thing too personally. Anytime there's a regime change at a business there's *bound* to be fallout.

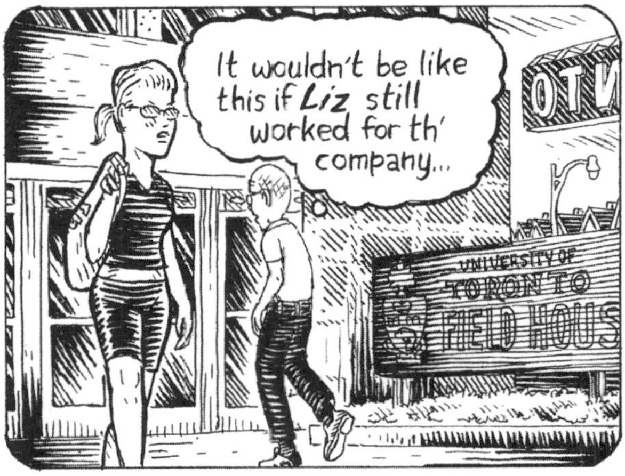
It wouldn't be like this if *Liz* still worked for th' company...
OTV
UNIVERSITY OF TORONTO FIELD HOUS

It was just that that day seemed to be a *culmination* of *months* of slights, real and perceived. All those unanswered emails...

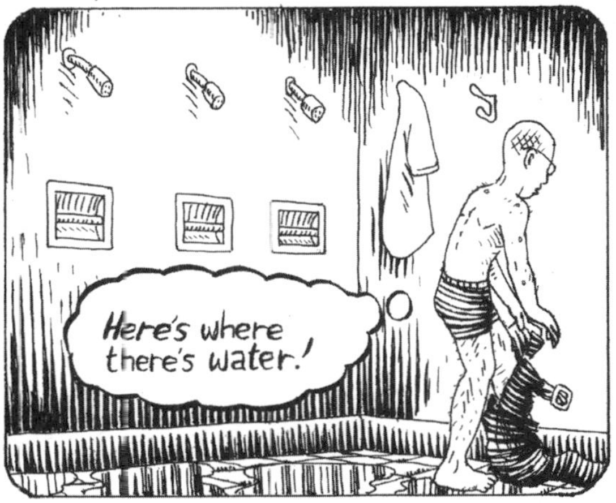
Here's where there's water!

My system requires a *lot of exercise*. Maybe it's a *dude* thing. Sometimes I go to schools as a parent/volunteer. And I see boys being made to sit still and quiet going *crazy*.

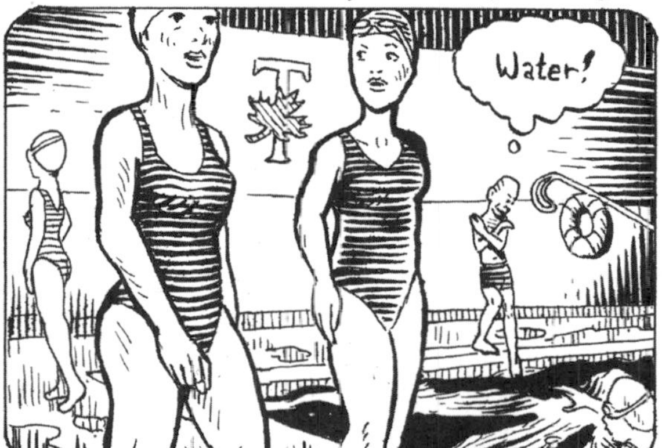
Water!

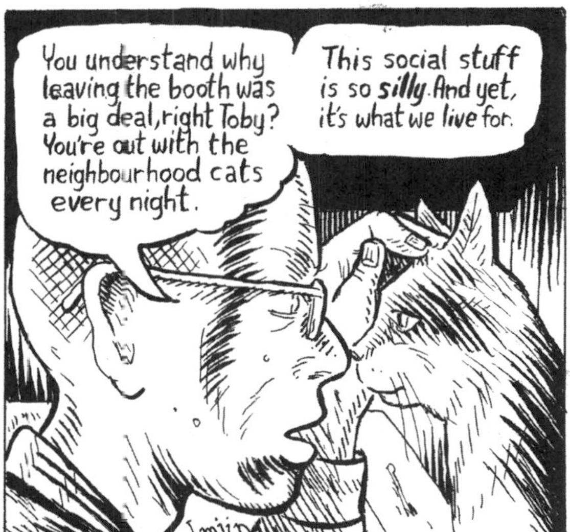
You understand why leaving the booth was a big deal, right Toby? You're out with the neighbourhood cats every night.
This social stuff is so *silly*. And yet, it's what we *live* for.
Imjin

"You wouldn't fight with the other cats in the alley so much, if you dealt with social stress by *swimming*."

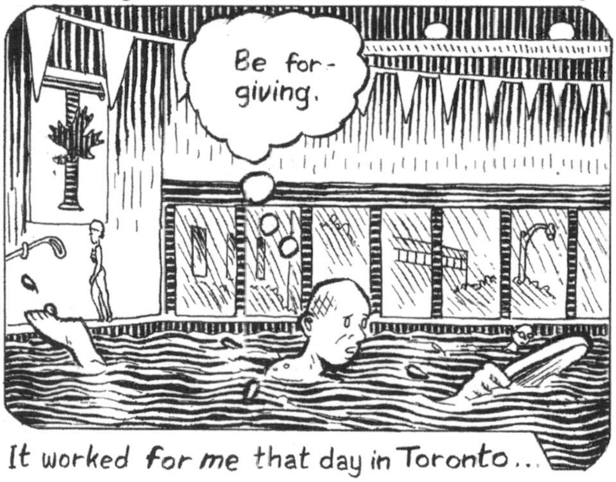
Be for-giving.

It worked *for me* that day in Toronto...

But not everyone was ready to reap the dividends of my meditative insights, then.

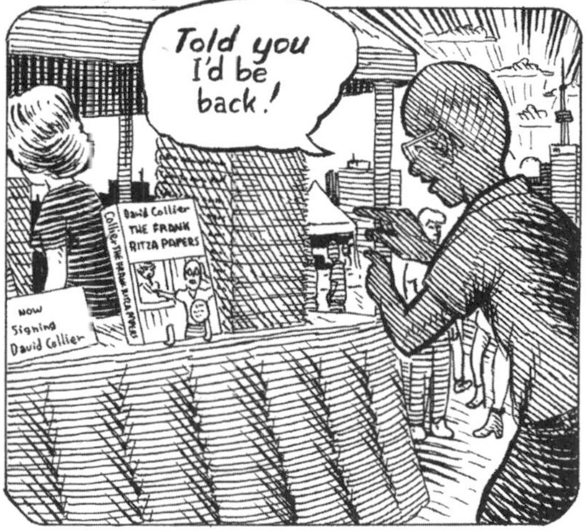
Told you I'd be back!
David Collier THE FRANK RITZA PAPERS
NOW Signing David Collier

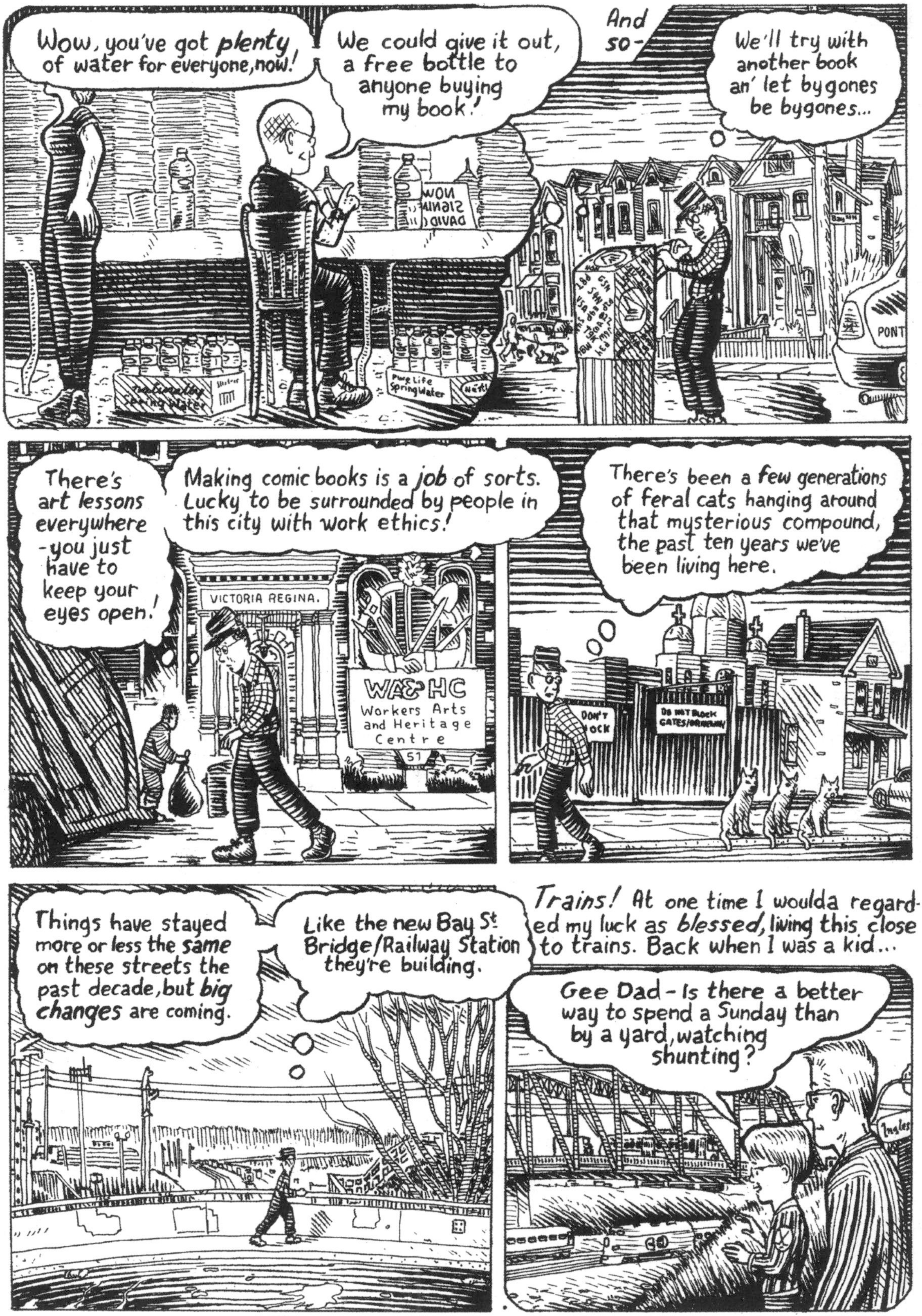
Wow, you've got plenty of water for everyone, now!
We could give it out, a free bottle to anyone buying my book!
And so-
We'll try with another book an' let bygones be bygones...
There's art lessons everywhere - you just have to keep your eyes open!
Making comic books is a job of sorts. Lucky to be surrounded by people in this city with work ethics!
VICTORIA REGINA.
WA&HC Workers Arts and Heritage Centre
51
There's been a few generations of feral cats hanging around that mysterious compound, the past ten years we've been living here.
DO NOT BLOCK GATES/DRIVEWAY
Things have stayed more or less the same on these streets the past decade, but big changes are coming.
Like the new Bay St. Bridge/Railway Station they're building.
Trains! At one time I woulda regarded my luck as blessed, living this close to trains. Back when I was a kid...
Gee Dad - Is there a better way to spend a Sunday than by a yard, watching shunting?

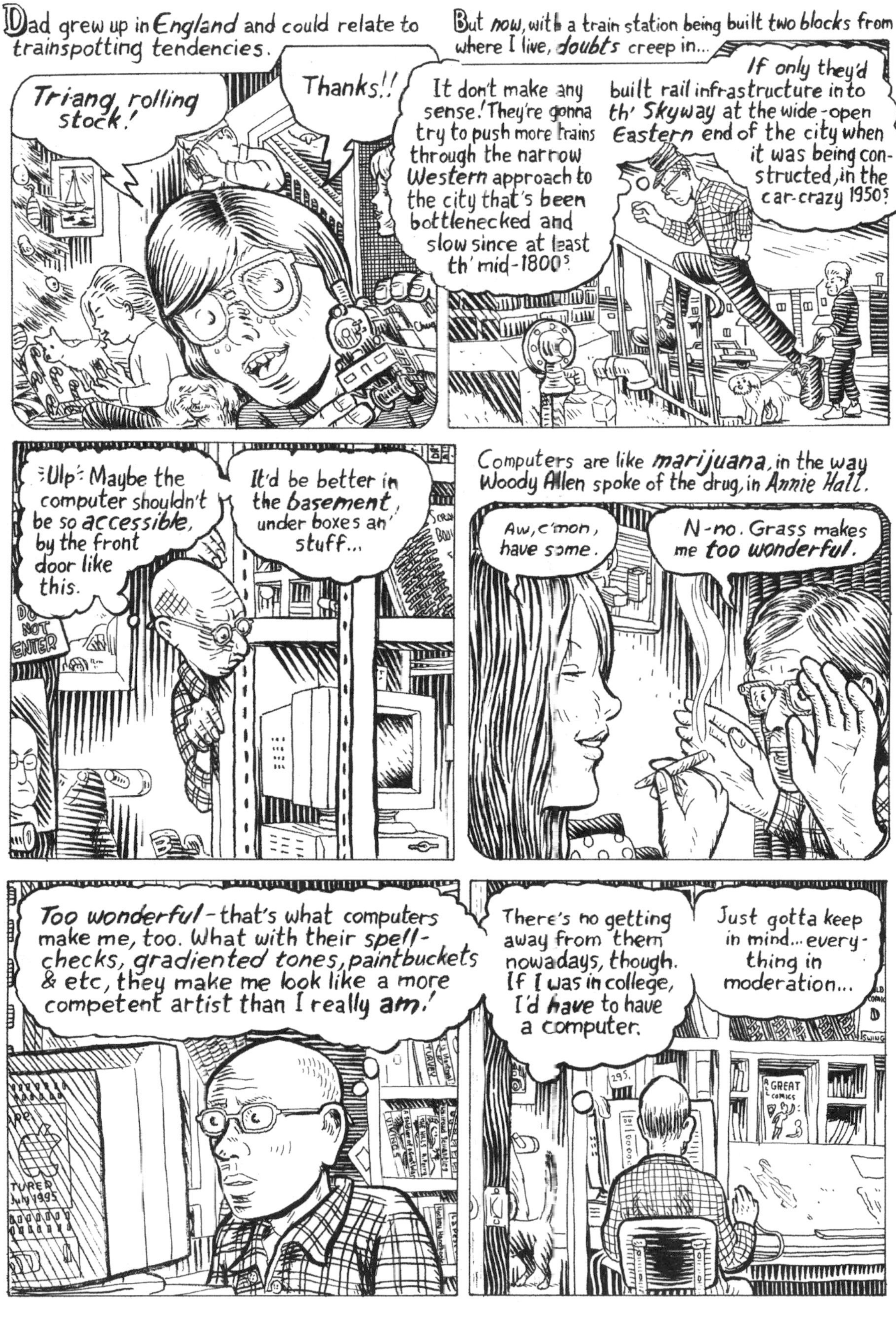
Dad grew up in England and could relate to trainspotting tendencies.
Tri·ang rolling stock!
Thanks!!
But now, with a train station being built two blocks from where I live, doubts creep in...
It don't make any sense! They're gonna try to push more trains through the narrow Western approach to the city that's been bottlenecked and slow since at least th' mid-1800s
If only they'd built rail infrastructure into th' Skyway at the wide-open Eastern end of the city when it was being constructed, in the car-crazy 1950s
:Ulp: Maybe the computer shouldn't be so accessible, by the front door like this.
It'd be better in the basement, under boxes an' stuff...
DO NOT ENTER
Computers are like marijuana, in the way Woody Allen spoke of the drug, in Annie Hall.
Aw, c'mon, have some.
N-no. Grass makes me too wonderful.
Too wonderful - that's what computers make me, too. What with their spell-checks, gradiented tones, paintbuckets & etc, they make me look like a more competent artist than I really am!
July 1995
There's no getting away from them nowadays, though. If I was in college, I'd have to have a computer.
Just gotta keep in mind... everything in moderation...
A GREAT COMICS

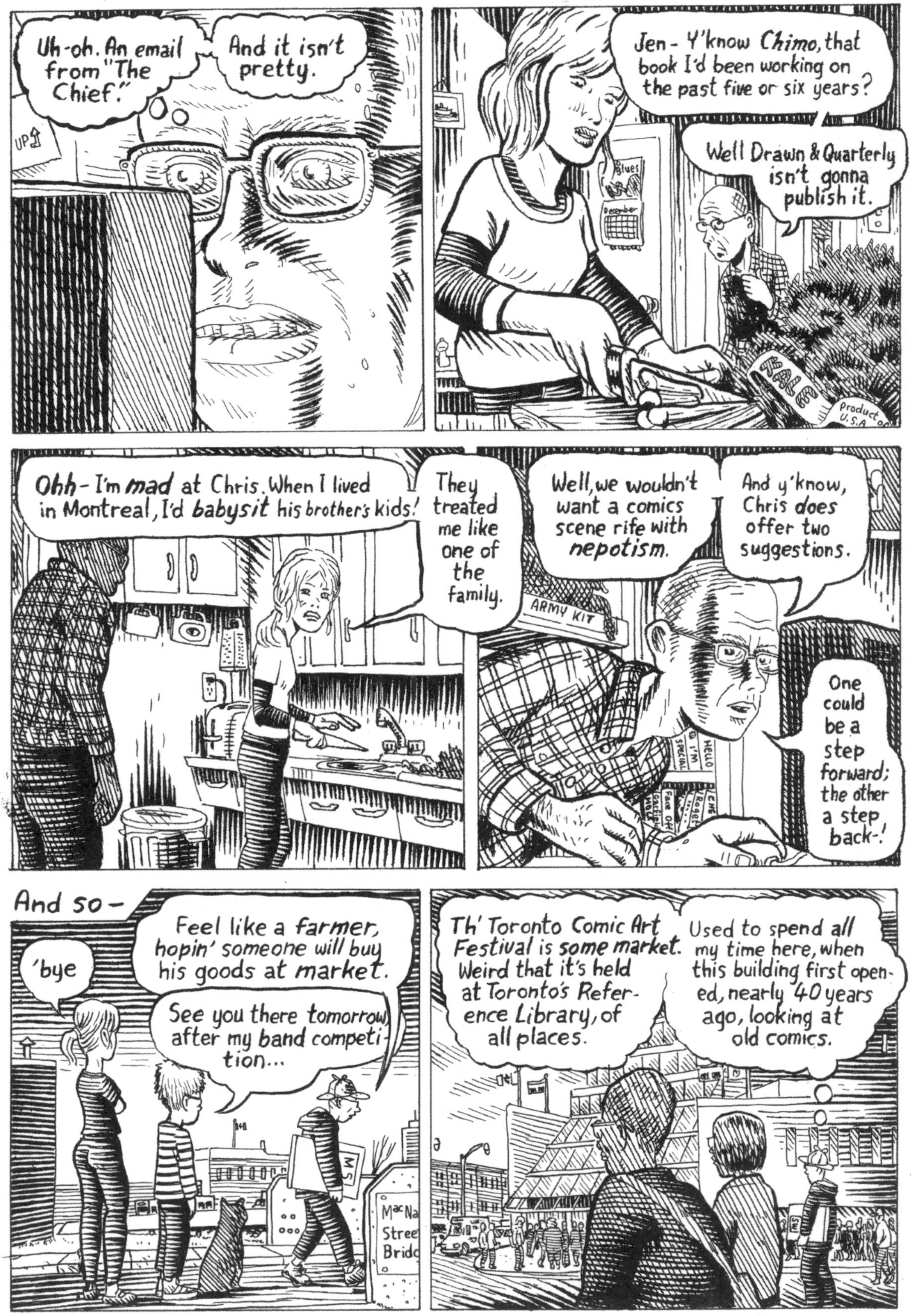

Uh-oh. An email from "The Chief."
And it isn't pretty.
UP
Jen- Y'know Chimo, that book I'd been working on the past five or six years?
Well Drawn & Quarterly isn't gonna publish it.
Blues
December
KALE
Product of U.S.A.
Ohh- I'm mad at Chris. When I lived in Montreal, I'd babysit his brother's kids!
They treated me like one of the family.
Well, we wouldn't want a comics scene rife with nepotism.
And y'know, Chris does offer two suggestions.
ARMY KIT
One could be a step forward; the other a step back-!
And so-
'bye
Feel like a farmer, hopin' someone will buy his goods at market.
See you there tomorrow after my band competition...
Th' Toronto Comic Art Festival is some market. Weird that it's held at Toronto's Reference Library, of all places.
Used to spend all my time here, when this building first opened, nearly 40 years ago, looking at old comics.

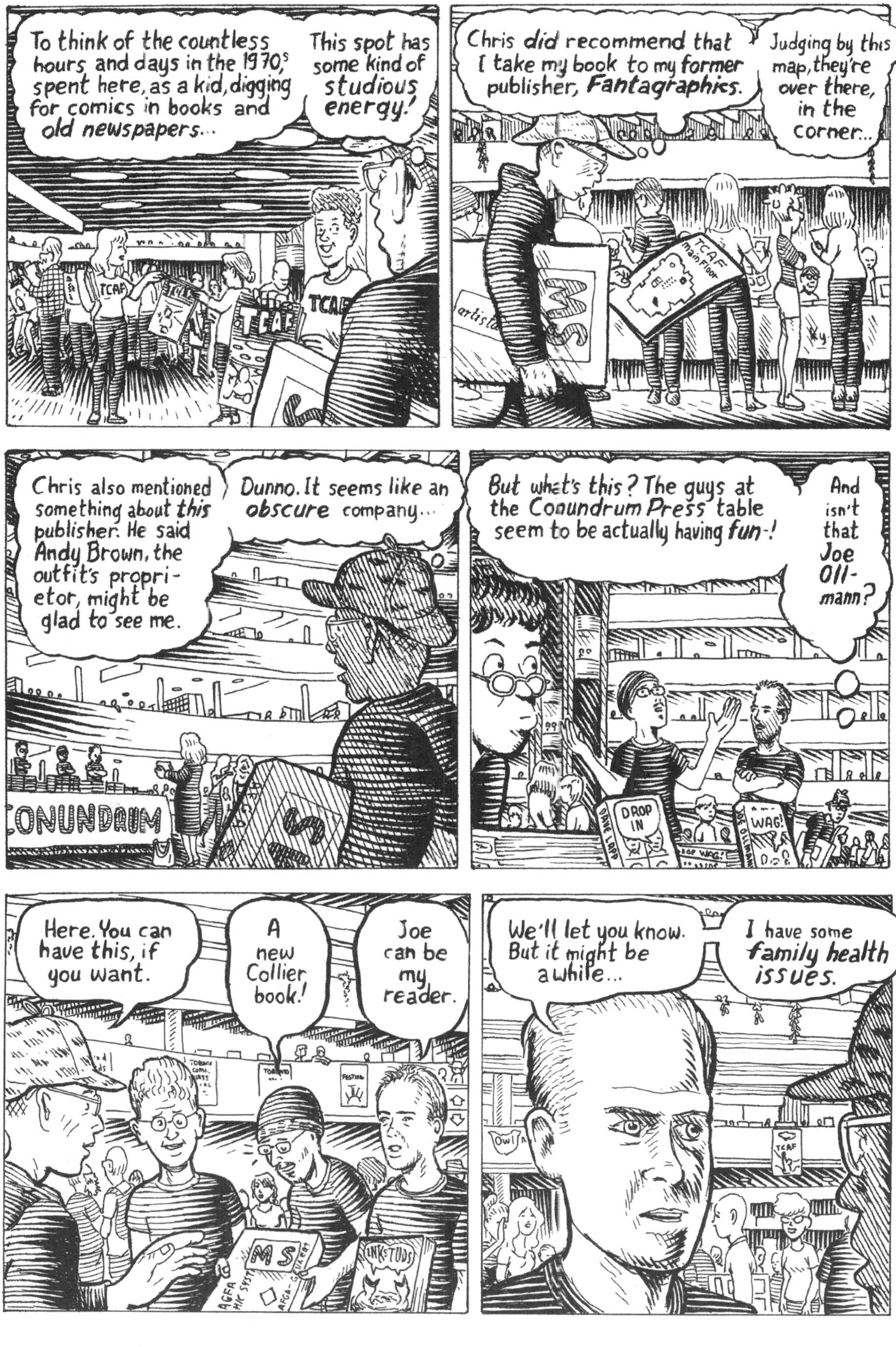
To think of the countless hours and days in the 1970s spent here, as a kid, digging for comics in books and old newspapers...
This spot has some kind of studious energy!
TCAF
Chris did recommend that I take my book to my former publisher, Fantagraphics.
Judging by this map, they're over there, in the corner...
TCAF main floor
Chris also mentioned something about this publisher. He said Andy Brown, the outfit's proprietor, might be glad to see me.
Dunno. It seems like an obscure company...
CONUNDRUM
But what's this? The guys at the Conundrum Press table seem to be actually having fun-!
And isn't that Joe Ollmann?
DROP IN
WAG!
Here. You can have this, if you want.
A new Collier book!
Joe can be my reader.
MS
INKSTUDS
We'll let you know. But it might be a while...
I have some family health issues.

The day of the big event arrives. **Aldershot**

The prompt publication of *Chimo* was too much to hope for.

Andy's spending a lot of time at Meg's bedside in the hospital.

VIA

VIA

Ottawa—!

Say, that box from the printer Gauvin Press... You wouldn't be delivering it to the War Museum...?

Yep.

Chimo!

GAUVIN PRESS

A little more than a month later, on a bitterly cold day in the Annapolis Valley, the writer Meg Sircom died at age 43.

Got to get her *sob* into the frozen ground, somehow.

And the car won't start.

How are we gonna get to her funeral?

Life is short.

Hey, remember you were talking 'bout us doing a big trip as a family?

There's a map of all the *train routes* here.

There's a little bit of *everything* in here. Stuff from before the internet!

Lakeshore
FUNDY
North Carolina
Time tables
Pamphlets
MAPS
CHICAGO

Information used to satisfy, in that it was *hard-won*. It was not *easy* to obtain a map of the affordable, U.S. Army Corps of Engineers campsites/ dams,

Coming off the road, this late at night-- one rarely has to pay at *all*.

STOP

for instance..

18

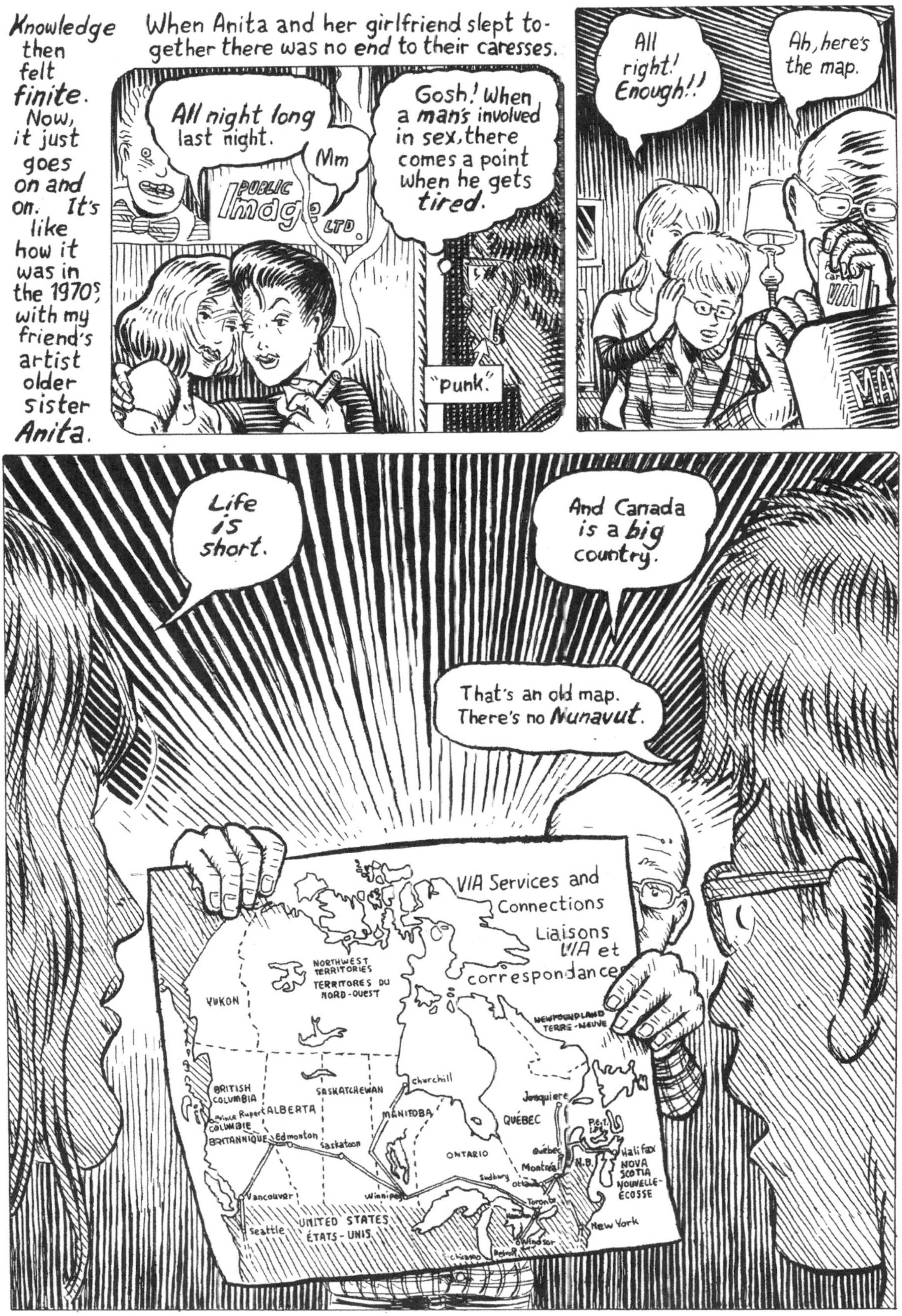
Knowledge then felt finite. Now, it just goes on and on. It's like how it was in the 1970s, with my friend's artist older sister Anita.
When Anita and her girlfriend slept together there was no end to their caresses.
All night long last night.
Mm
PUBLIC Image LTD.
Gosh! When a man's involved in sex, there comes a point when he gets tired.
"punk."
All right! Enough!!
Ah, here's the map.
Life is short.
And Canada is a big country.
That's an old map. There's no Nunavut.
VIA Services and Connections
Liaisons VIA et correspondances
NORTHWEST TERRITORIES
TERRITORES DU NORD-OUEST
YUKON
NEWFOUNDLAND TERRE-NEUVE
BRITISH COLUMBIA
ALBERTA
SASKATCHEWAN
MANITOBA
Churchill
Jonquiere
QUÉBEC
Prince Rupert
COLUMBIE BRITANNIQUE
Edmonton
Saskatoon
ONTARIO
Québec
Montréal
N.B.
Halifax
NOVA SCOTIA NOUVELLE-ÉCOSSE
Sudbury
Ottawa
Vancouver
Winnipeg
Toronto
UNITED STATES
ÉTATS-UNIS
Seattle
New York
Windsor

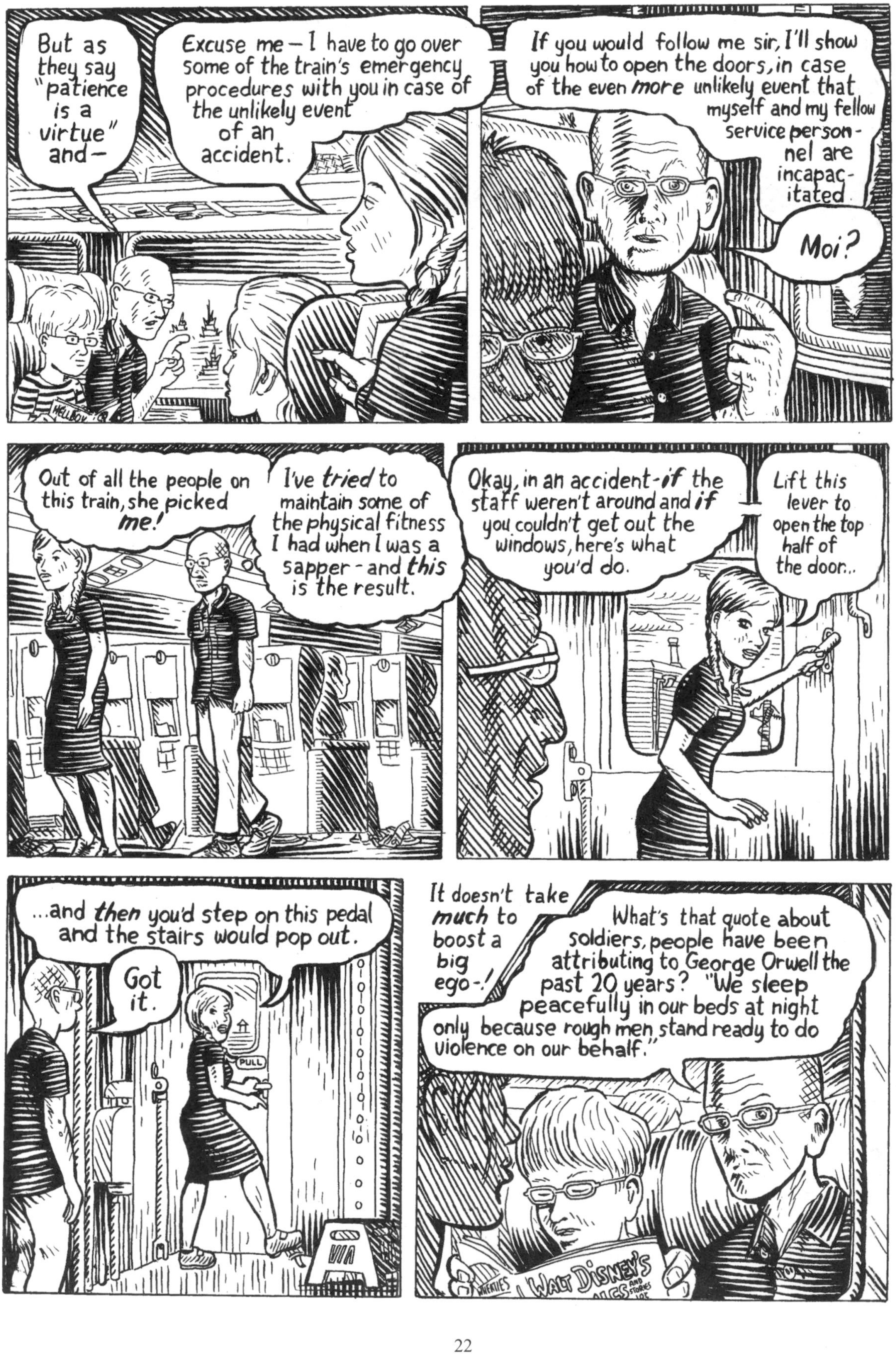
But as they say "patience is a virtue" and—
Excuse me—I have to go over some of the train's emergency procedures with you in case of the unlikely event of an accident.
HELLBOY
If you would follow me sir, I'll show you how to open the doors, in case of the even more unlikely event that myself and my fellow service personnel are incapacitated.
Moi?
Out of all the people on this train, she picked me!
I've tried to maintain some of the physical fitness I had when I was a sapper - and this is the result.
Okay, in an accident-if the staff weren't around and if you couldn't get out the windows, here's what you'd do.
Lift this lever to open the top half of the door..
...and then you'd step on this pedal and the stairs would pop out.
Got it.
PULL
VIA
It doesn't take much to boost a big ego-!
What's that quote about soldiers, people have been attributing to George Orwell the past 20 years? "We sleep peacefully in our beds at night only because rough men stand ready to do violence on our behalf."
WALT DISNEY'S

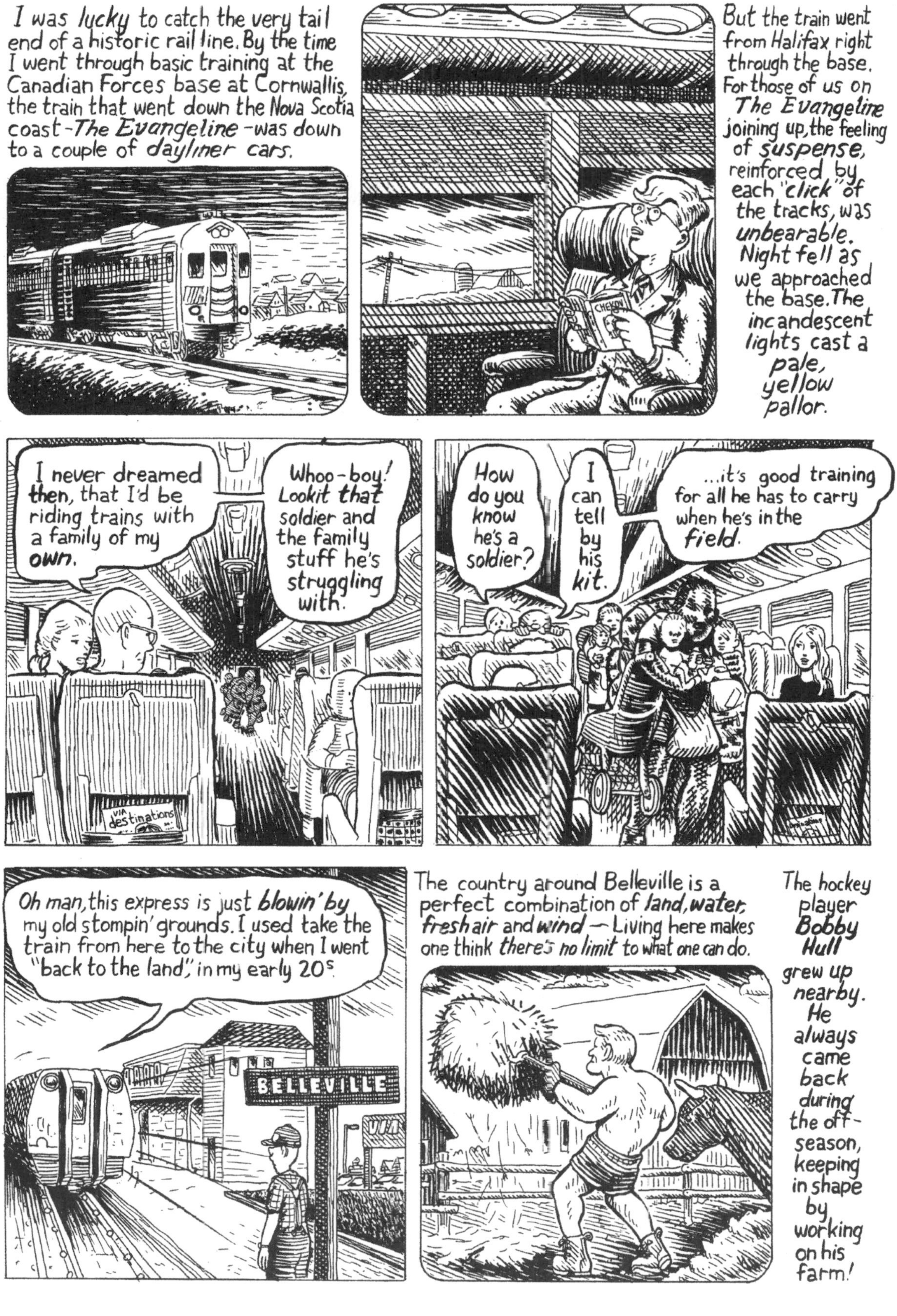
I was lucky to catch the very tail end of a historic rail line. By the time I went through basic training at the Canadian Forces base at Cornwallis, the train that went down the Nova Scotia coast - The Evangeline - was down to a couple of dayliner cars.
But the train went from Halifax right through the base. For those of us on The Evangeline joining up, the feeling of suspense, reinforced by each "click" of the tracks, was unbearable. Night fell as we approached the base. The incandescent lights cast a pale, yellow pallor.
CHEKOV
I never dreamed then, that I'd be riding trains with a family of my own.
Whoo-boy! Lookit that soldier and the family stuff he's struggling with.
VIA destinations
How do you know he's a soldier?
I can tell by his kit.
...it's good training for all he has to carry when he's in the field.
Oh man, this express is just blowin' by my old stompin' grounds. I used take the train from here to the city when I went "back to the land," in my early 20s.
BELLEVILLE
VIA
The country around Belleville is a perfect combination of land, water, fresh air and wind — Living here makes one think there's no limit to what one can do.
The hockey player Bobby Hull grew up nearby. He always came back during the off-season, keeping in shape by working on his farm!

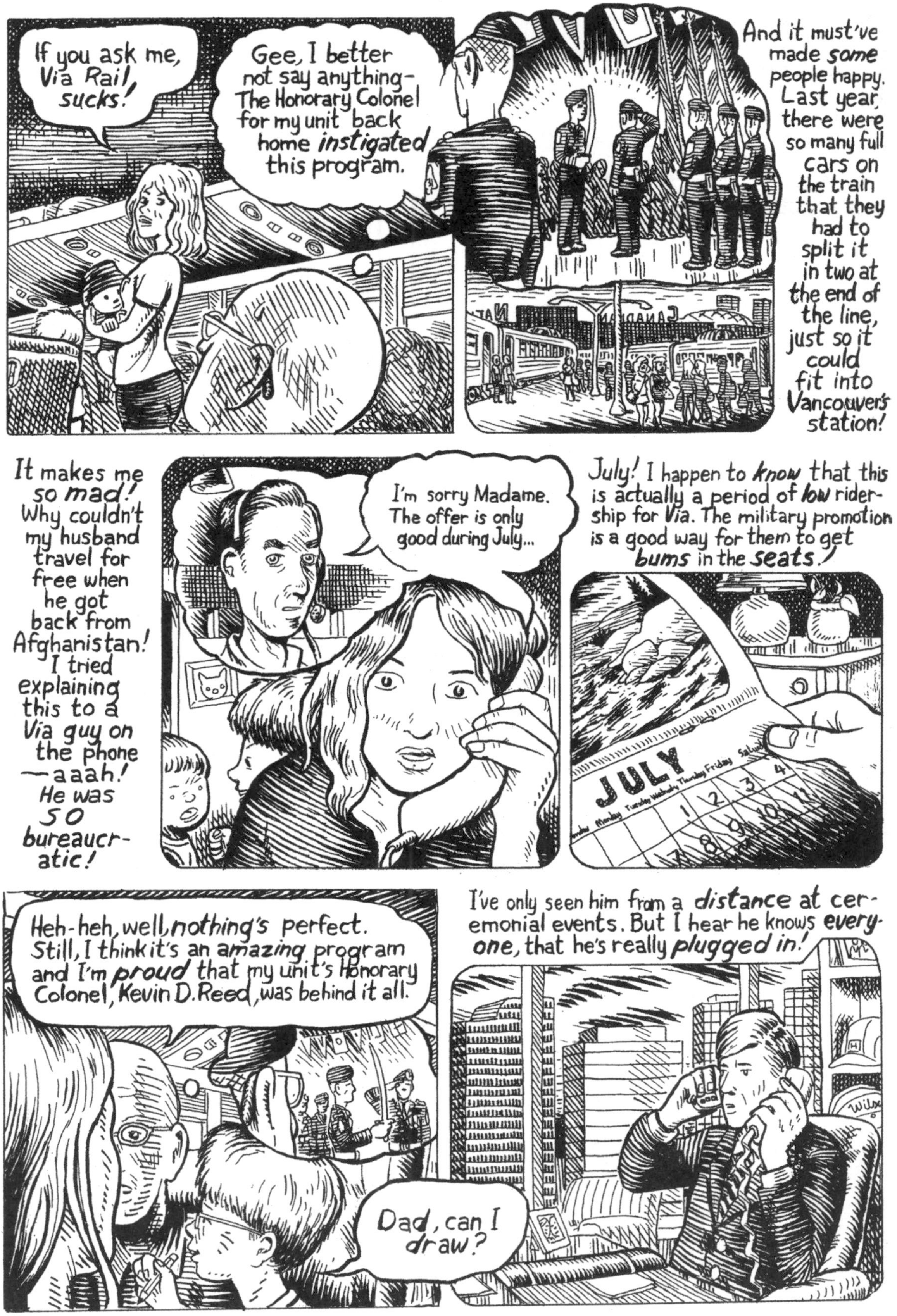
If you ask me, Via Rail, sucks!
Gee, I better not say anything- The Honorary Colonel for my unit back home instigated this program.
And it must've made some people happy. Last year, there were so many full cars on the train that they had to split it in two at the end of the line, just so it could fit into Vancouver's station!
It makes me so mad! Why couldn't my husband travel for free when he got back from Afghanistan! I tried explaining this to a Via guy on the phone —aaah! He was SO bureaucr-atic!
I'm sorry Madame. The offer is only good during July...
July! I happen to know that this is actually a period of low rider-ship for Via. The military promotion is a good way for them to get bums in the seats!
JULY
Heh-heh, well, nothing's perfect. Still, I think it's an amazing program and I'm proud that my unit's Honorary Colonel, Kevin D. Reed, was behind it all.
I've only seen him from a distance at cer-emonial events. But I hear he knows every-one, that he's really plugged in!
Dad, can I draw?

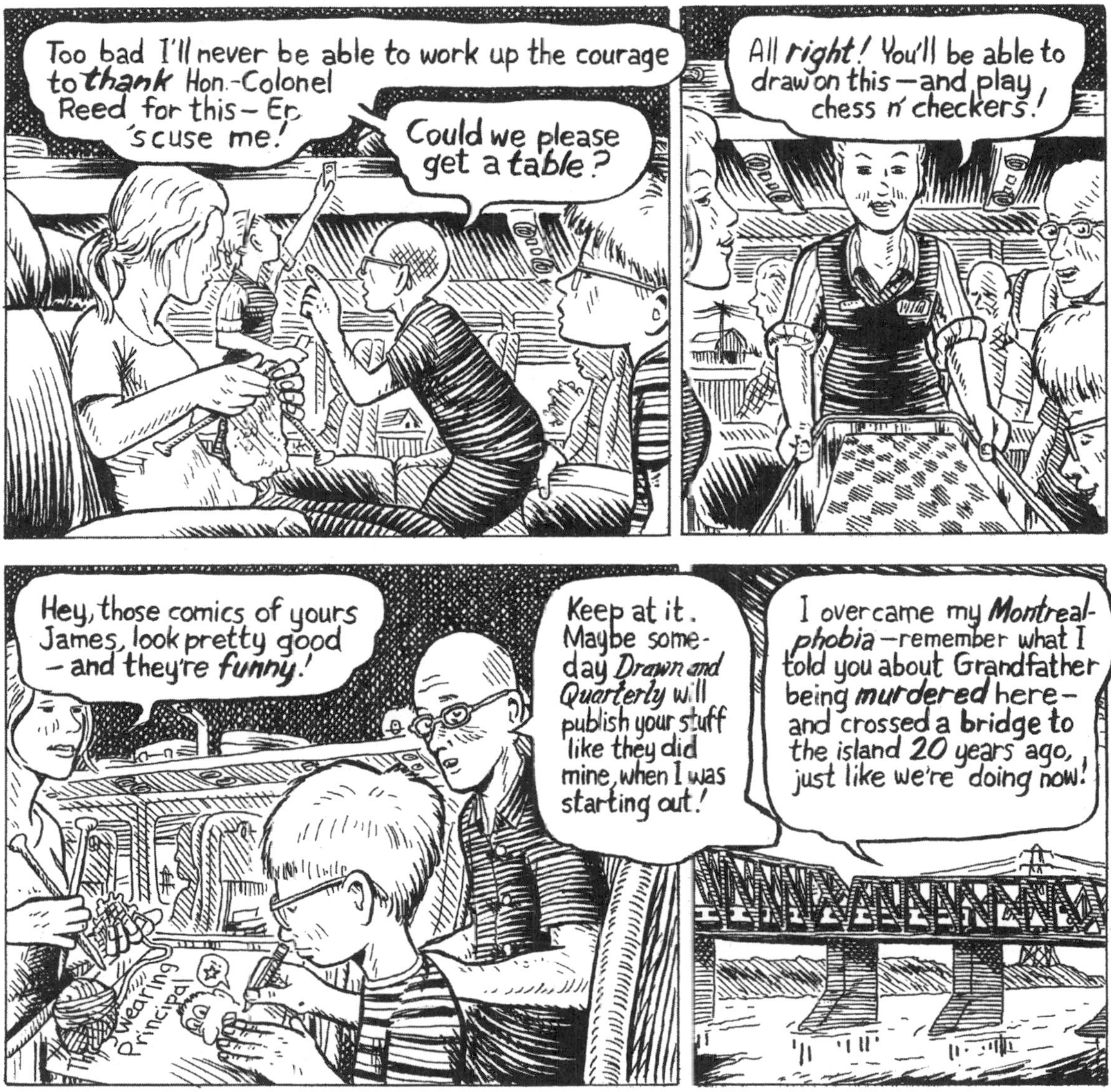
Too bad I'll never be able to work up the courage to *thank* Hon.-Colonel Reed for this—Er 'scuse me!
Could we please get a *table*?
All *right*! You'll be able to draw on this—and play chess n' checkers!
Hey, those comics of yours James, look pretty good —and they're *funny*!
Keep at it. Maybe someday *Drawn and Quarterly* will publish your stuff like they did mine, when I was starting out!
I overcame my *Montreal-phobia*—remember what I told you about Grandfather being *murdered* here—and crossed a **bridge** to the island 20 years ago, just like we're doing now!

I visited Drawn & Quarterly's publisher Chris Oliveros and his wife Marina Lesenko at their first apartment.

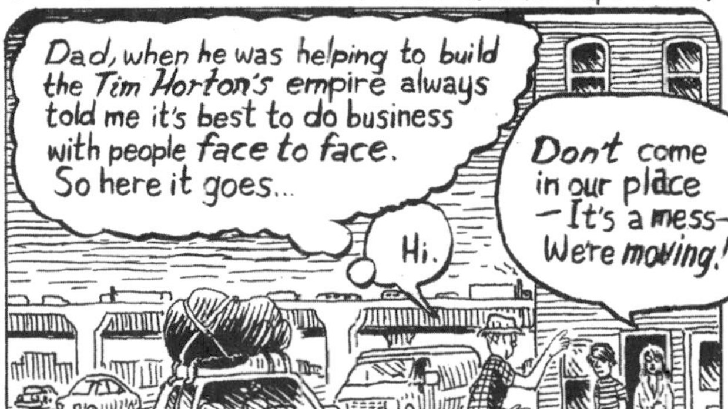
Dad, when he was helping to build the *Tim Horton's* empire always told me it's best to do business with people *face to face*. So here it goes...
Hi.
Don't come in our place —It's a mess— We're *moving*!

They were young and it was before *noon*—they were still in their *bedclothes*.

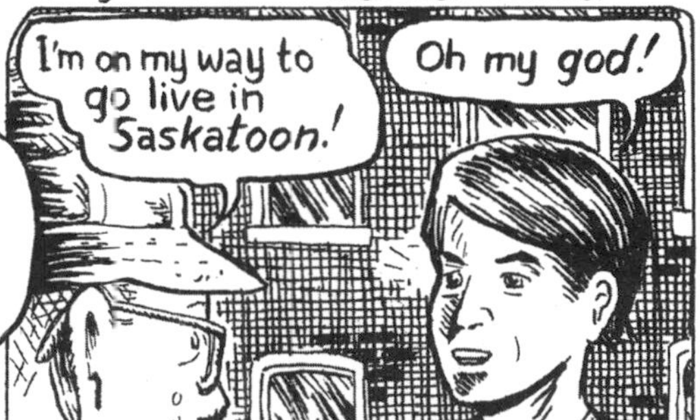
I'm on my way to go live in Saskatoon!
Oh my *god*!

Chris has always had *strong opinions*.

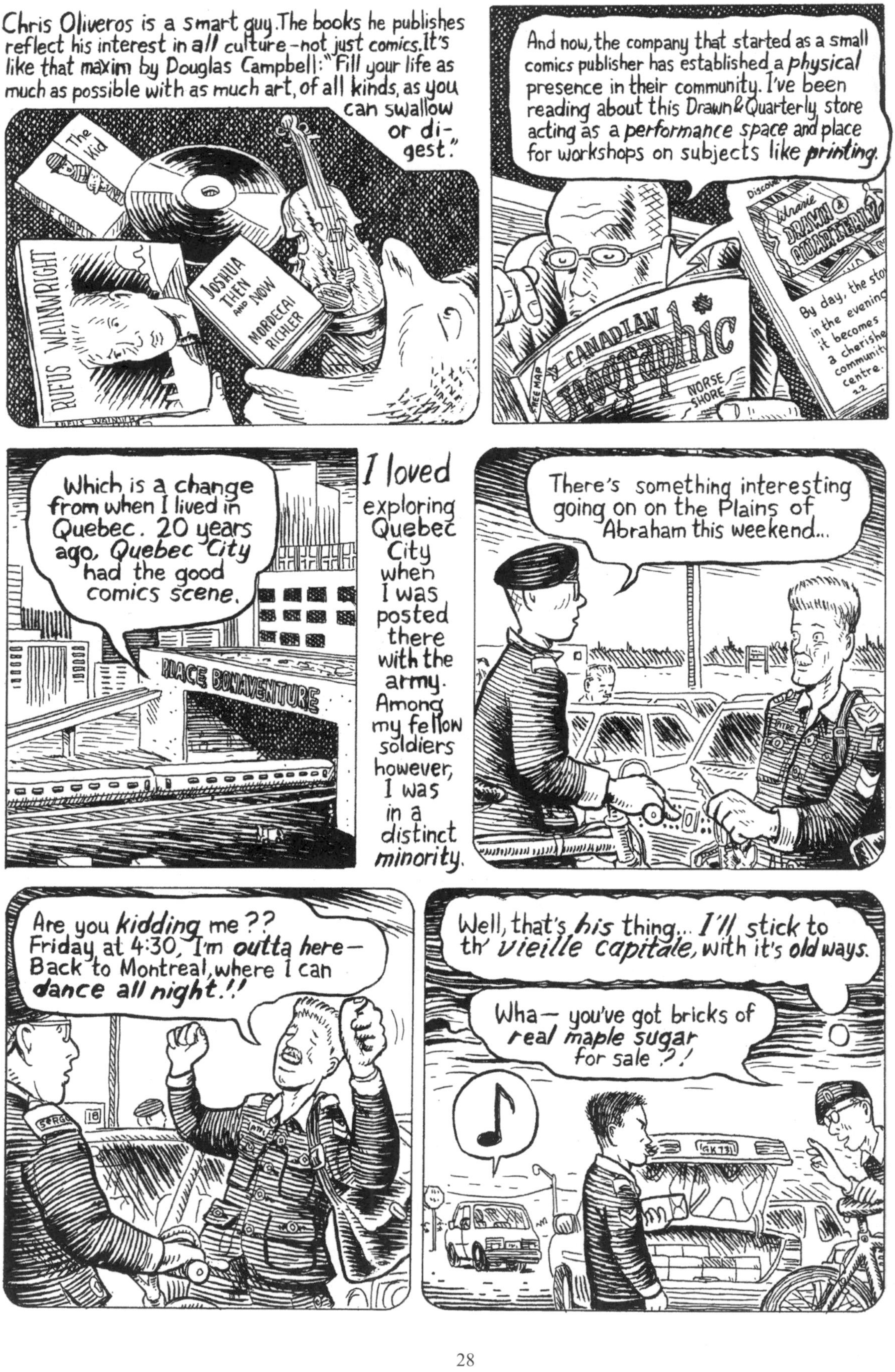
Chris Oliveros is a smart guy. The books he publishes reflect his interest in all culture - not just comics. It's like that maxim by Douglas Campbell: "Fill your life as much as possible with as much art, of all kinds, as you can swallow or digest."
The Kid
Charlie Chaplin
Rufus Wainwright
Joshua Then and Now
Mordecai Richler
And now, the company that started as a small comics publisher has established a physical presence in their community. I've been reading about this Drawn & Quarterly store acting as a performance space and place for workshops on subjects like printing.
Canadian Geographic
Norse Shore
Librairie Drawn & Quarterly
Which is a change from when I lived in Quebec. 20 years ago, Quebec City had the good comics scene.
Place Bonaventure
I loved exploring Quebec City when I was posted there with the army. Among my fellow soldiers however, I was in a distinct minority.
There's something interesting going on on the Plains of Abraham this weekend...
Are you kidding me?? Friday at 4:30, I'm outta here - Back to Montreal, where I can dance all night!!
Well, that's his thing... I'll stick to th' vieille capitale, with it's old ways.
Wha— you've got bricks of real maple sugar for sale?!

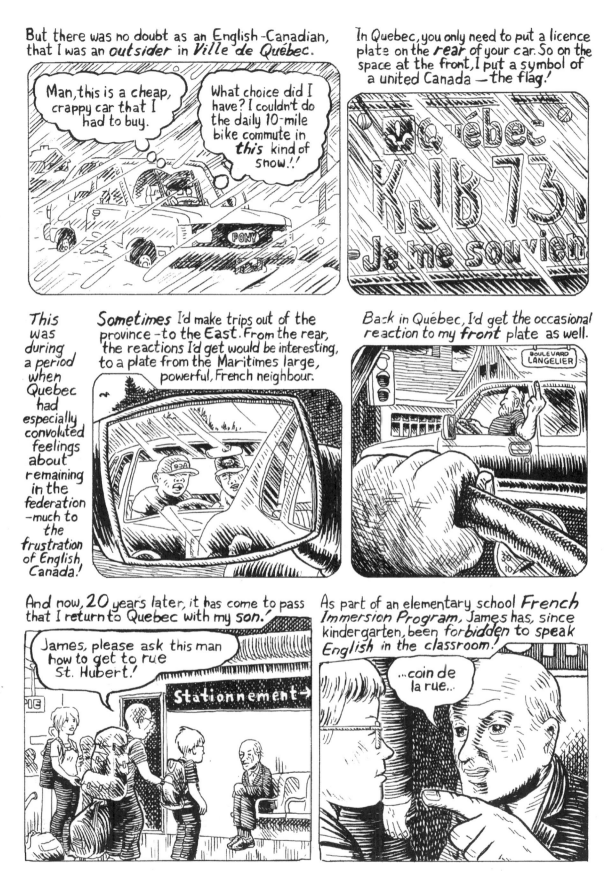

But there was no doubt as an English-Canadian, that I was an *outsider* in *Ville de Québec.*

Man, this is a cheap, crappy car that I had to buy.

What choice did I have? I couldn't do the daily 10-mile bike commute in *this* kind of snow!!

PONY

In Quebec, you only need to put a licence plate on the *rear* of your car. So on the space at the front, I put a symbol of a united Canada — the flag!

Québec KJB 73 — Je me souviens

This was during a period when Quebec had especially convoluted feelings about remaining in the federation — much to the frustration of English Canada!

Sometimes I'd make trips out of the province — to the East. From the rear, the reactions I'd get would be interesting, to a plate from the Maritimes large, powerful, French neighbour.

Back in Québec, I'd get the occasional reaction to my *front* plate as well.

BOULEVARD LANGELIER

And now, 20 years later, it has come to pass that I return to Quebec with my *son.*

James, please ask this man how to get to rue St. Hubert!

Stationnement →

As part of an elementary school *French Immersion Program,* James has, since kindergarten, been *forbidden* to speak *English* in the classroom!

...coin de la rue...

29

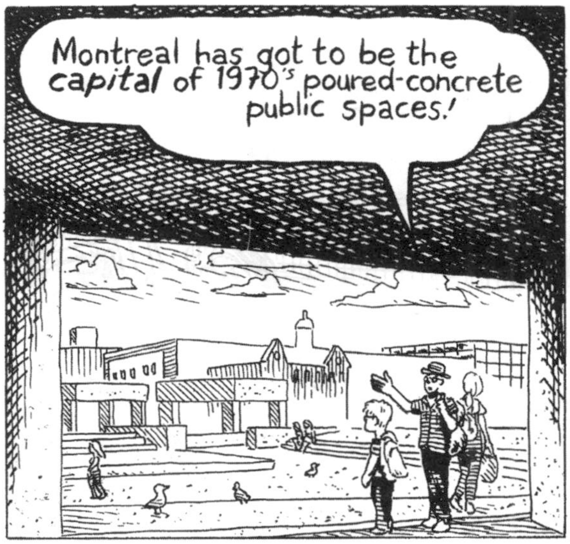
Montreal has got to be the capital of 1970's poured-concrete public spaces!

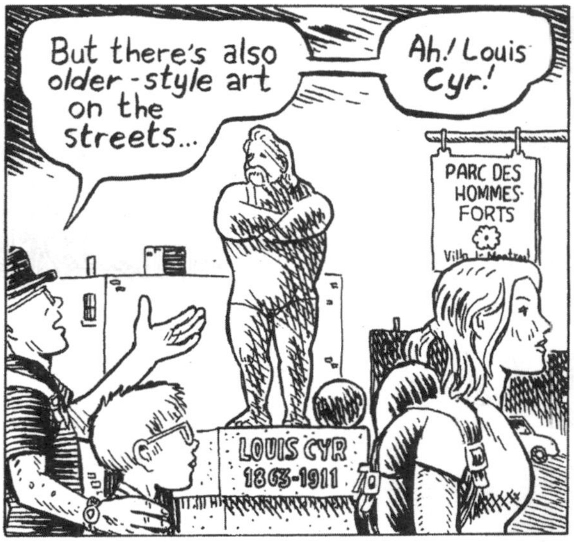
But there's also older-style art on the streets...
Ah! Louis Cyr!
PARC DES HOMMES-FORTS
LOUIS CYR
1863-1911

You ever hear of the *strong man Louis Cyr*? He was born in the farm country South of Montreal and moved to the big city in the early 1880's. In Montreal, he worked as a policeman.

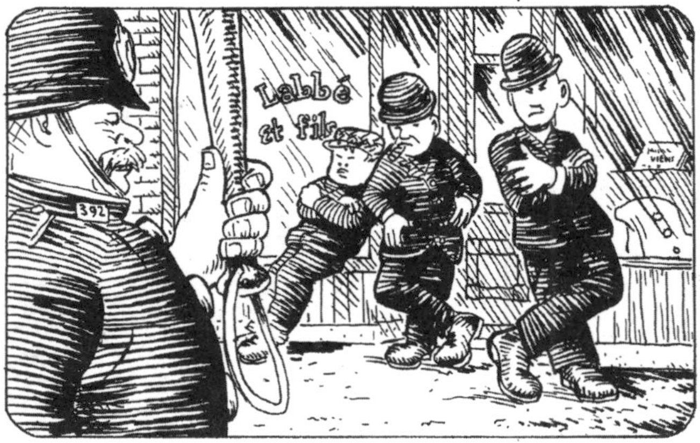
Labbé et fils
392

Cyr started to attract the world's attention after the New York papers published an article about him arresting *three* heavy louts and carrying them to the station house!

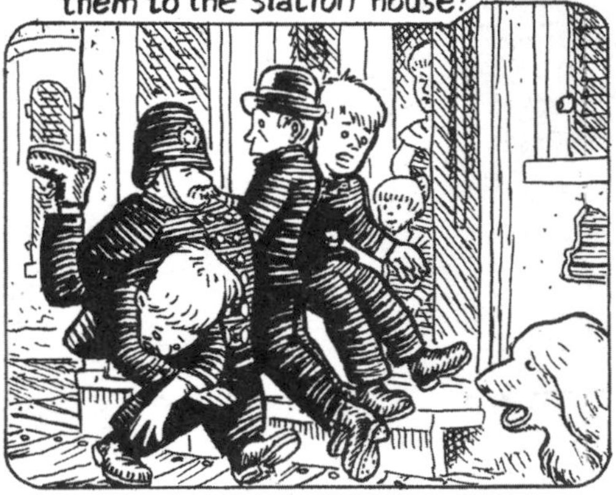

Travel and fame followed. Cyr would show how he could lift 500 pounds with one finger. His stock-in-trade was getting a dozen or so fat men from the audience to stand on a platform and hoisting the whole thing!

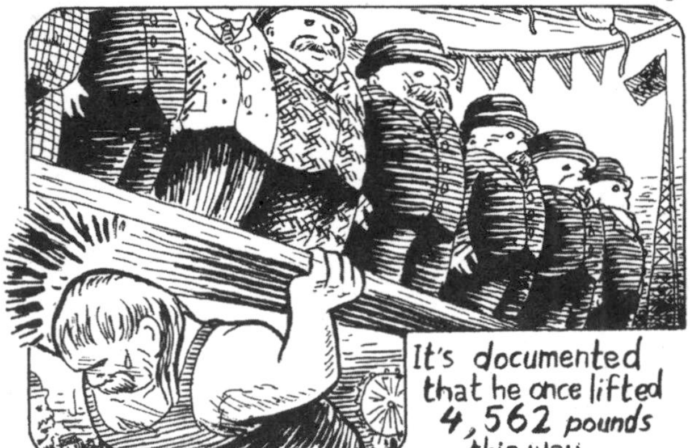
It's documented that he once lifted 4,562 pounds this way.

But *strength* wasn't the *only* thing he was known for. He could *eat* like almost no one else. Cyr and his friend, Curé Labelle, would descend on restaurants near the courthouse and consume a whole suckling pig - *each*!

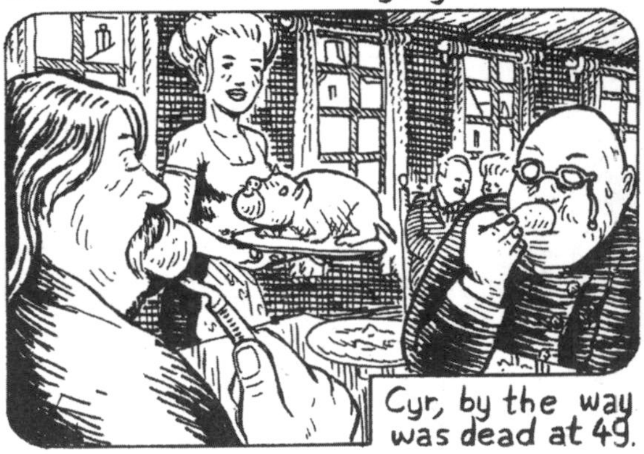
Cyr, by the way was dead at 49.

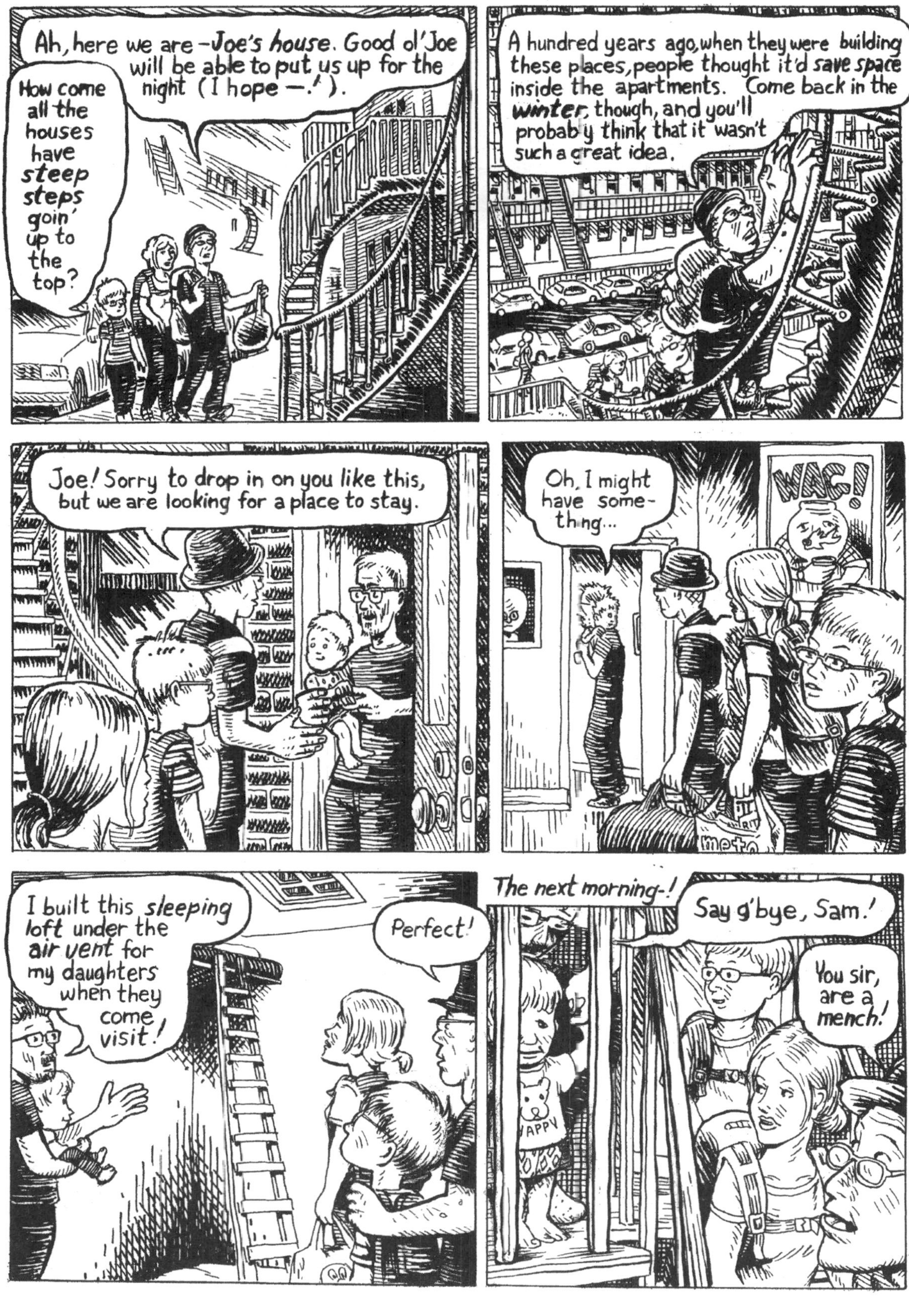
Ah, here we are –Joe's house. Good ol' Joe will be able to put us up for the night (I hope –!).
How come all the houses have steep steps goin' up to the top?
A hundred years ago, when they were building these places, people thought it'd save space inside the apartments. Come back in the winter, though, and you'll probably think that it wasn't such a great idea.
Joe! Sorry to drop in on you like this, but we are looking for a place to stay.
Oh, I might have some-thing...
WAG!
I built this sleeping loft under the air vent for my daughters when they come visit!
Perfect!
The next morning-!
Say g'bye, Sam!
You sir, are a mench!

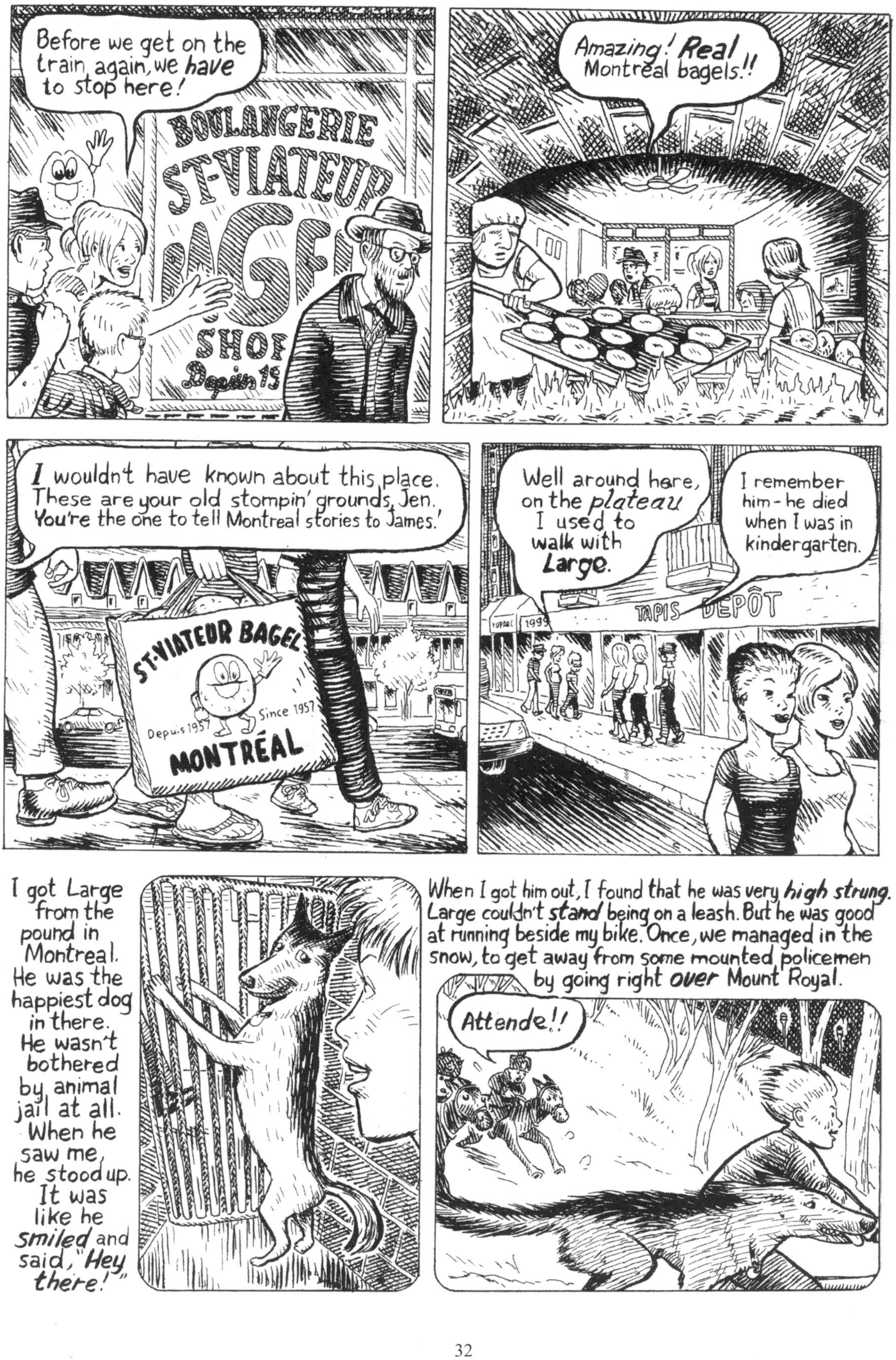
Before we get on the train again, we *have* to stop here!
BOULANGERIE
ST-VIATEUR
Amazing! **Real** Montreal bagels!!
I wouldn't have known about this place. These are your old stompin' grounds, Jen. You're the one to tell Montreal stories to James.
ST-VIATEUR BAGEL
Depuis 1957
Since 1957
MONTRÉAL
Well around here, on the *plateau* I used to walk with **Large**.
I remember him - he died when I was in kindergarten.
TAPIS DÉPÔT
I got Large from the pound in Montreal. He was the happiest dog in there. He wasn't bothered by animal jail at all. When he saw me, he stood up. It was like he *smiled* and said, "*Hey there!*"
When I got him out, I found that he was very ***high strung***. Large couldn't *stand* being on a leash. But he was good at running beside my bike. Once, we managed in the snow, to get away from some mounted policemen by going right ***over*** Mount Royal.
Attende!!

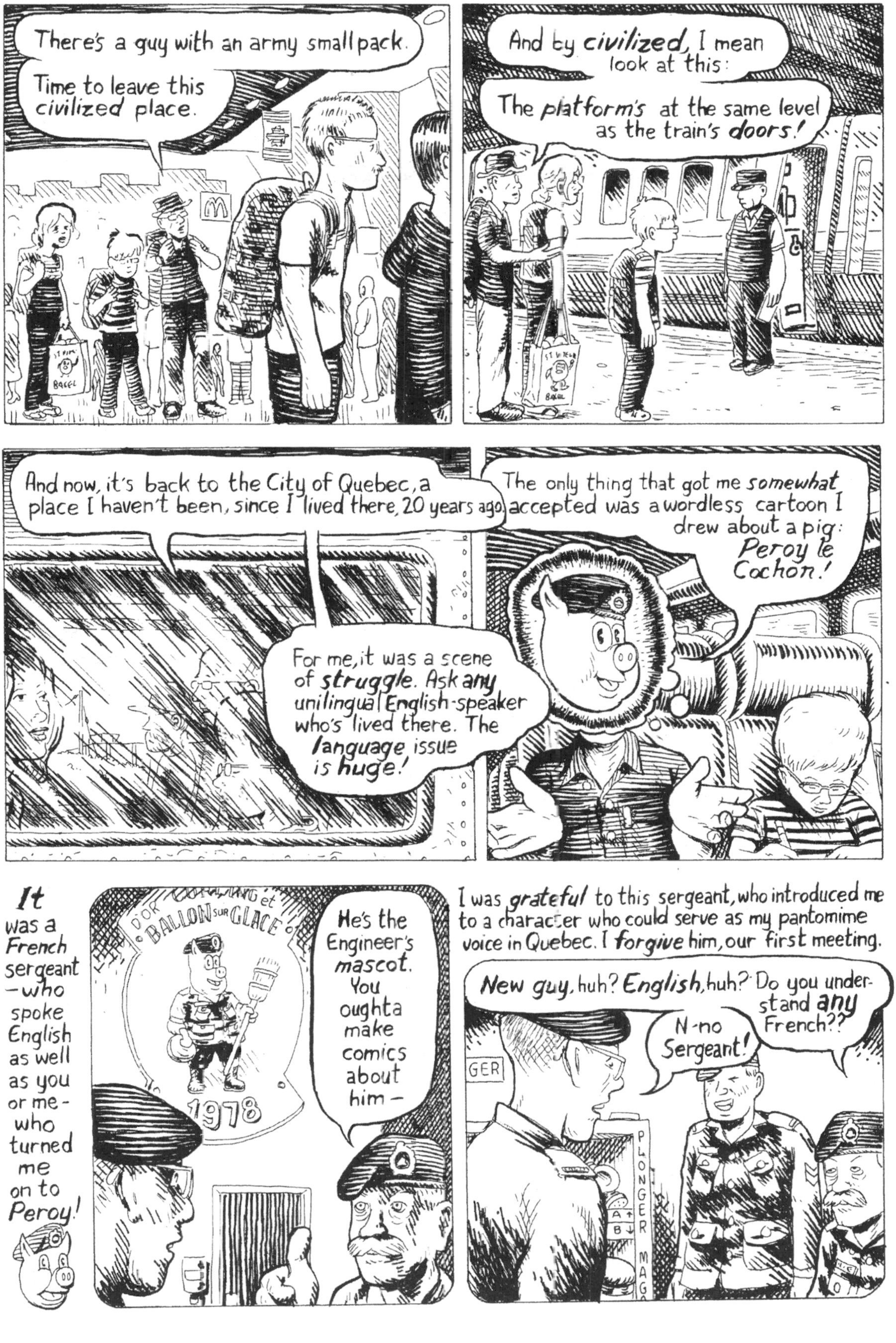
There's a guy with an army smallpack.
Time to leave this civilized place.
And by civilized, I mean look at this:
The platform's at the same level as the train's doors!
And now, it's back to the City of Quebec, a place I haven't been, since I lived there, 20 years ago.
For me, it was a scene of struggle. Ask any unilingual English-speaker who's lived there. The language issue is huge!
The only thing that got me somewhat accepted was a wordless cartoon I drew about a pig: Peroy le Cochon!
It was a French sergeant — who spoke English as well as you or me — who turned me on to Peroy!
BALLON SUR GLACE
1978
He's the Engineer's mascot. You oughta make comics about him —
I was grateful to this sergeant, who introduced me to a character who could serve as my pantomime voice in Quebec. I forgive him, our first meeting.
New guy, huh? English, huh? Do you understand any French??
N-no Sergeant!
GER
PLONGER MAG

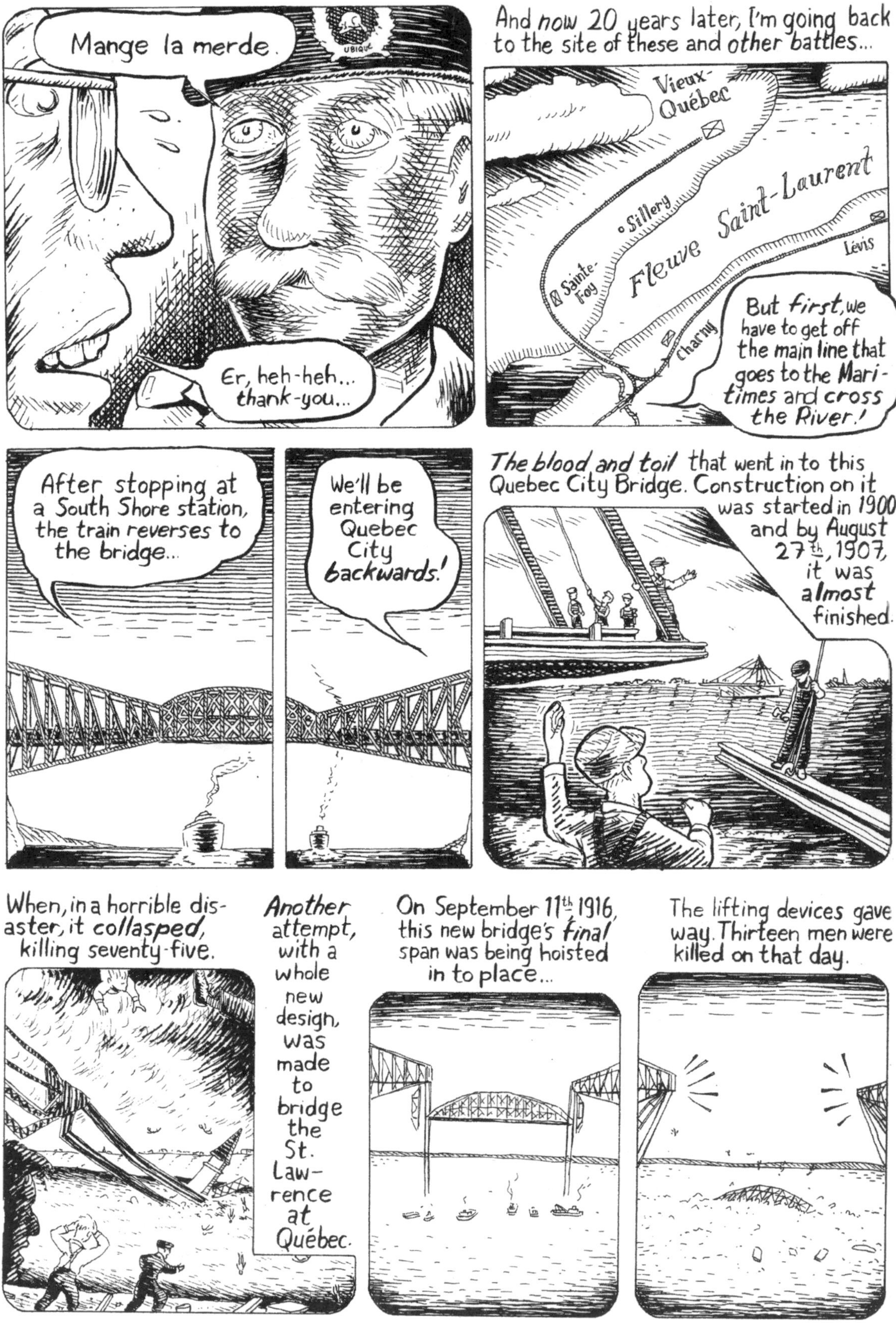
Mange la merde.
UBIQUE
Er, heh-heh... thank-you...
And now 20 years later, I'm going back to the site of these and other battles...
Vieux-Québec
Sillery
Fleuve Saint-Laurent
Lévis
Sainte-Foy
Charny
But first, we have to get off the main line that goes to the Maritimes and cross the River!
After stopping at a South Shore station, the train reverses to the bridge...
We'll be entering Quebec City backwards!
The blood and toil that went in to this Quebec City Bridge. Construction on it was started in 1900 and by August 27th, 1907, it was almost finished.
When, in a horrible disaster, it collasped, killing seventy-five.
Another attempt, with a whole new design, was made to bridge the St. Lawrence at Québec.
On September 11th 1916, this new bridge's final span was being hoisted in to place...
The lifting devices gave way. Thirteen men were killed on that day.

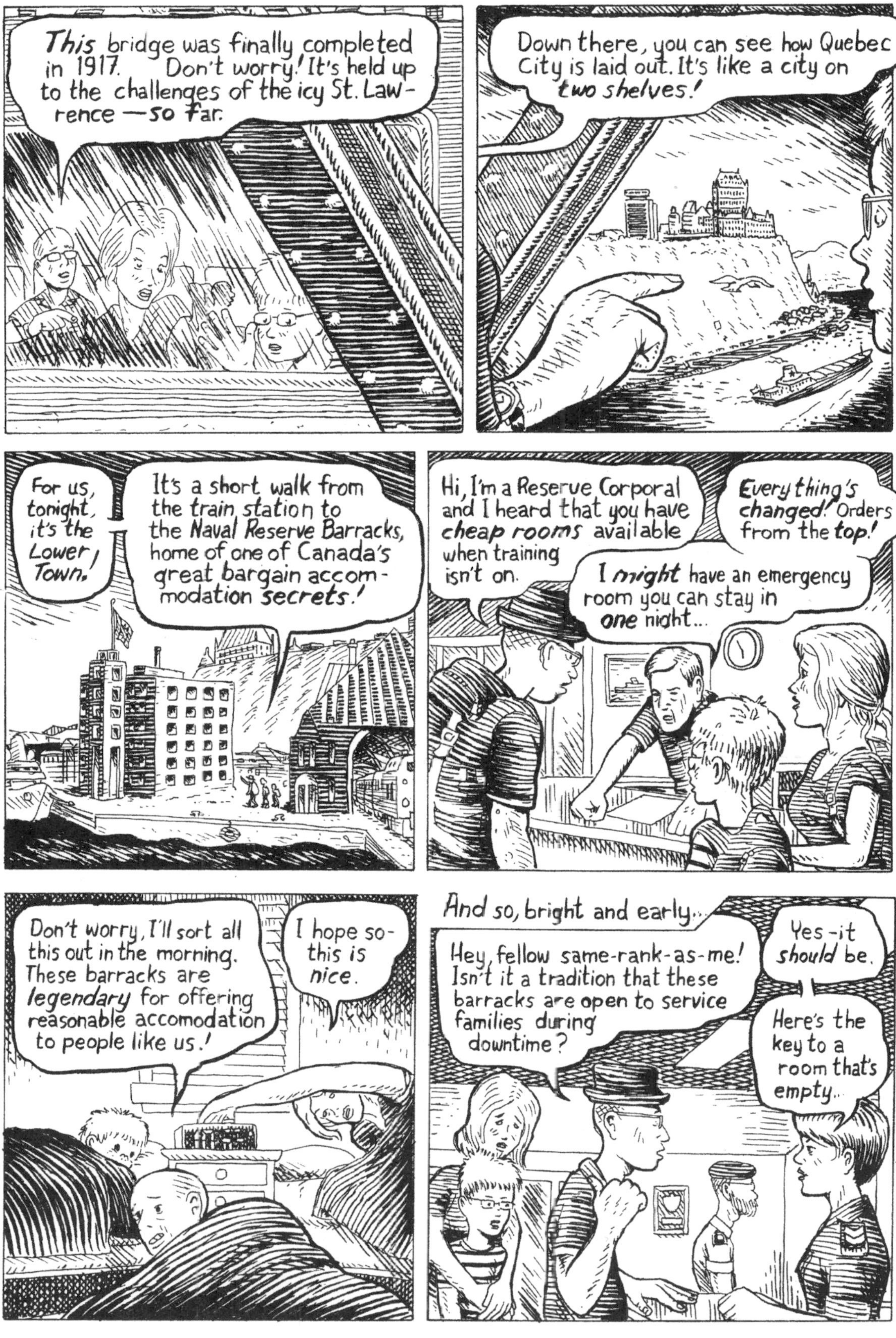
This bridge was finally completed in 1917. Don't worry! It's held up to the challenges of the icy St. Lawrence —so far.
Down there, you can see how Quebec City is laid out. It's like a city on two shelves!
For us, tonight, it's the Lower Town!
It's a short walk from the train station to the Naval Reserve Barracks, home of one of Canada's great bargain accommodation secrets!
Hi, I'm a Reserve Corporal and I heard that you have cheap rooms available when training isn't on.
Everything's changed! Orders from the top!
I might have an emergency room you can stay in one night...
Don't worry, I'll sort all this out in the morning. These barracks are legendary for offering reasonable accomodation to people like us!
I hope so- this is nice.
And so, bright and early...
Hey, fellow same-rank-as-me! Isn't it a tradition that these barracks are open to service families during downtime?
Yes-it should be.
Here's the key to a room that's empty...

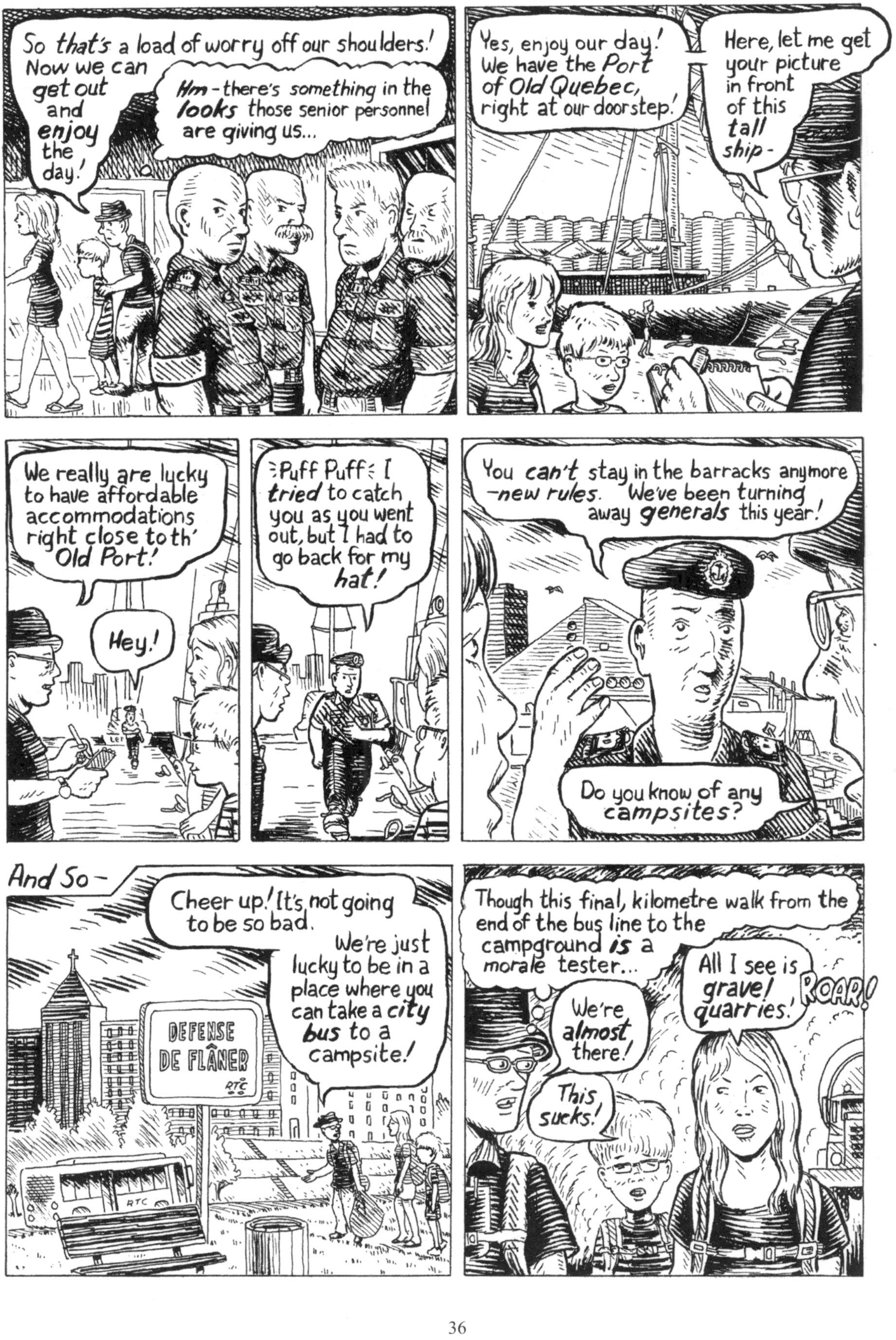
So that's a load of worry off our shoulders! Now we can get out and enjoy the day!
Hm - there's something in the looks those senior personnel are giving us...
Yes, enjoy our day! We have the Port of Old Quebec, right at our doorstep!
Here, let me get your picture in front of this tall ship -
We really are lucky to have affordable accommodations right close to th' Old Port!
Hey!
Puff Puff I tried to catch you as you went out, but I had to go back for my hat!
You can't stay in the barracks anymore - new rules. We've been turning away generals this year!
Do you know of any campsites?
And So -
Cheer up! It's not going to be so bad.
We're just lucky to be in a place where you can take a city bus to a campsite!
DEFENSE DE FLÂNER
RTC
Though this final, kilometre walk from the end of the bus line to the campground is a morale tester...
We're almost there!
This sucks!
All I see is gravel quarries!
ROAR!

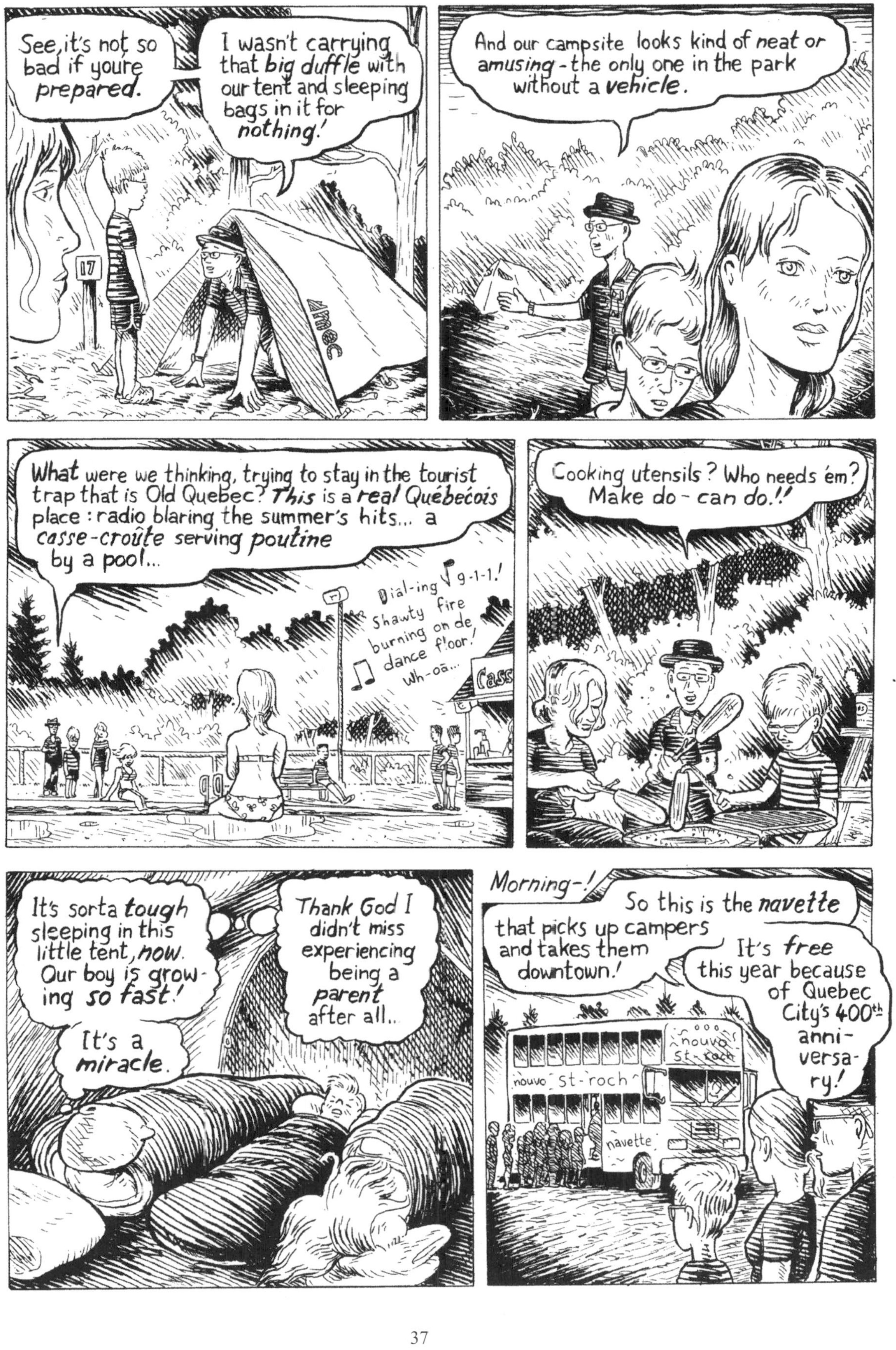
See, it's not so bad if you're prepared.
I wasn't carrying that big duffle with our tent and sleeping bags in it for nothing!
17
mec
And our campsite looks kind of neat or amusing - the only one in the park without a vehicle.
What were we thinking, trying to stay in the tourist trap that is Old Quebec? This is a real Québécois place: radio blaring the summer's hits... a casse-croûte serving poutine by a pool...
Dial-ing 9-1-1! Shawty fire burning on de dance floor! Wh-oa...
Cass
Cooking utensils? Who needs 'em? Make do - can do.!!
It's sorta tough sleeping in this little tent, now. Our boy is growing so fast!
It's a miracle.
Thank God I didn't miss experiencing being a parent after all..
Morning-!
So this is the navette that picks up campers and takes them downtown!
It's free this year because of Quebec City's 400th anniversary!
nouvo st-roch
navette

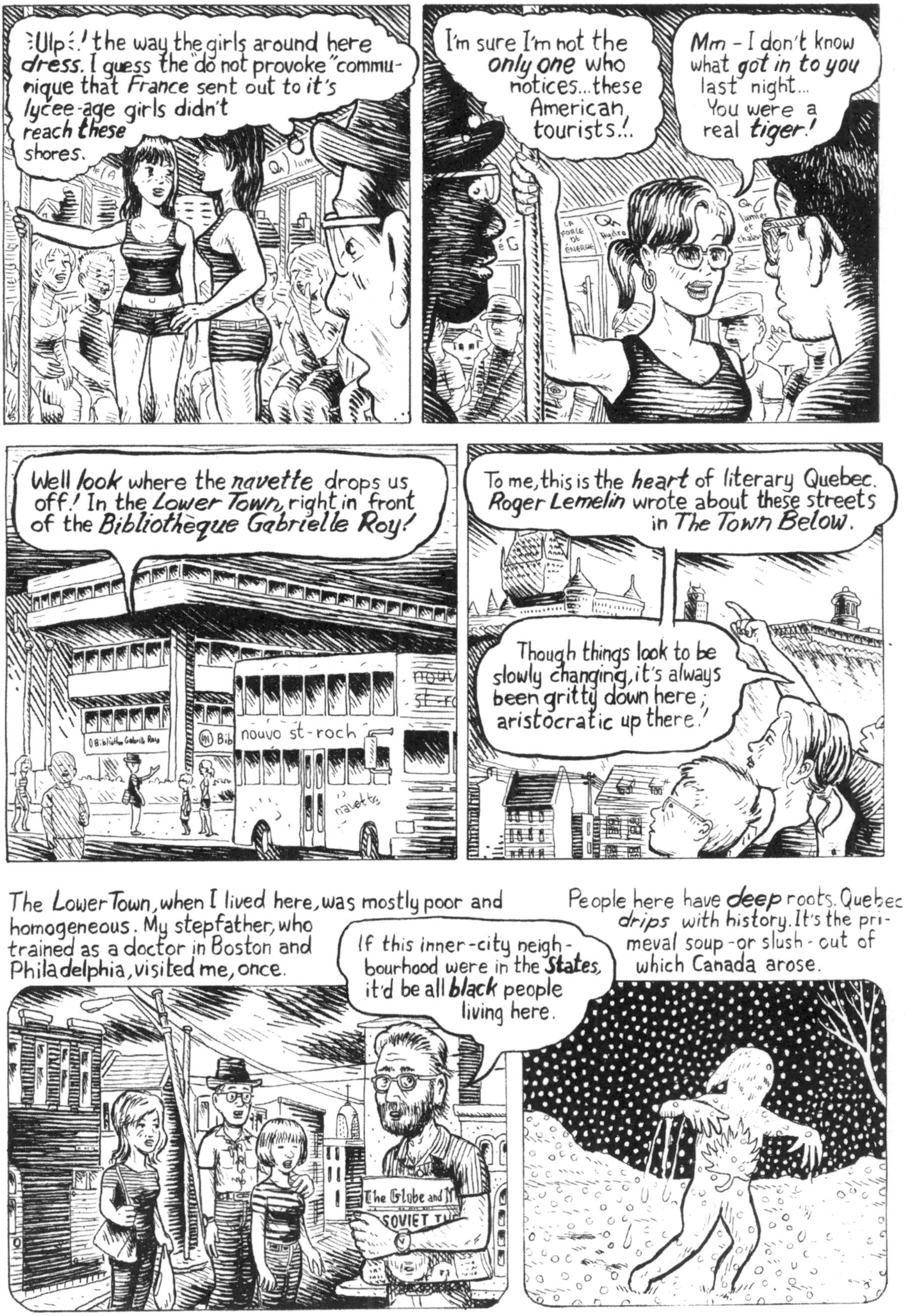

:Ulp:! the way the girls around here *dress*. I guess the "do not provoke" communique that *France* sent out to *it's* lycee-age girls didn't reach *these* shores.
I'm sure I'm not the *only one* who notices... these American tourists!.
Mm - I don't know what *got in to you* last night... You were a real *tiger*!
Well *look* where the *navette* drops us off! In the *Lower Town*, right in front of the *Bibliothèque Gabrielle Roy*!
nouvo st-roch
To me, this is the *heart* of literary Quebec. *Roger Lemelin* wrote about these streets in *The Town Below*.
Though things look to be slowly changing, it's always been gritty down here; aristocratic up there.
The *Lower Town*, when I lived here, was mostly poor and homogeneous. My stepfather, who trained as a doctor in Boston and Philadelphia, visited me, once.
If this inner-city neighbourhood were in the *States*, it'd be all *black* people living here.
People here have *deep* roots. Quebec *drips* with history. It's the primeval soup - or slush - out of which Canada arose.

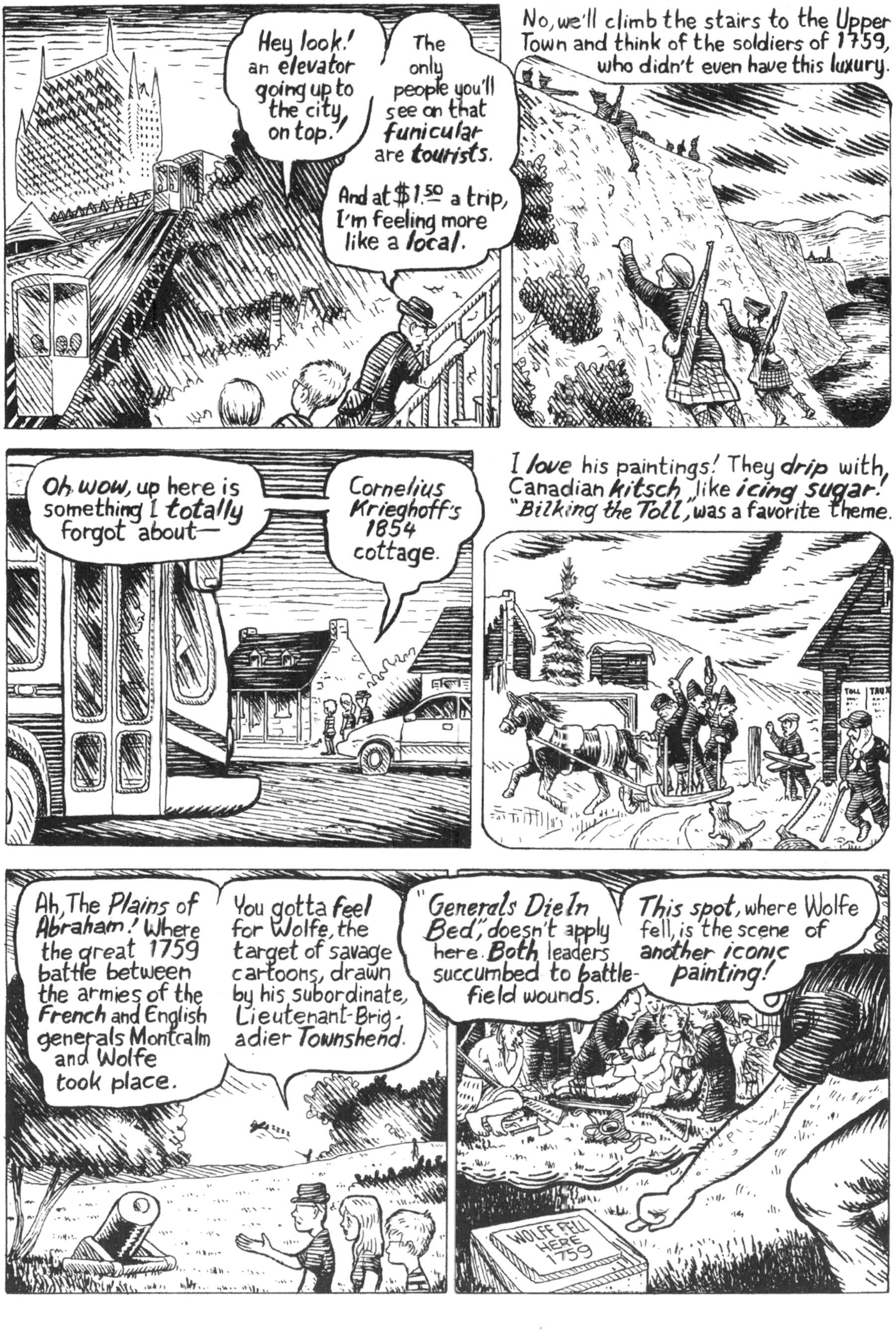
Hey look! an elevator going up to the city, on top.
The only people you'll see on that funicular are tourists.
And at $1.50 a trip, I'm feeling more like a local.
No, we'll climb the stairs to the Upper Town and think of the soldiers of 1759, who didn't even have this luxury.
Oh, wow, up here is something I totally forgot about—
Cornelius Krieghoff's 1854 cottage.
I love his paintings! They drip with Canadian kitsch, like icing sugar! "Bilking the Toll," was a favorite theme.
TOLL
Ah, The Plains of Abraham! Where the great 1759 battle between the armies of the French and English generals Montcalm and Wolfe took place.
You gotta feel for Wolfe, the target of savage cartoons, drawn by his subordinate, Lieutenant-Brigadier Townshend.
"Generals Die In Bed," doesn't apply here. Both leaders succumbed to battle-field wounds.
This spot, where Wolfe fell, is the scene of another iconic painting!
WOLFE FELL HERE 1759

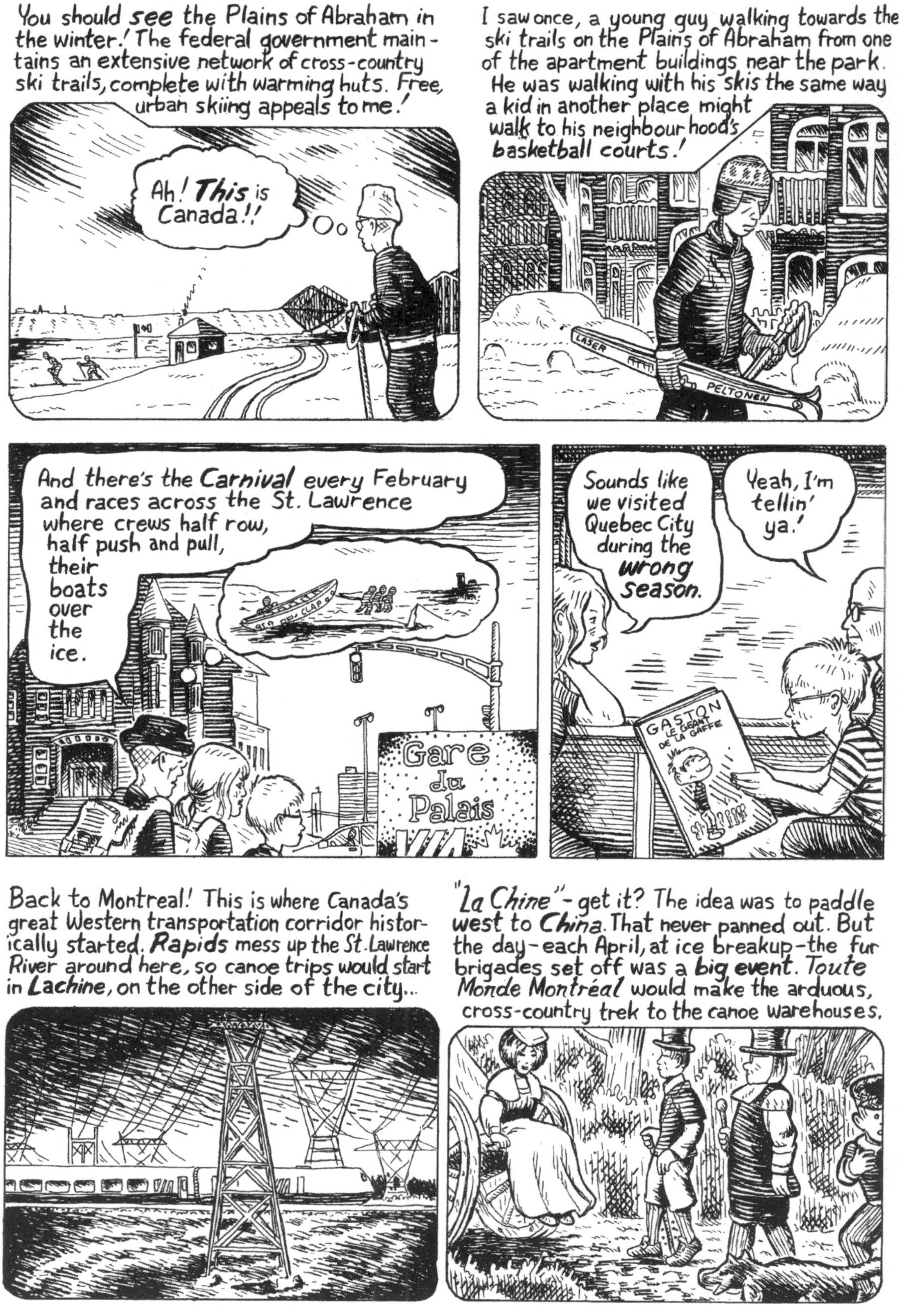
You should see the Plains of Abraham in the winter! The federal government maintains an extensive network of cross-country ski trails, complete with warming huts. Free, urban skiing appeals to me!
Ah! This is Canada!!
I saw once, a young guy walking towards the ski trails on the Plains of Abraham from one of the apartment buildings near the park. He was walking with his skis the same way a kid in another place might walk to his neighbourhood's basketball courts!
LASER
PELTONEN
And there's the Carnival every February and races across the St. Lawrence where crews half row, half push and pull, their boats over the ice.
Gare du Palais
VIA
Sounds like we visited Quebec City during the wrong season.
Yeah, I'm tellin' ya!
GASTON LE GEANT DE LA GAFFE
Back to Montreal! This is where Canada's great Western transportation corridor historically started. Rapids mess up the St. Lawrence River around here, so canoe trips would start in Lachine, on the other side of the city...
"La Chine" - get it? The idea was to paddle west to China. That never panned out. But the day - each April, at ice breakup - the fur brigades set off was a big event. Toute Monde Montréal would make the arduous, cross-country trek to the canoe warehouses.

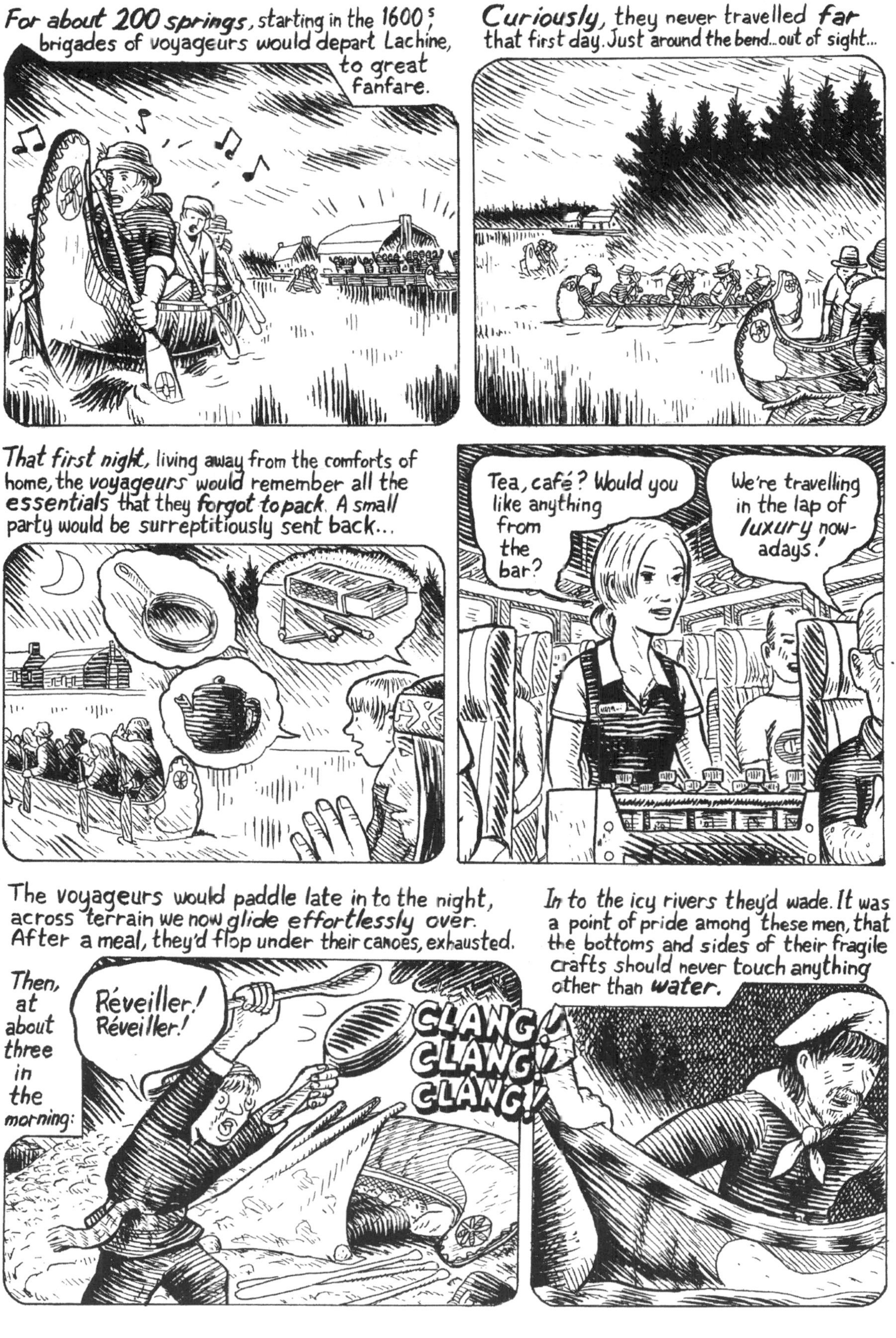
For about 200 springs, starting in the 1600s, brigades of voyageurs would depart Lachine, to great fanfare.
Curiously, they never travelled far that first day. Just around the bend...out of sight...
That first night, living away from the comforts of home, the voyageurs would remember all the essentials that they forgot to pack. A small party would be surreptitiously sent back...
Tea, café? Would you like anything from the bar?
We're travelling in the lap of luxury nowadays!
The voyageurs would paddle late in to the night, across terrain we now glide effortlessly over. After a meal, they'd flop under their canoes, exhausted.
Then, at about three in the morning:
Réveiller! Réveiller!
CLANG! CLANG! CLANG!
In to the icy rivers they'd wade. It was a point of pride among these men, that the bottoms and sides of their fragile crafts should never touch anything other than water.

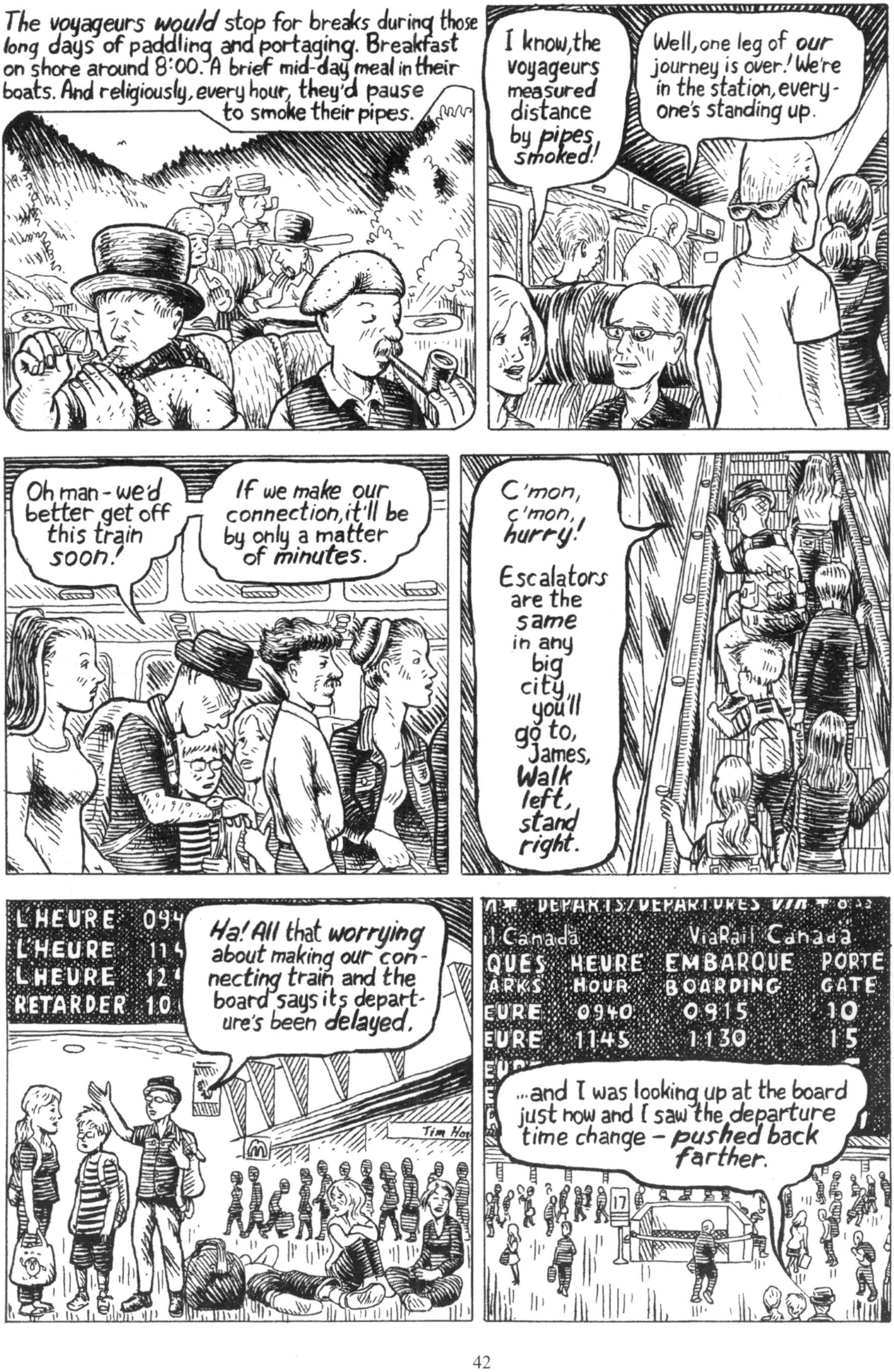

The voyageurs would stop for breaks during those long days of paddling and portaging. Breakfast on shore around 8:00. A brief mid-day meal in their boats. And religiously, every hour, they'd pause to smoke their pipes.
I know, the voyageurs measured distance by pipes smoked!
Well, one leg of our journey is over! We're in the station, everyone's standing up.
Oh man - we'd better get off this train soon!
If we make our connection, it'll be by only a matter of minutes.
C'mon, c'mon, hurry!
Escalators are the same in any big city you'll go to, James. Walk left, stand right.
L'HEURE 094
L'HEURE 114
L'HEURE 124
RETARDER 10
Ha! All that worrying about making our connecting train and the board says its departure's been delayed.
Tim Ho
DEPARTS/DEPARTURES VIA
ViaRail Canada
QUES HEURE EMBARQUE PORTE
ARKS HOUR BOARDING GATE
EURE 0940 0915 10
EURE 1145 1130 15
...and I was looking up at the board just now and I saw the departure time change - pushed back farther.
17

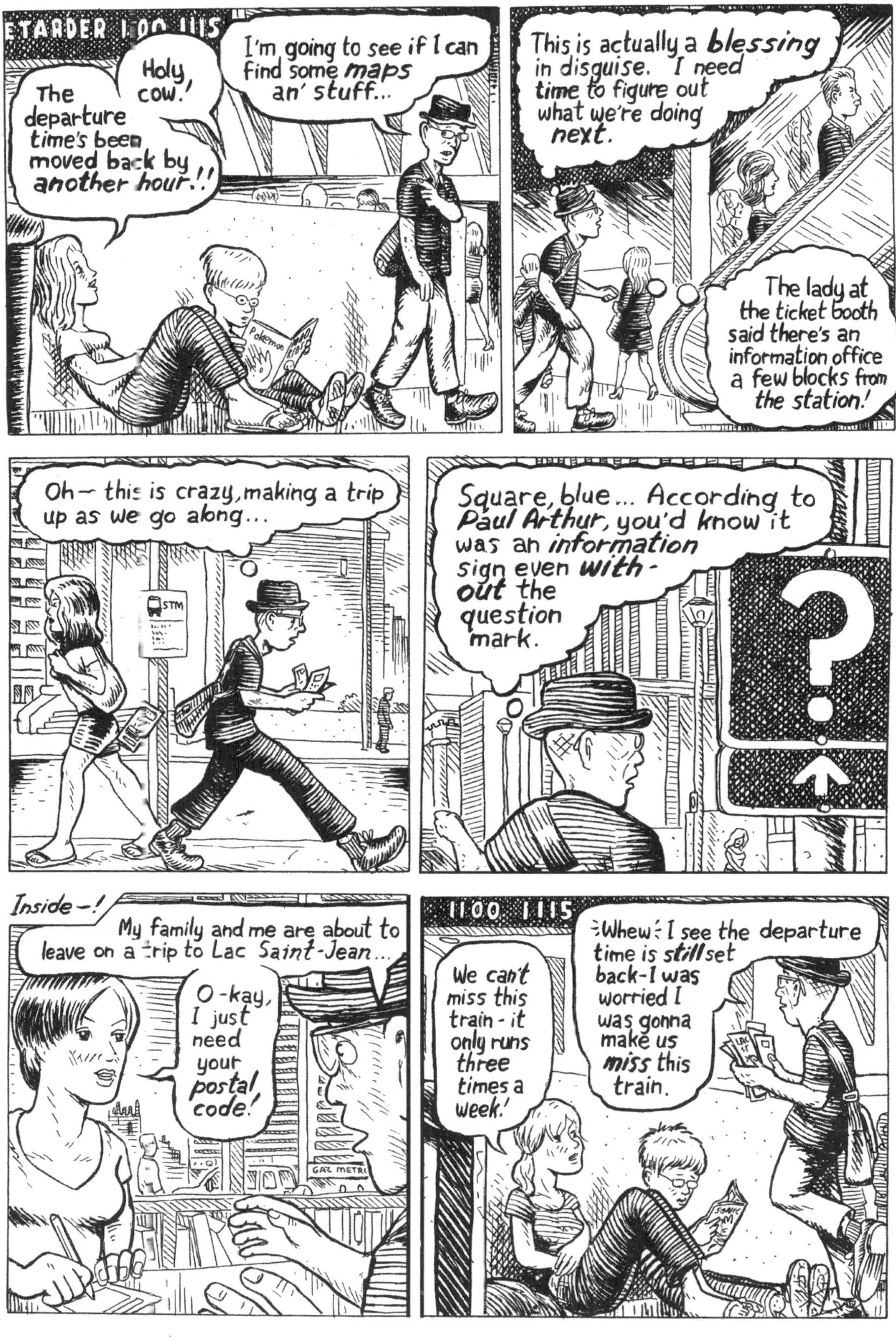
ETARDER 1100 1115
Holy, cow.!
The departure time's been moved back by another hour.!!
I'm going to see if I can find some maps an' stuff...
Pokemon
This is actually a blessing in disguise. I need time to figure out what we're doing next.
The lady at the ticket booth said there's an information office a few blocks from the station!
Oh — this is crazy, making a trip up as we go along...
STM
Square, blue... According to Paul Arthur, you'd know it was an information sign even with-out the question mark.
?
Inside —!
My family and me are about to leave on a trip to Lac Saint-Jean...
O-kay, I just need your postal code!
GAZ METRO
1100 1115
We can't miss this train - it only runs three times a week!
Whew! I see the departure time is still set back-I was worried I was gonna make us miss this train.

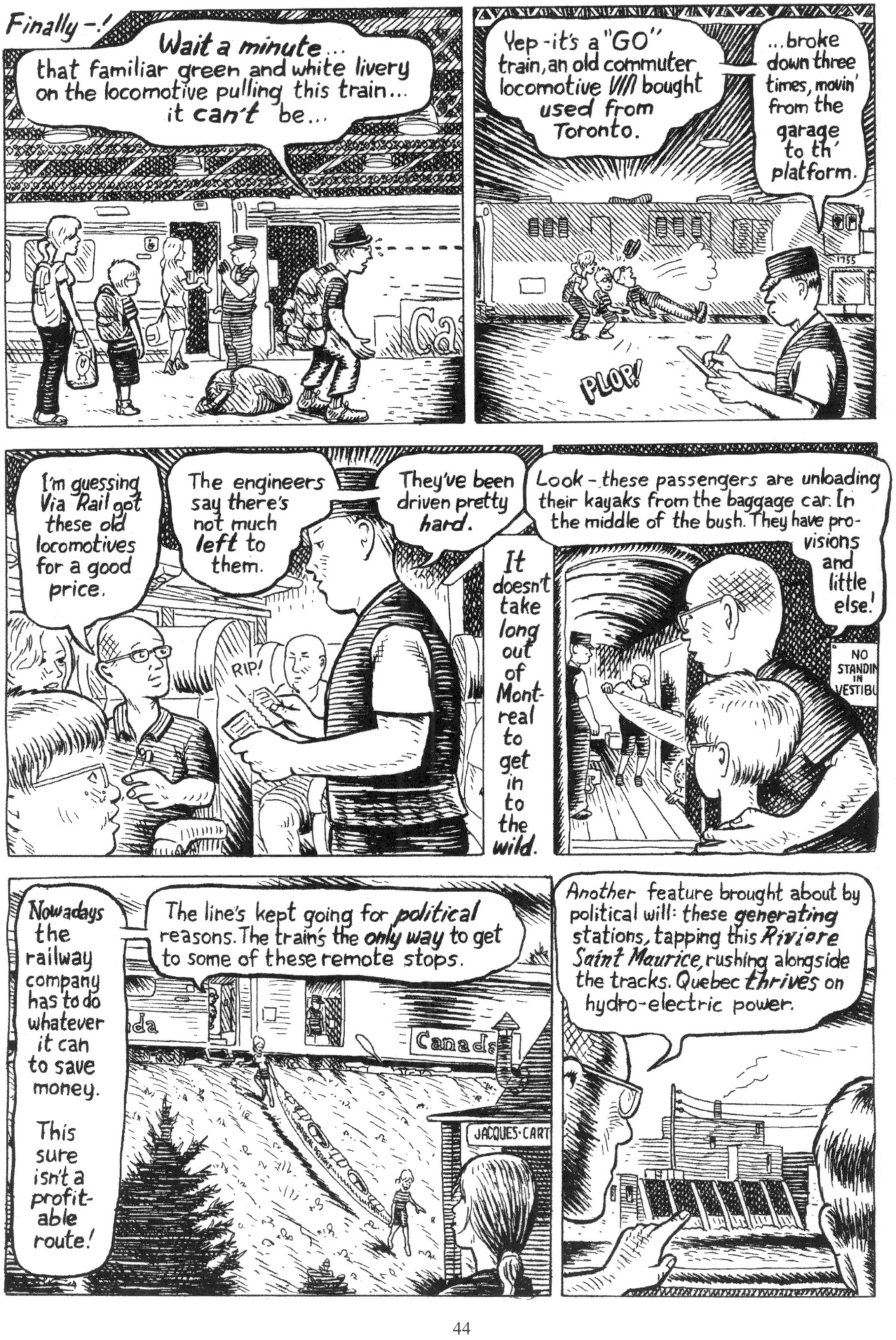
Finally-!
Wait a minute... that familiar green and white livery on the locomotive pulling this train... it can't be...
Yep-it's a "GO" train, an old commuter locomotive VIA bought used from Toronto.
...broke down three times, movin' from the garage to th' platform.
PLOP!
I'm guessing Via Rail got these old locomotives for a good price.
The engineers say there's not much left to them.
They've been driven pretty hard.
RIP!
It doesn't take long out of Montreal to get in to the wild.
Look-these passengers are unloading their kayaks from the baggage car. In the middle of the bush. They have provisions and little else!
NO STANDIN IN VESTIBU
Nowadays the railway company has to do whatever it can to save money.
This sure isn't a profitable route!
The line's kept going for political reasons. The train's the only way to get to some of these remote stops.
Canada
JACQUES-CART
Another feature brought about by political will: these generating stations, tapping this Riviere Saint Maurice, rushing alongside the tracks. Quebec thrives on hydro-electric power.

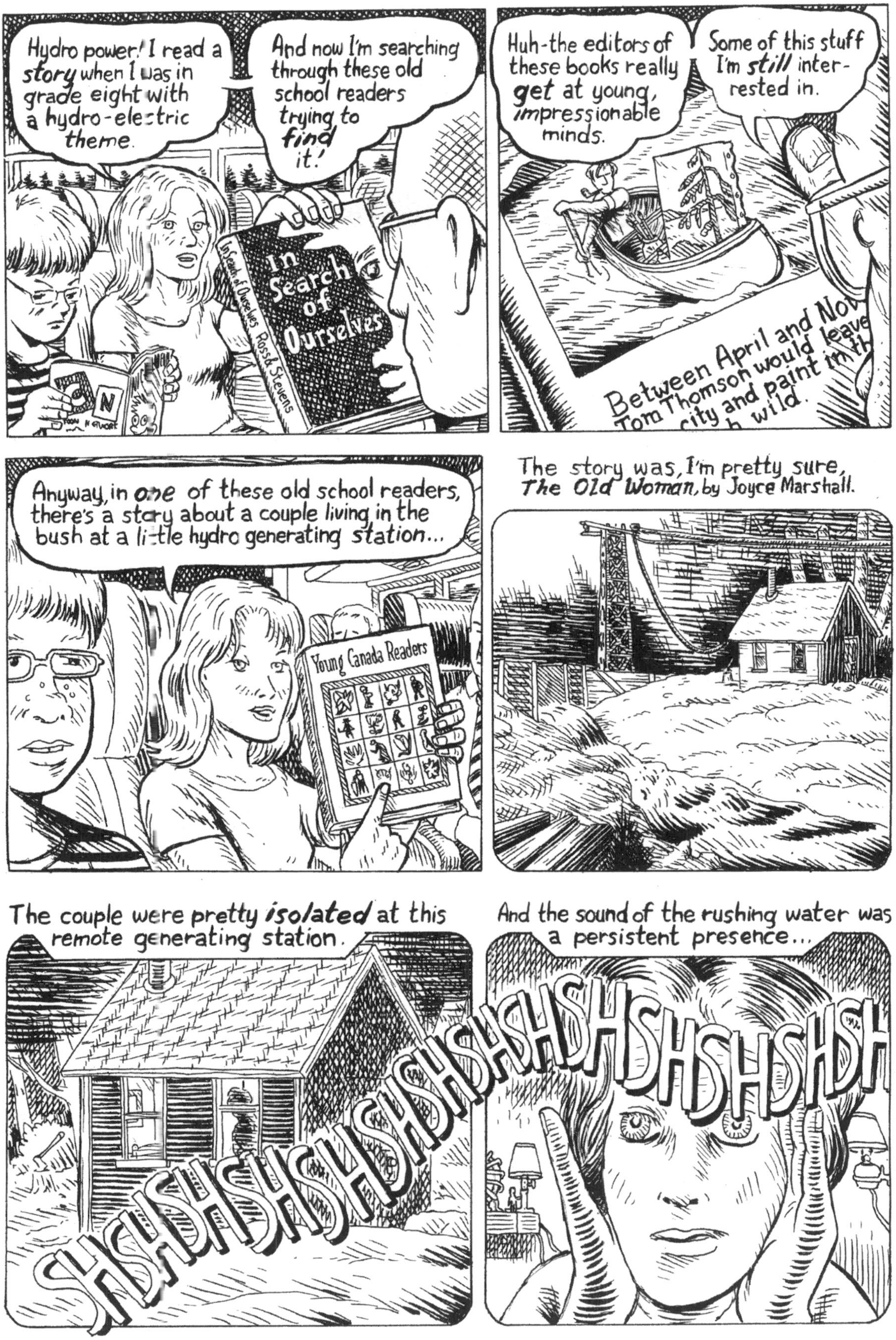
Hydro power! I read a story when I was in grade eight with a hydro-electric theme.
And now I'm searching through these old school readers trying to find it!
In Search of Ourselves
Ross & Stevens
Huh-the editors of these books really get at young, impressionable minds.
Some of this stuff I'm still interested in.
Between April and Nov
Tom Thomson would leave
city and paint in th
Anyway, in one of these old school readers, there's a story about a couple living in the bush at a little hydro generating station...
Young Canada Readers
The story was, I'm pretty sure, The Old Woman, by Joyce Marshall.
The couple were pretty isolated at this remote generating station.
SHSHSHSHSHSHSHSHSHSHSHSHSHSHSH
And the sound of the rushing water was a persistent presence...

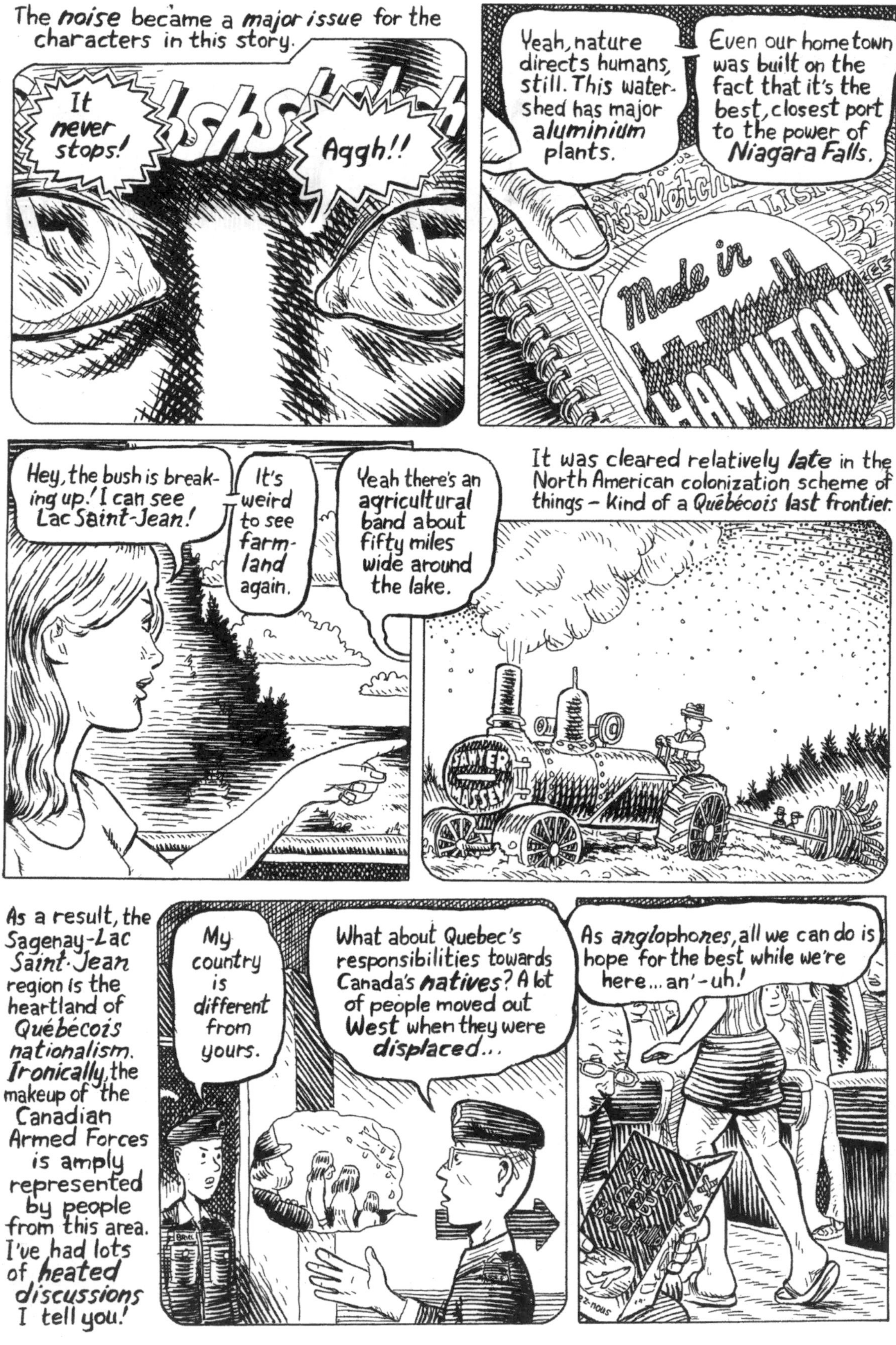
The noise became a major issue for the characters in this story.
It never stops!
Aggh!!
Yeah, nature directs humans, still. This watershed has major aluminium plants.
Even our hometown was built on the fact that it's the best, closest port to the power of Niagara Falls.
Made in HAMILTON
Hey, the bush is breaking up! I can see Lac Saint-Jean!
It's weird to see farmland again.
Yeah there's an agricultural band about fifty miles wide around the lake.
It was cleared relatively late in the North American colonization scheme of things – kind of a Québécois last frontier.
SAWYER MASSEY
As a result, the Sagenay-Lac Saint-Jean region is the heartland of Québécois nationalism. Ironically, the makeup of the Canadian Armed Forces is amply represented by people from this area. I've had lots of heated discussions I tell you!
My country is different from yours.
What about Quebec's responsibilities towards Canada's natives? A lot of people moved out West when they were displaced...
As anglophones, all we can do is hope for the best while we're here... an'-uh!

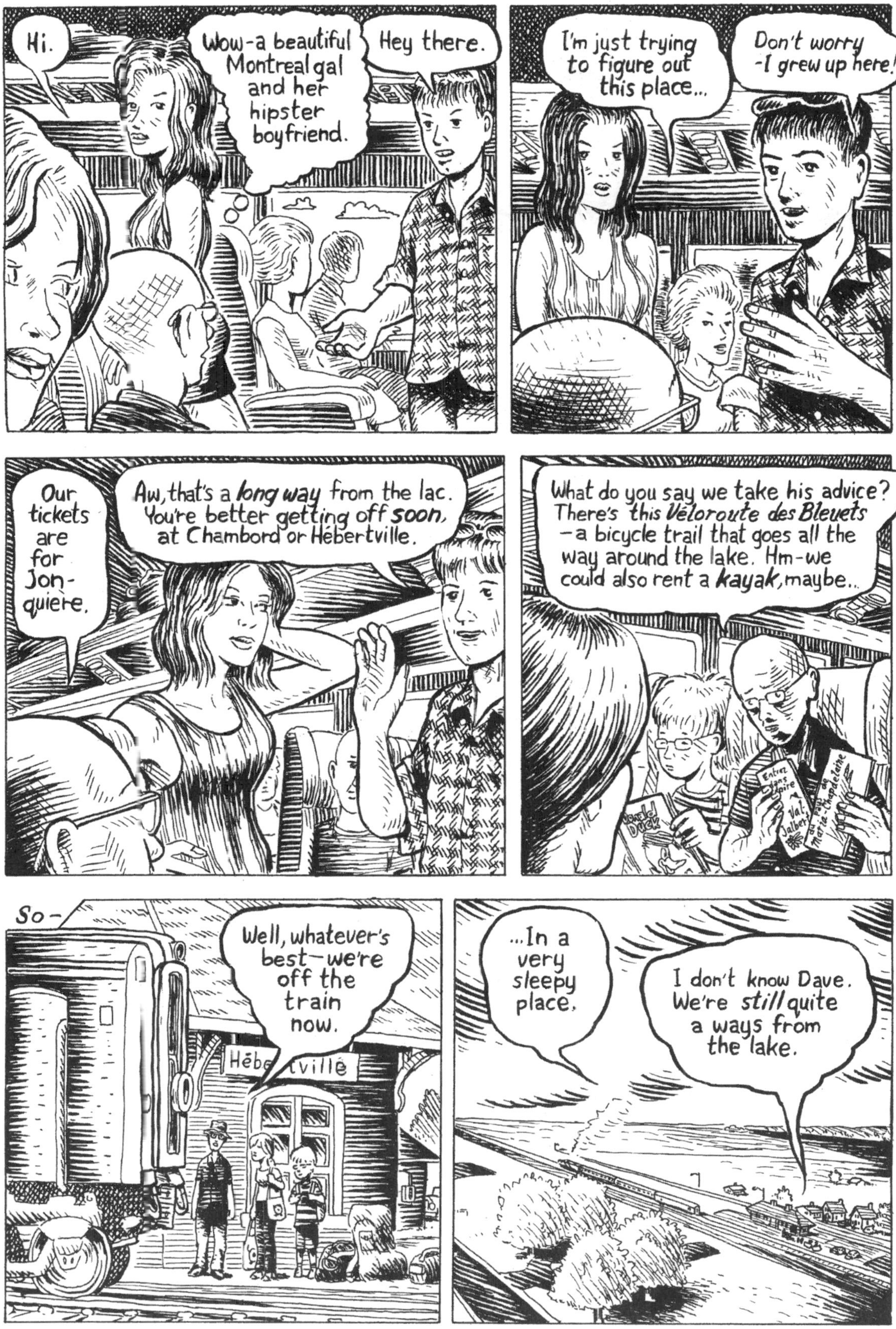
Hi.
Wow-a beautiful Montreal gal and her hipster boyfriend.
Hey there.
I'm just trying to figure out this place...
Don't worry -I grew up here!
Our tickets are for Jon-quière.
Aw, that's a *long way* from the lac. You're better getting off *soon*, at Chambord or Hébertville.
What do you say we take his advice? There's this *Véloroute des Bleuets* -a bicycle trail that goes all the way around the lake. Hm-we could also rent a *kayak*, maybe...
So-
Well, whatever's best-we're off the train now.
...In a very sleepy place.
I don't know Dave. We're *still* quite a ways from the lake.

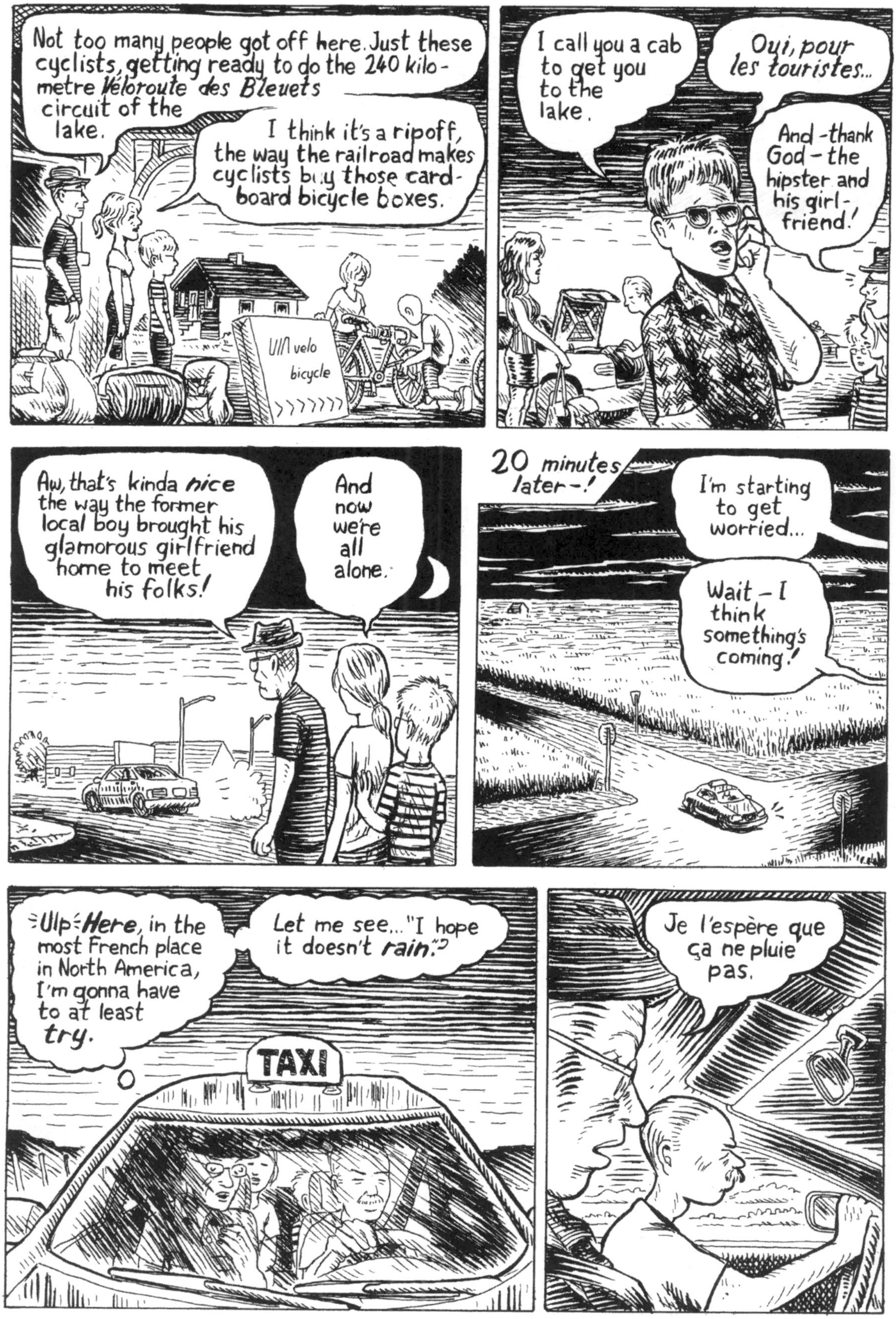
Not too many people got off here. Just these cyclists, getting ready to do the 240 kilometre Véloroute des Bleuets circuit of the lake.
I think it's a ripoff, the way the railroad makes cyclists buy those cardboard bicycle boxes.
velo
bicycle
I call you a cab to get you to the lake.
Oui, pour les touristes...
And -thank God - the hipster and his girlfriend!
Aw, that's kinda nice the way the former local boy brought his glamorous girlfriend home to meet his folks!
And now we're all alone.
20 minutes later-!
I'm starting to get worried...
Wait - I think something's coming!
Ulp Here, in the most French place in North America, I'm gonna have to at least try.
Let me see..."I hope it doesn't rain."?
TAXI
Je l'espère que ça ne pluie pas.

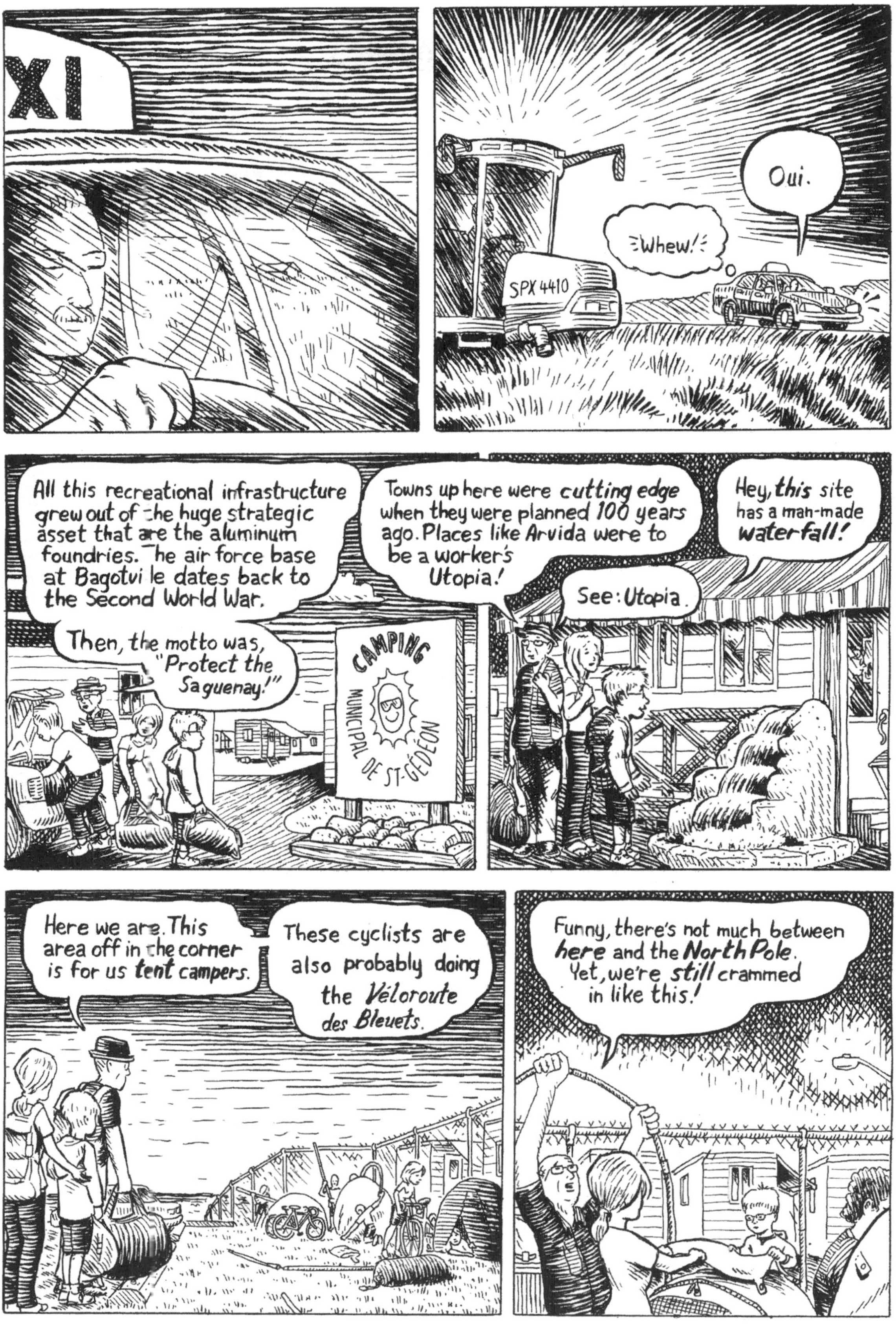
XI
Oui.
Whew!
SPX 4410
All this recreational infrastructure grew out of the huge strategic asset that are the aluminum foundries. The air force base at Bagotville dates back to the Second World War.
Then, the motto was, "Protect the Saguenay!"
CAMPING MUNICIPAL DE ST-GÉDEON
Towns up here were cutting edge when they were planned 100 years ago. Places like Arvida were to be a worker's Utopia!
See: Utopia.
Hey, this site has a man-made waterfall!
Here we are. This area off in the corner is for us tent campers.
These cyclists are also probably doing the Véloroute des Bleuets.
Funny, there's not much between here and the North Pole. Yet, we're still crammed in like this!

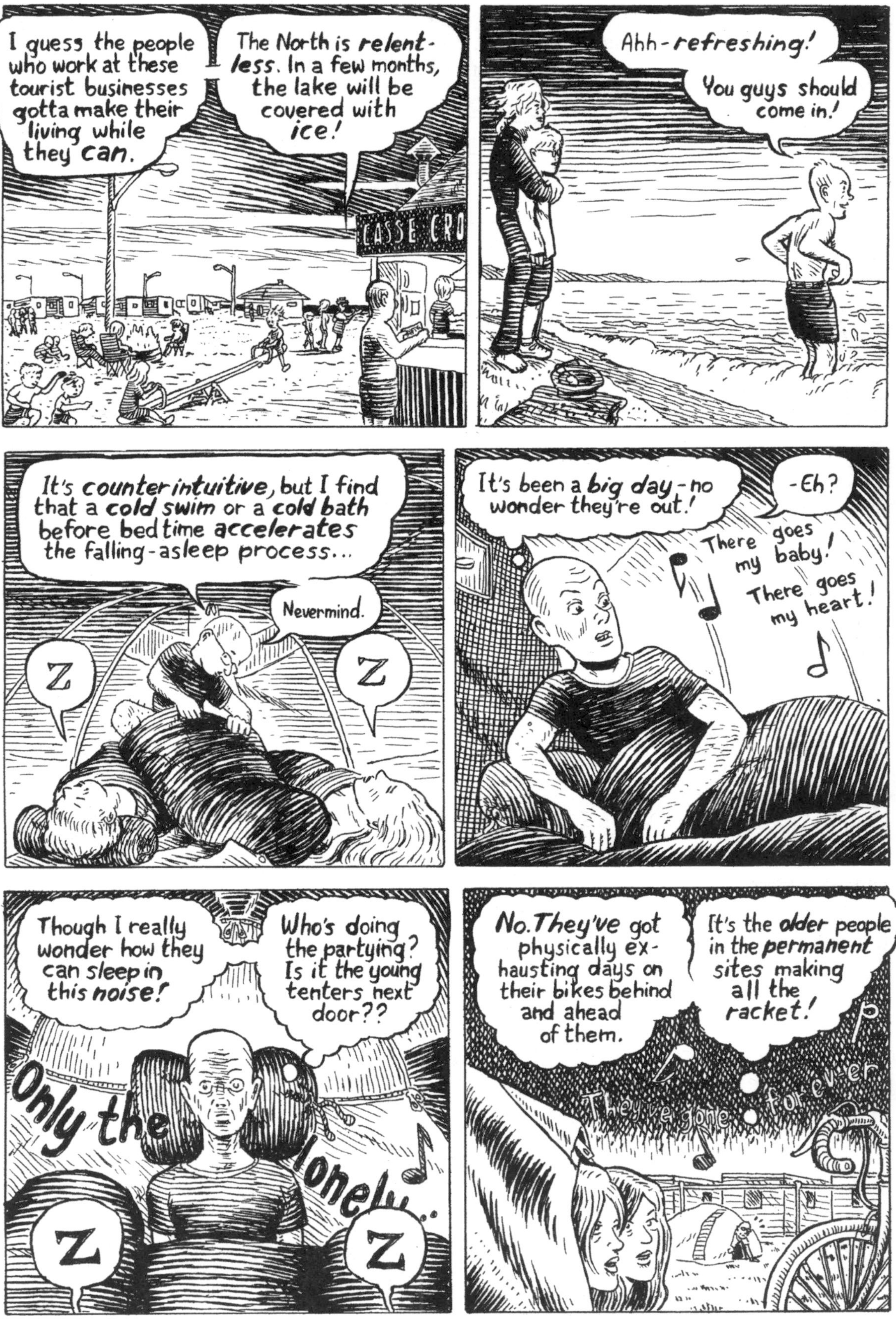
I guess the people who work at these tourist businesses gotta make their living while they can.
The North is relentless. In a few months, the lake will be covered with ice!
CASSE CRO
Ahh-refreshing!
You guys should come in!
It's counterintuitive, but I find that a cold swim or a cold bath before bedtime accelerates the falling-asleep process...
Nevermind.
Z
Z
It's been a big day-no wonder they're out!
-Eh?
There goes my baby!
There goes my heart!
Though I really wonder how they can sleep in this noise!
Who's doing the partying? Is it the young tenters next door??
Only the lonely..
Z
Z
No. They've got physically exhausting days on their bikes behind and ahead of them.
It's the older people in the permanent sites making all the racket!
They've gone for-e-ver

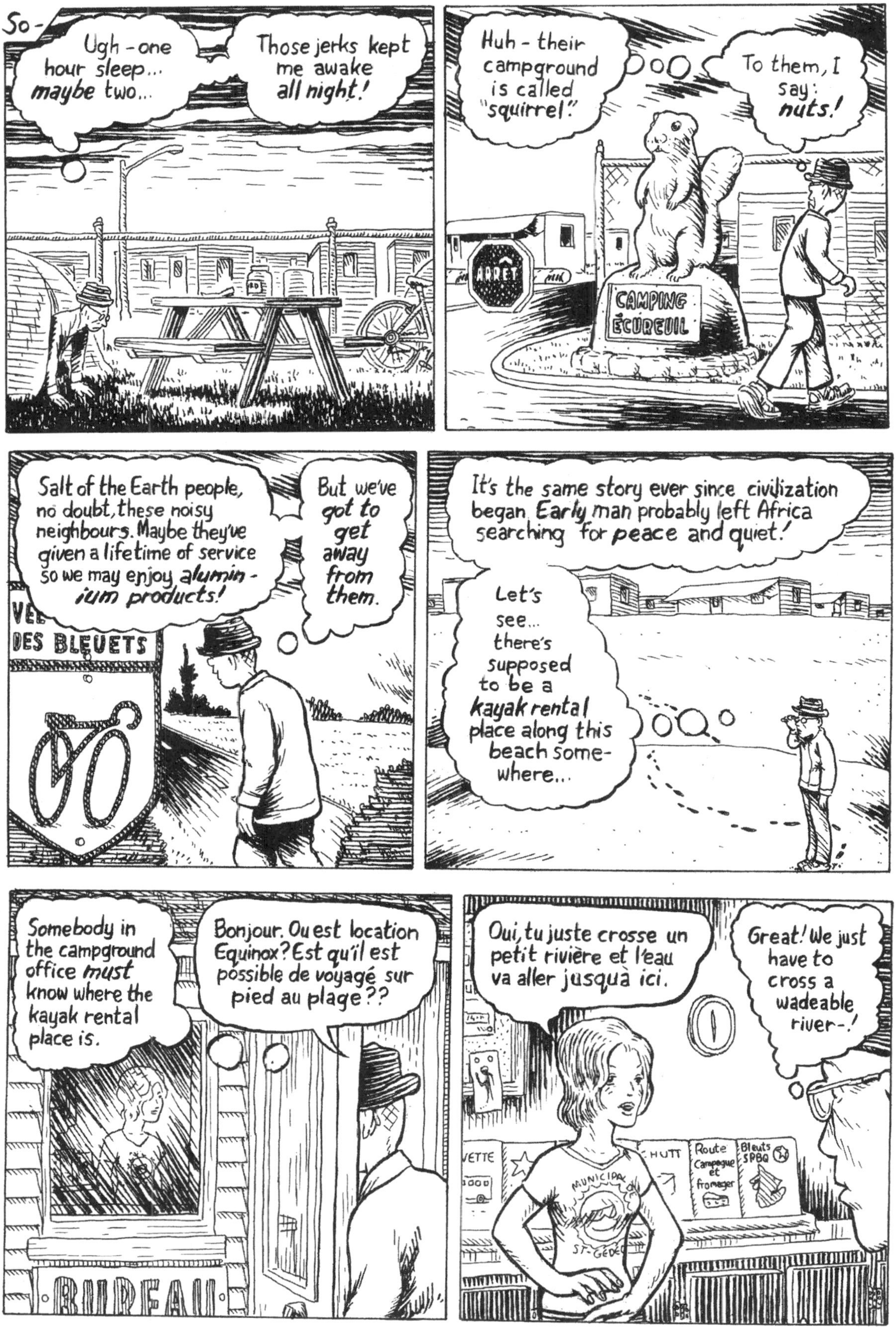
So-
Ugh - one hour sleep... maybe two...
Those jerks kept me awake all night!
Huh - their campground is called "squirrel."
To them, I say: nuts!
ARRÊT
CAMPING ÉCUREUIL
Salt of the Earth people, no doubt, these noisy neighbours. Maybe they've given a lifetime of service so we may enjoy aluminium products!
But we've got to get away from them.
DES BLEUETS
It's the same story ever since civilization began. Early man probably left Africa searching for peace and quiet!
Let's see... there's supposed to be a kayak rental place along this beach somewhere...
Somebody in the campground office must know where the kayak rental place is.
Bonjour. Ou est location Equinox? Est qu'il est possible de voyagé sur pied au plage??
BUREAU
Oui, tu juste crosse un petit rivière et l'eau va aller jusquà ici.
Great! We just have to cross a wadeable river-!
MUNICIPAL
ST-GÉDÉO
Route Campagne et fromager
Bleuets SPBQ

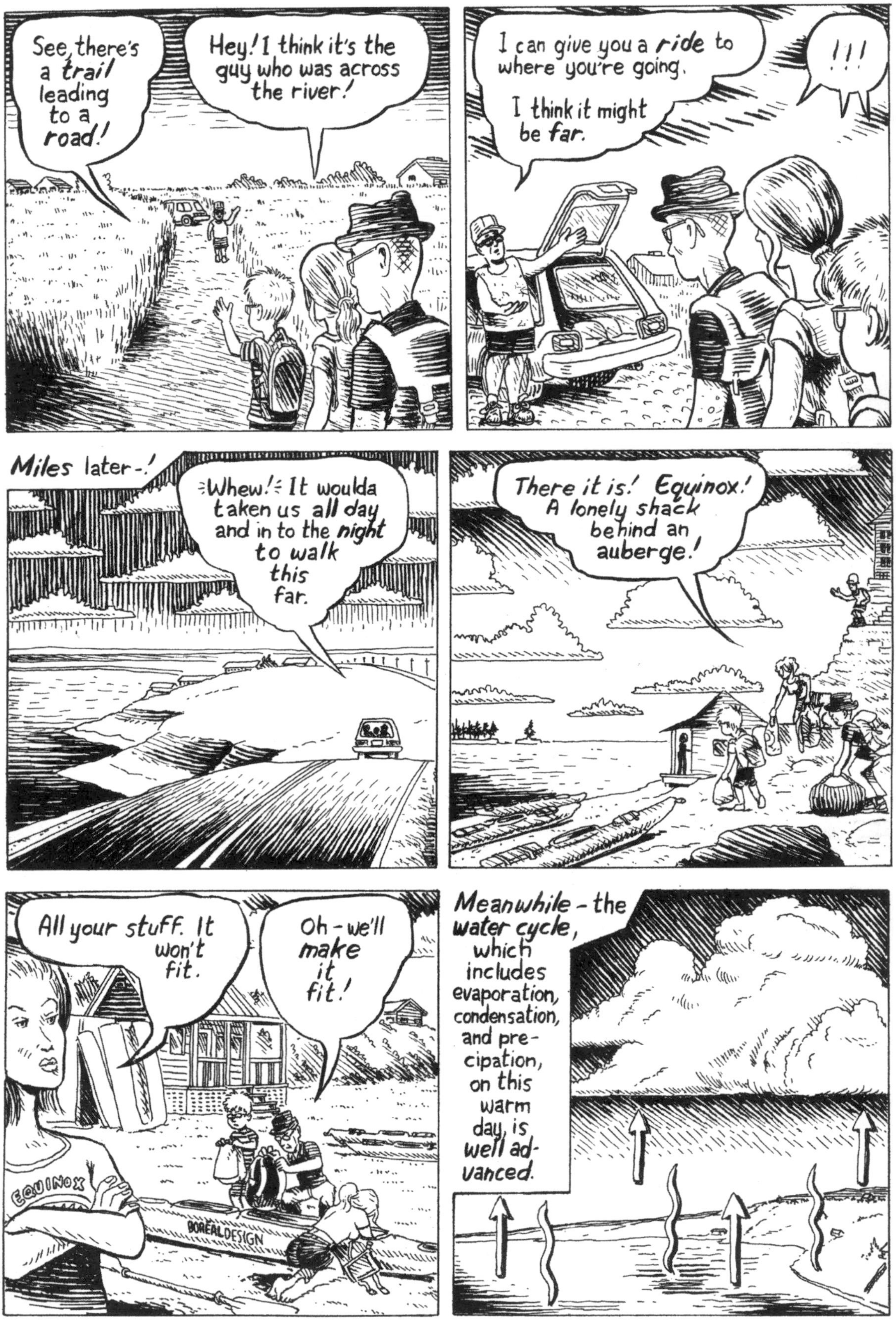
See, there's a trail leading to a road!
Hey! I think it's the guy who was across the river!
I can give you a ride to where you're going.
I think it might be far.
!!!
Miles later-!
Whew! It woulda taken us all day and in to the night to walk this far.
There it is! Equinox! A lonely shack behind an auberge!
All your stuff. It won't fit.
Oh-we'll make it fit!
EQUINOX
BOREAL DESIGN
Meanwhile - the water cycle, which includes evaporation, condensation, and precipitation, on this warm day, is well advanced.

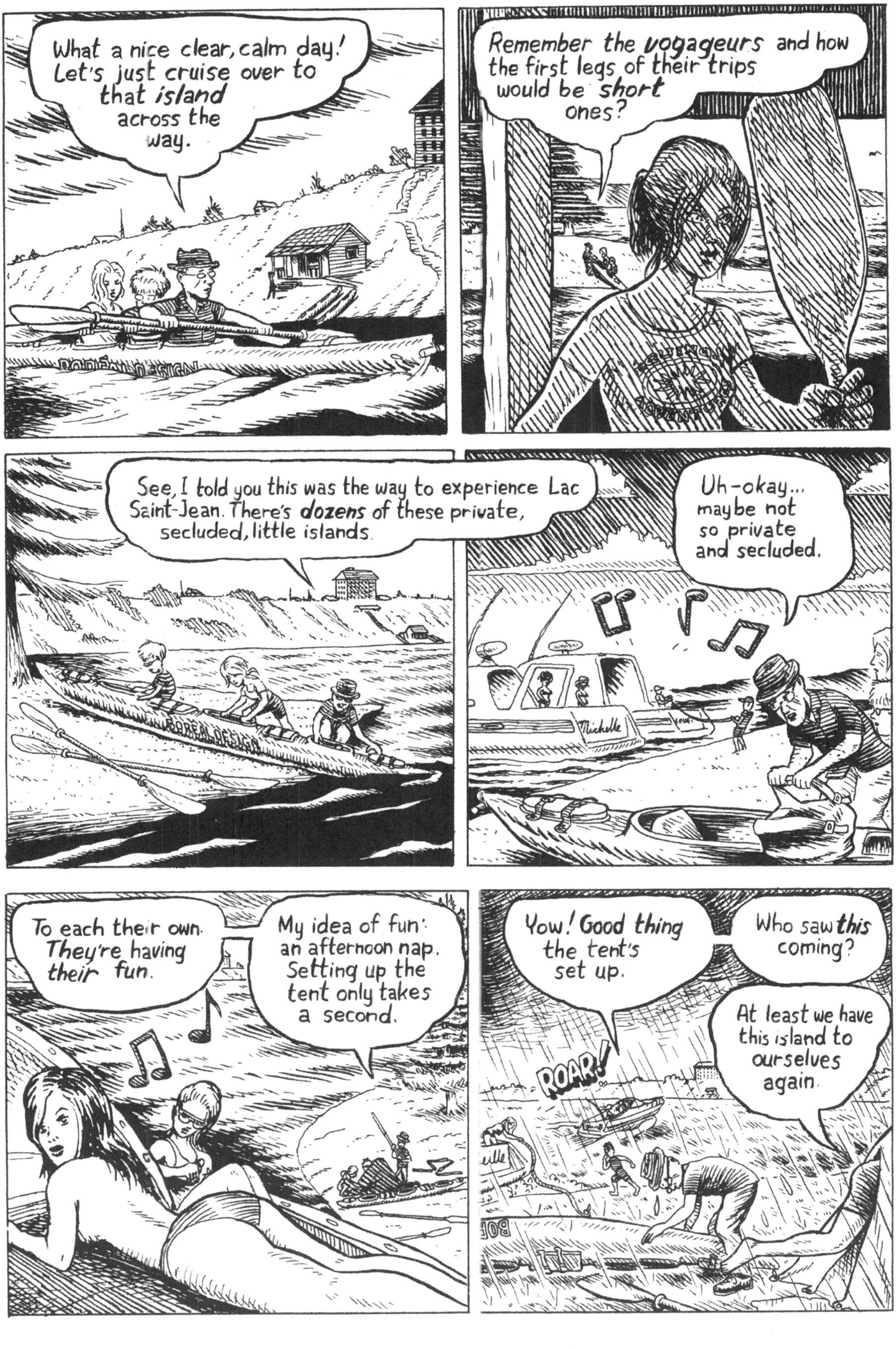
What a nice clear, calm day! Let's just cruise over to that island across the way.
BOREAL DESIGN
Remember the voyageurs and how the first legs of their trips would be short ones?
See, I told you this was the way to experience Lac Saint-Jean. There's dozens of these private, secluded, little islands.
BOREAL DESIGN
Uh-okay... maybe not so private and secluded.
Michelle
To each their own. They're having their fun.
My idea of fun: an afternoon nap. Setting up the tent only takes a second.
Yow! Good thing the tent's set up.
Who saw this coming?
At least we have this island to ourselves again.
ROAR!

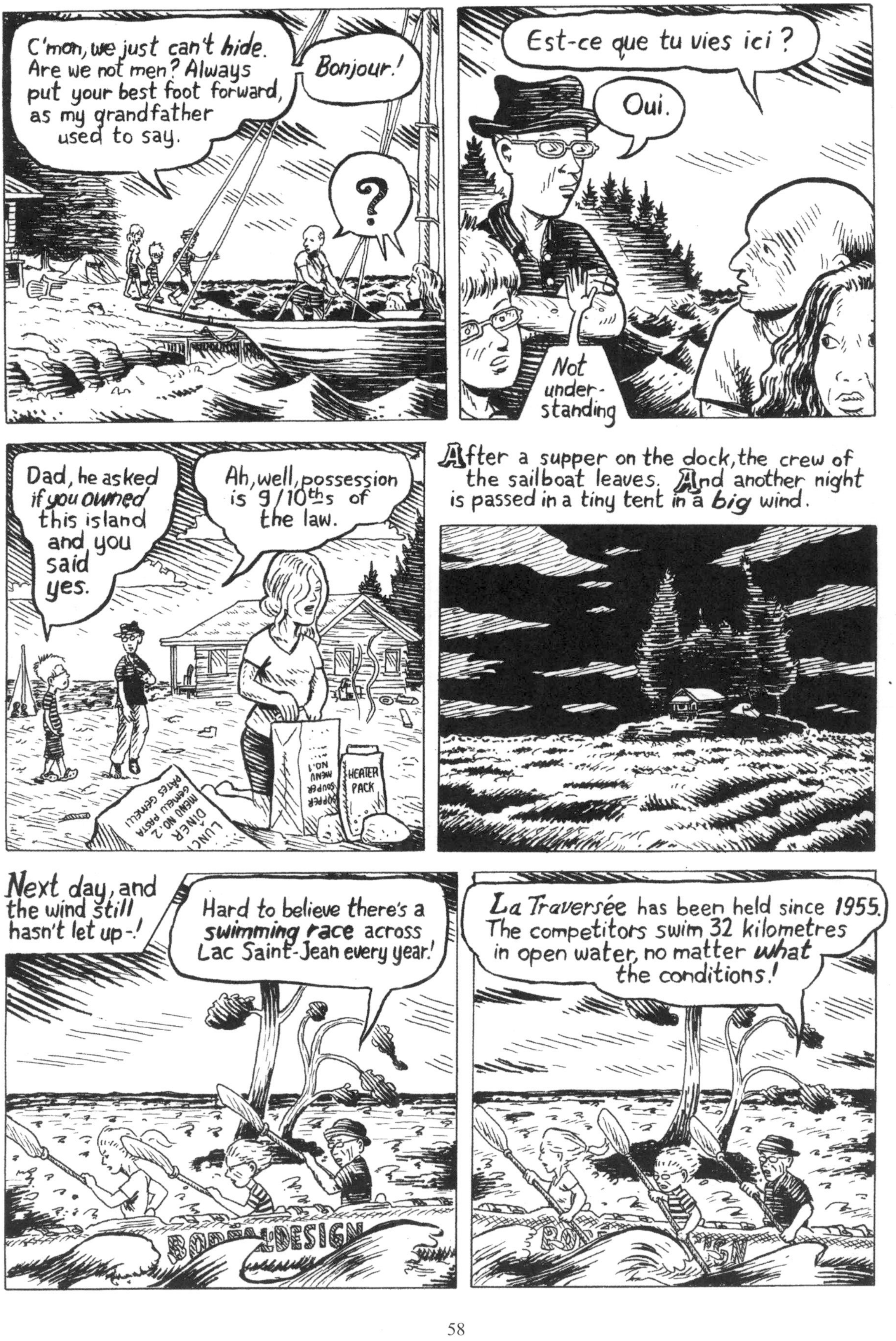

C'mon, we just can't hide. Are we not men? Always put your best foot forward, as my grandfather used to say.
Bonjour!
?
Est-ce que tu vies ici?
Oui.
Not under-standing
Dad, he asked if you owned this island and you said yes.
Ah, well, possession is 9/10ths of the law.
HEATER PACK
After a supper on the dock, the crew of the sailboat leaves. And another night is passed in a tiny tent in a big wind.
Next day, and the wind still hasn't let up-!
Hard to believe there's a swimming race across Lac Saint-Jean every year!
La Traversée has been held since 1955. The competitors swim 32 kilometres in open water, no matter what the conditions!

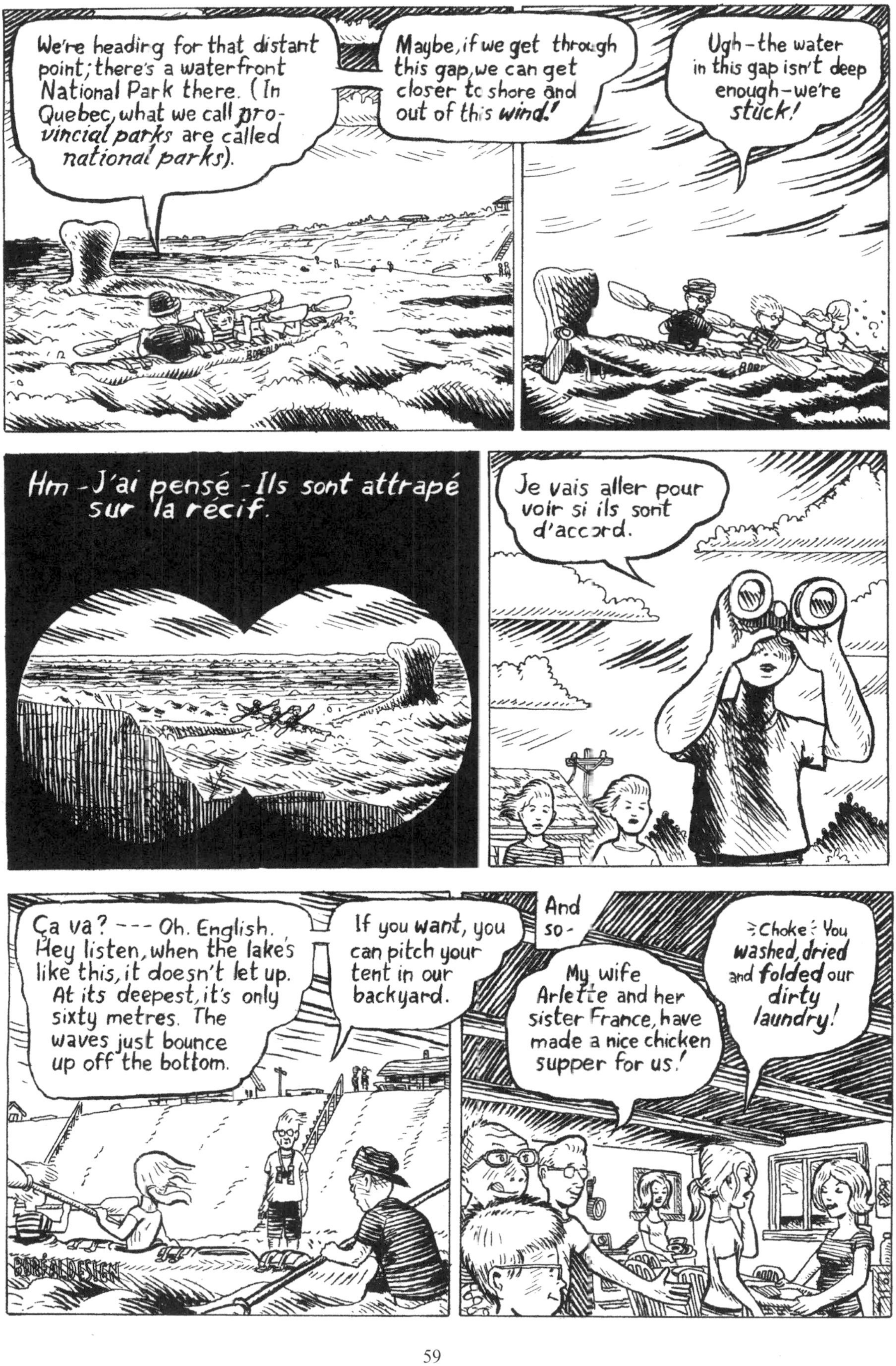

We're heading for that distant point; there's a waterfront National Park there. (In Quebec, what we call provincial parks are called national parks).
Maybe, if we get through this gap, we can get closer to shore and out of this wind!
Ugh – the water in this gap isn't deep enough – we're stuck!
Hm – J'ai pensé – Ils sont attrapé sur la récif.
Je vais aller pour voir si ils sont d'accord.
Ça va? --- Oh. English. Hey listen, when the lake's like this, it doesn't let up. At its deepest, it's only sixty metres. The waves just bounce up off the bottom.
If you want, you can pitch your tent in our backyard.
And so-
My wife Arlette and her sister France, have made a nice chicken supper for us!
Choke You washed, dried and folded our dirty laundry!

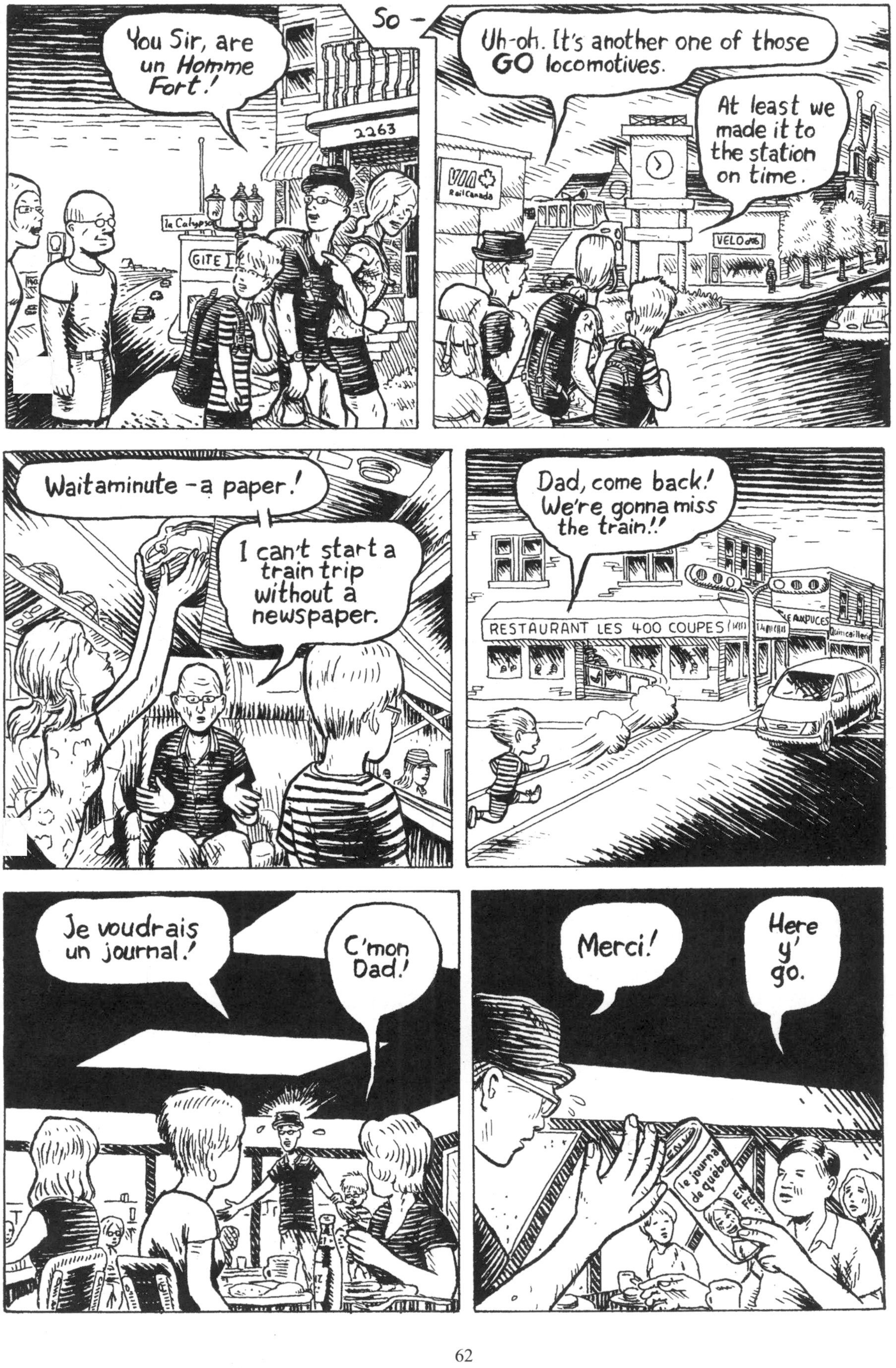
You Sir, are un Homme Fort!
2263
la Calypso
GITE
So –
Uh-oh. It's another one of those GO locomotives.
At least we made it to the station on time.
VIA Rail Canada
Waitaminute – a paper!
I can't start a train trip without a newspaper.
Dad, come back! We're gonna miss the train!!
RESTAURANT LES 400 COUPES
Je voudrais un journal!
C'mon Dad!
Merci!
Here y' go.
le journal de québec

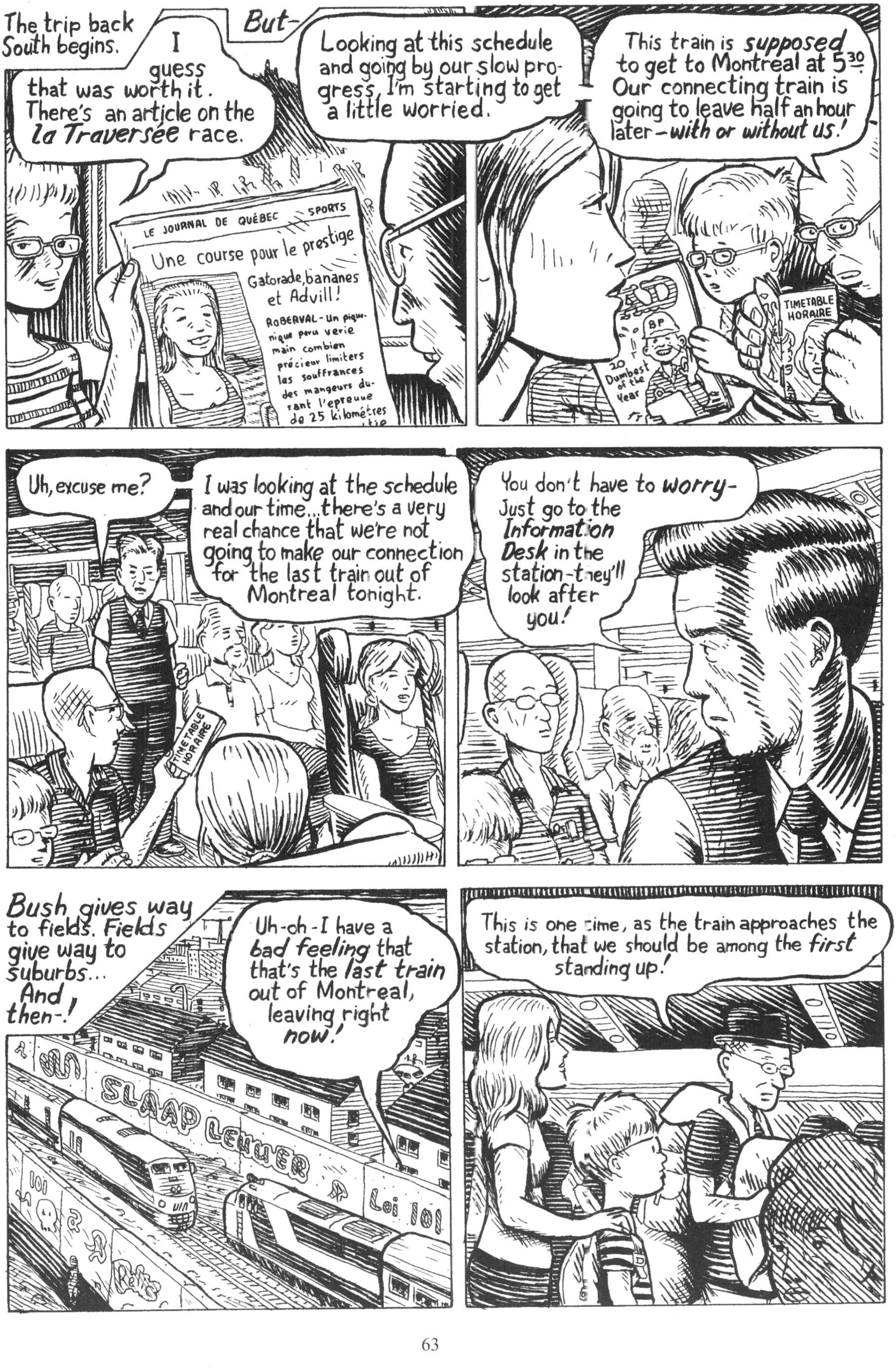

The trip back South begins.
I guess that was worth it. There's an article on the *la Traversée* race.
LE JOURNAL DE QUÉBEC
SPORTS
Une course pour le prestige
Gatorade, bananes et Advill!
But-
Looking at this schedule and going by our slow progress, I'm starting to get a little worried.
This train is *supposed* to get to Montreal at 5^{30}. Our connecting train is going to leave half an hour later—*with or without us!*
BP
20 Dumbest of the Year
TIMETABLE HORAIRE
Uh, excuse me?
I was looking at the schedule and our time... there's a very real chance that we're not going to make our connection for the last train out of Montreal tonight.
TIMETABLE HORAIRE
You don't have to *worry*- Just go to the *Information Desk* in the station-they'll look after you!
Bush gives way to fields. Fields give way to suburbs... And then-!
Uh-oh-I have a *bad feeling* that that's the *last train* out of Montreal, leaving right *now!*
Loi 101
VIA
This is one time, as the train approaches the station, that we should be among the *first* standing up!

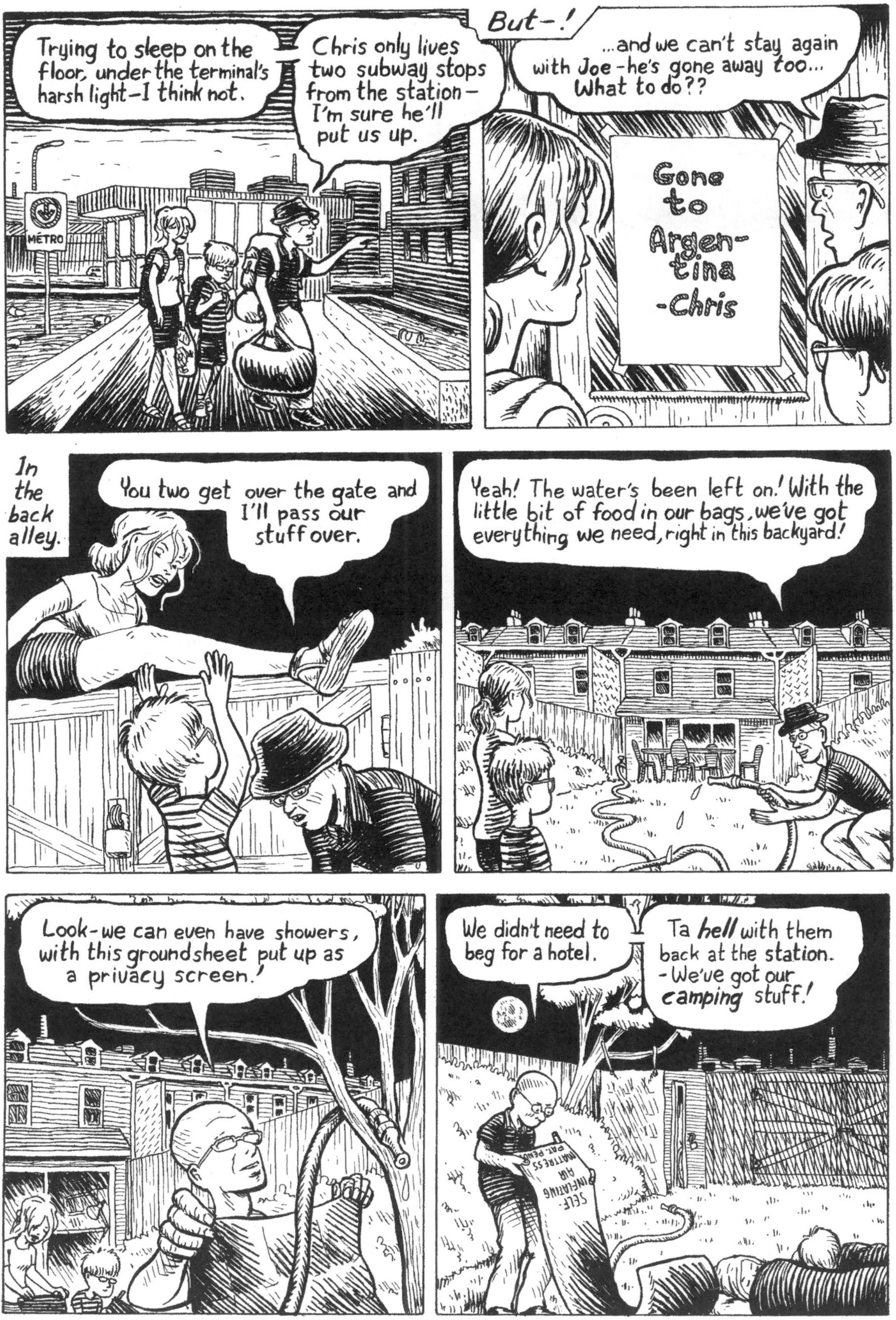
Trying to sleep on the floor, under the terminal's harsh light—I think not.
Chris only lives two subway stops from the station—I'm sure he'll put us up.
MÉTRO
But—!
...and we can't stay again with Joe—he's gone away too... What to do??
Gone to Argen-tina -Chris
In the back alley.
You two get over the gate and I'll pass our stuff over.
Yeah! The water's been left on! With the little bit of food in our bags, we've got everything we need, right in this backyard!
Look—we can even have showers, with this groundsheet put up as a privacy screen!
We didn't need to beg for a hotel.
Ta hell with them back at the station. -We've got our camping stuff!
SELF-INFLATING AIR MATTRESS PAT. PEND.

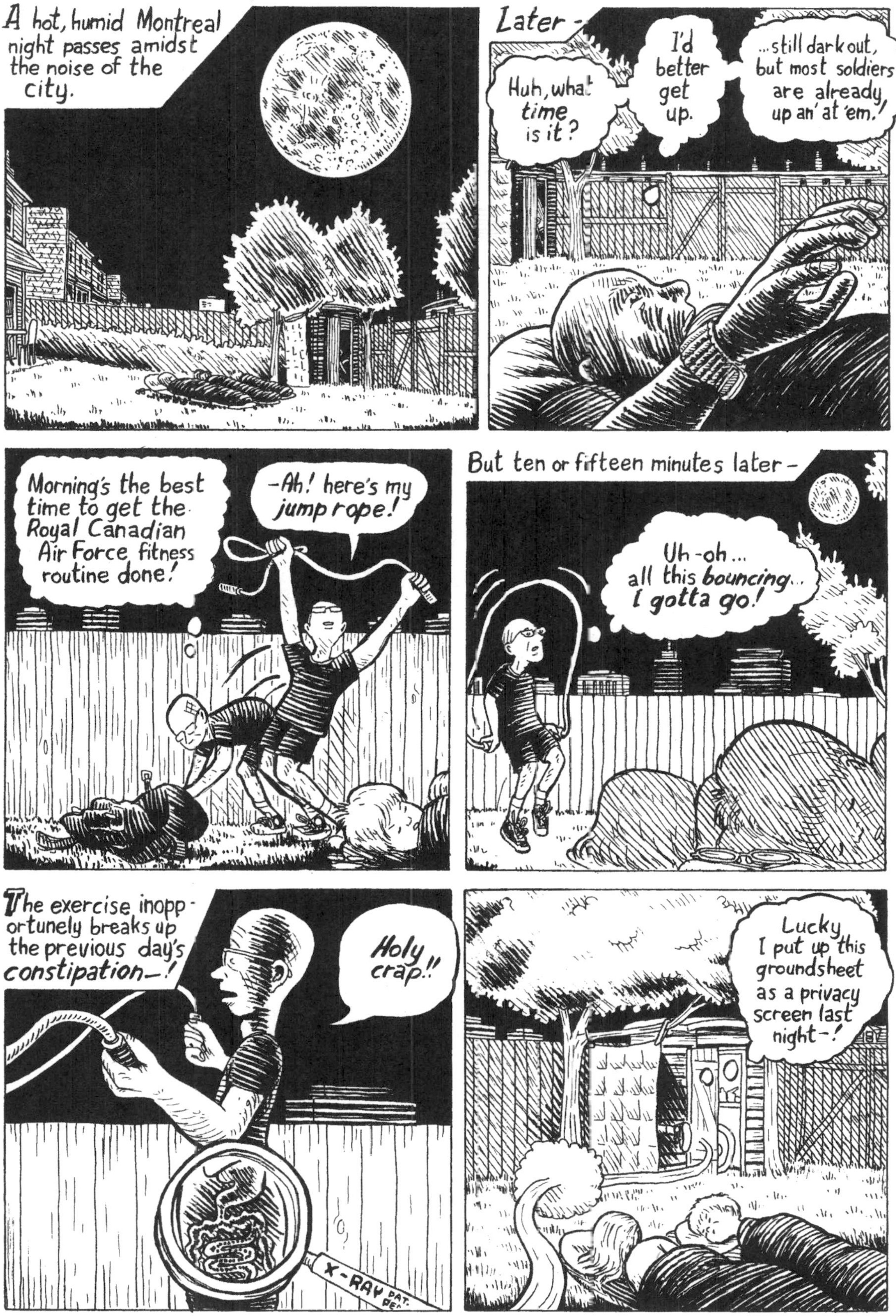
A hot, humid Montreal night passes amidst the noise of the city.
Later -
Huh, what time is it?
I'd better get up.
...still dark out, but most soldiers are already up an' at 'em!
Morning's the best time to get the Royal Canadian Air Force fitness routine done!
-Ah! here's my jump rope!
But ten or fifteen minutes later -
Uh-oh... all this bouncing... I gotta go!
The exercise inopportunely breaks up the previous day's constipation -!
Holy crap!!
X-RAY
Lucky I put up this groundsheet as a privacy screen last night -!

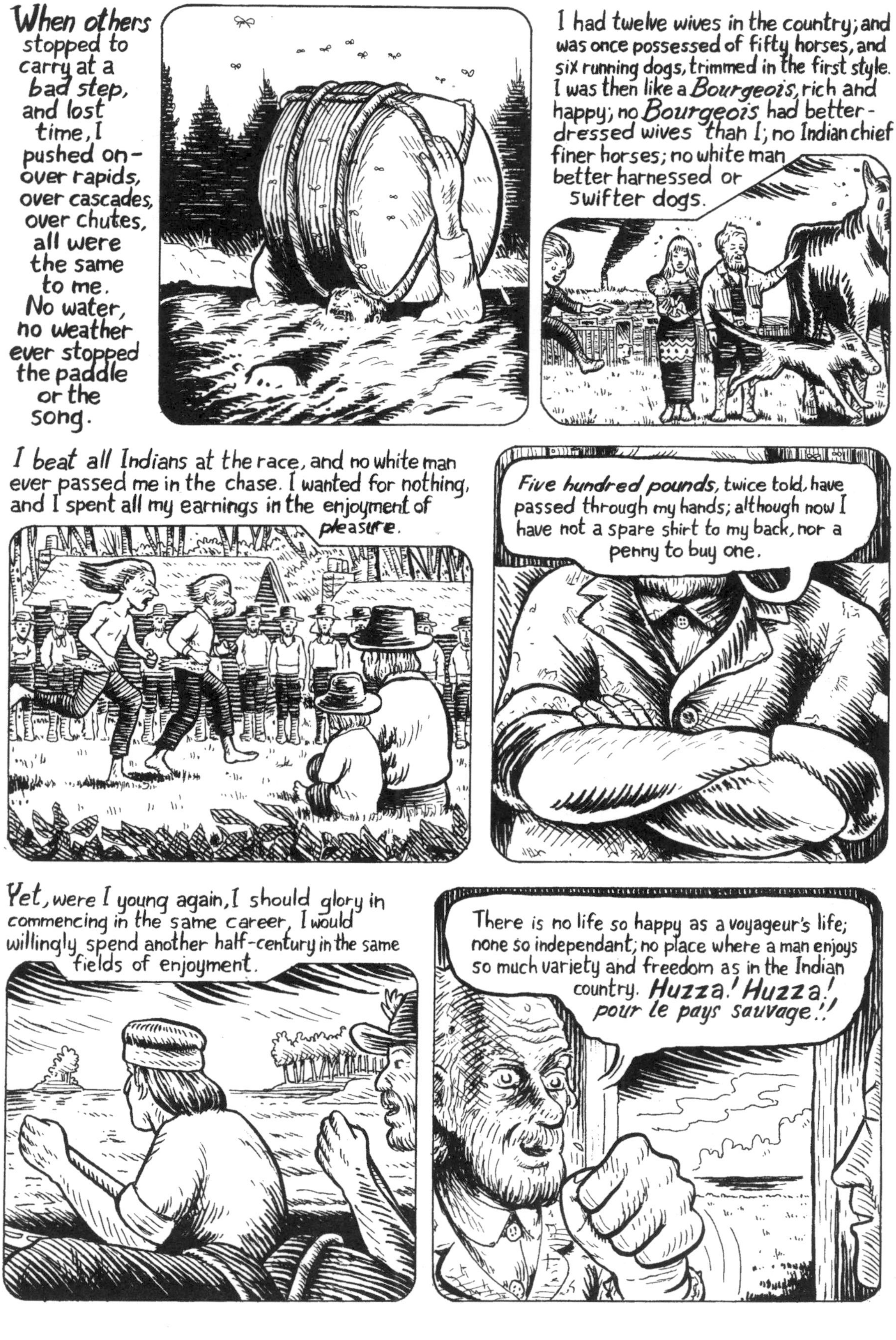
When others stopped to carry at a bad step, and lost time, I pushed on– over rapids, over cascades, over chutes, all were the same to me. No water, no weather ever stopped the paddle or the song.
I had twelve wives in the country; and was once possessed of fifty horses, and six running dogs, trimmed in the first style. I was then like a Bourgeois, rich and happy; no Bourgeois had better-dressed wives than I; no Indian chief finer horses; no white man better harnessed or swifter dogs.
I beat all Indians at the race, and no white man ever passed me in the chase. I wanted for nothing, and I spent all my earnings in the enjoyment of pleasure.
Five hundred pounds, twice told, have passed through my hands; although now I have not a spare shirt to my back, nor a penny to buy one.
Yet, were I young again, I should glory in commencing in the same career, I would willingly spend another half-century in the same fields of enjoyment.
There is no life so happy as a voyageur's life; none so independant; no place where a man enjoys so much variety and freedom as in the Indian country. Huzza! Huzza! pour le pays sauvage!!

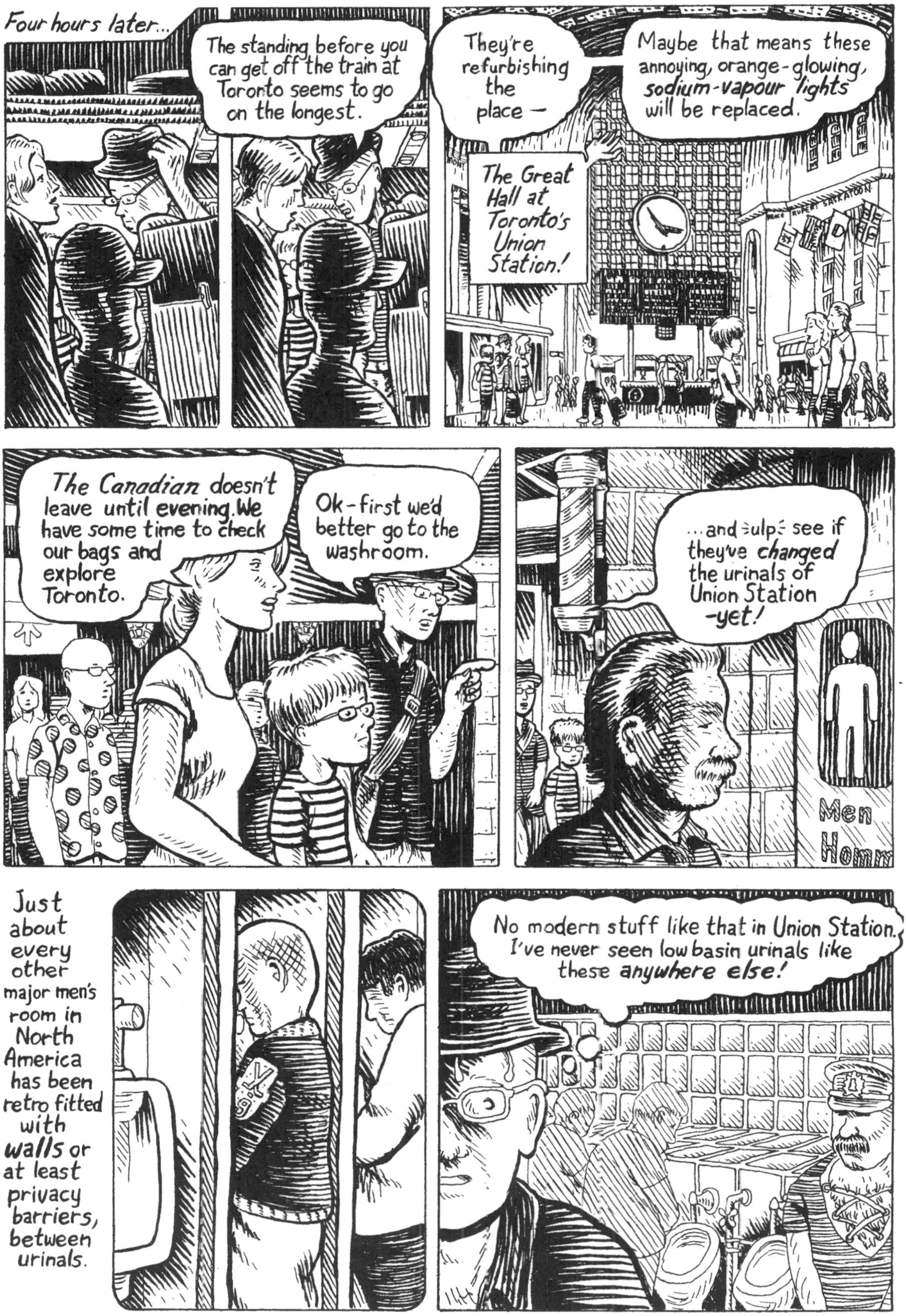
Four hours later...
The standing before you can get off the train at Toronto seems to go on the longest.
They're refurbishing the place —
Maybe that means these annoying, orange-glowing, sodium-vapour lights will be replaced.
The Great Hall at Toronto's Union Station!
The Canadian doesn't leave until evening. We have some time to check our bags and explore Toronto.
Ok - first we'd better go to the washroom.
...and :gulp: see if they've changed the urinals of Union Station -yet!
Men
Just about every other major men's room in North America has been retro fitted with walls or at least privacy barriers, between urinals.
No modern stuff like that in Union Station. I've never seen low basin urinals like these anywhere else!

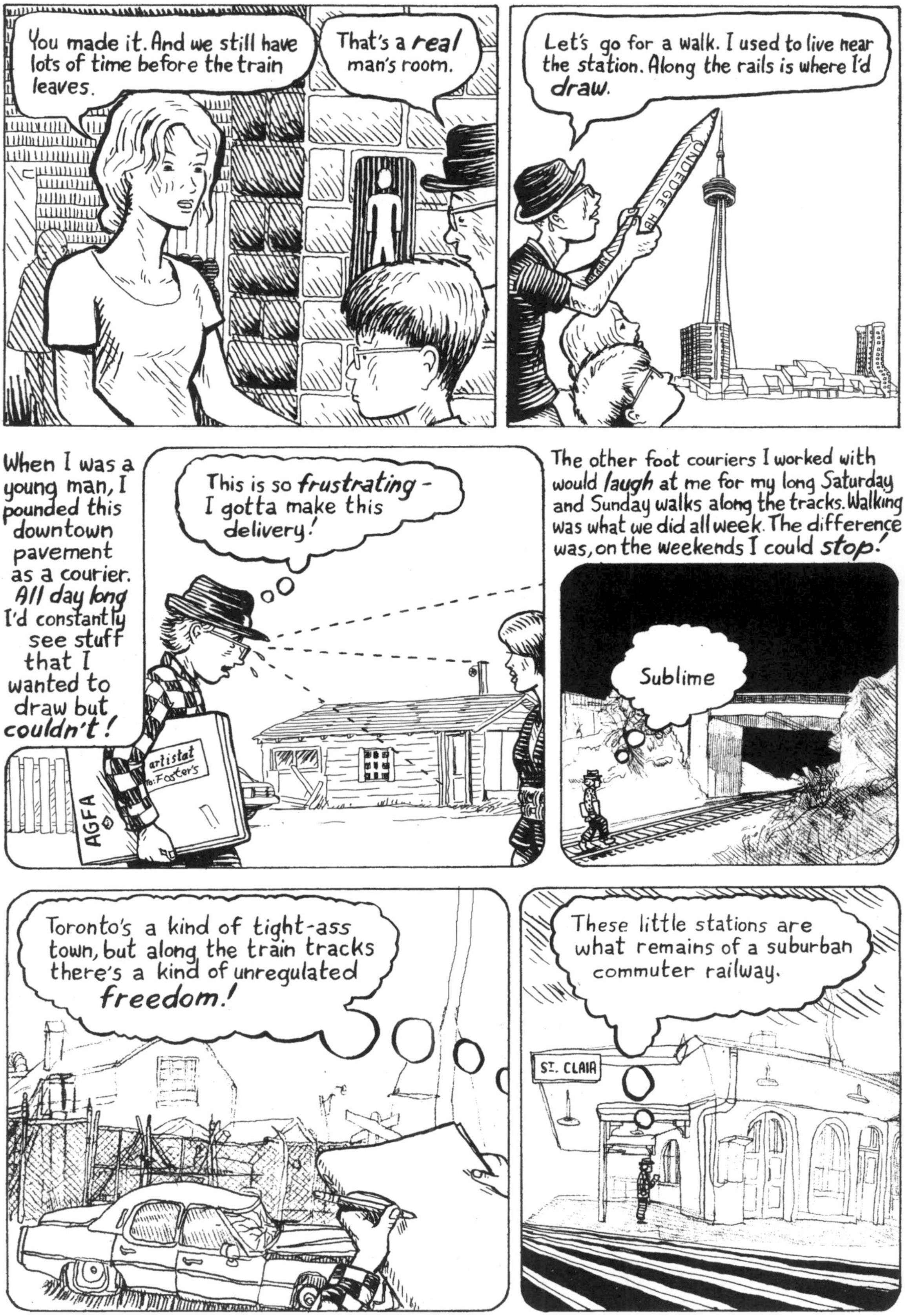
You made it. And we still have lots of time before the train leaves.
That's a real man's room.
Let's go for a walk. I used to live near the station. Along the rails is where I'd draw.
UNDEDGE HB
When I was a young man, I pounded this downtown pavement as a courier. All day long I'd constantly see stuff that I wanted to draw but couldn't!
This is so frustrating - I gotta make this delivery!
artistat
To: Foster's
AGFA
The other foot couriers I worked with would laugh at me for my long Saturday and Sunday walks along the tracks. Walking was what we did all week. The difference was, on the weekends I could stop!
Sublime
Toronto's a kind of tight-ass town, but along the train tracks there's a kind of unregulated freedom!
These little stations are what remains of a suburban commuter railway.
ST. CLAIR

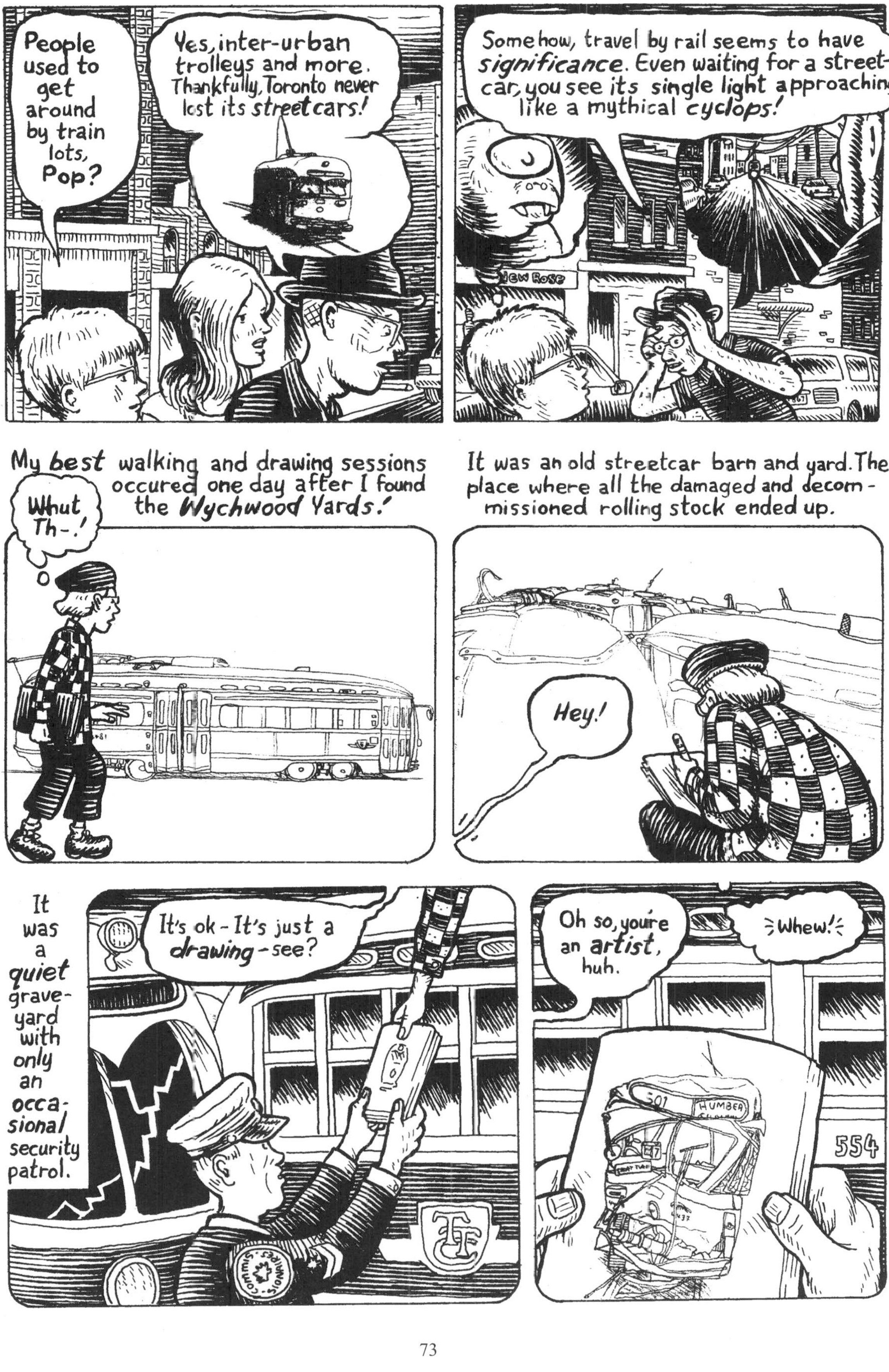
People used to get around by train lots, Pop?
Yes, inter-urban trolleys and more. Thankfully, Toronto never lost its *streetcars!*
Somehow, travel by rail seems to have *significance*. Even waiting for a street-car, you see its single light approaching like a mythical *cyclops!*
My *best* walking and drawing sessions occured one day after I found the *Wychwood Yards!*
Whut Th-!
It was an old streetcar barn and yard. The place where all the damaged and decom-missioned rolling stock ended up.
Hey!
It was a *quiet* grave-yard with only an occasional security patrol.
It's ok - It's just a *drawing* - see?
Oh so, you're an *artist*, huh.
Whew!
554

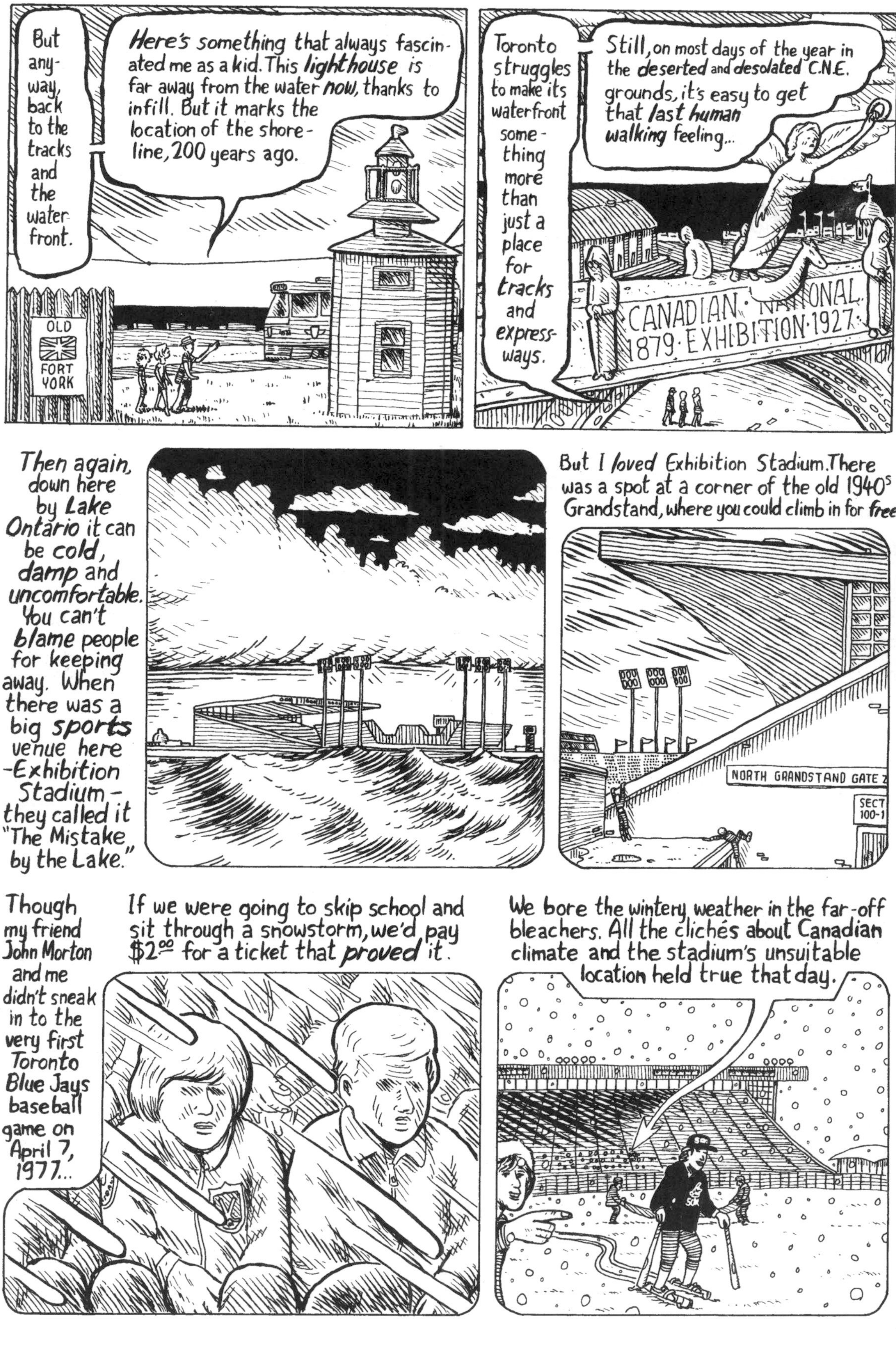

But anyway, back to the tracks and the waterfront.
Here's something that always fascinated me as a kid. This lighthouse is far away from the water now, thanks to infill. But it marks the location of the shoreline, 200 years ago.
OLD FORT YORK
Toronto struggles to make its waterfront something more than just a place for tracks and expressways.
Still, on most days of the year in the deserted and desolated C.N.E. grounds, it's easy to get that last human walking feeling...
CANADIAN NATIONAL 1879 · EXHIBITION · 1927
Then again, down here by Lake Ontario it can be cold, damp and uncomfortable. You can't blame people for keeping away. When there was a big sports venue here - Exhibition Stadium - they called it "The Mistake by the Lake."
But I loved Exhibition Stadium. There was a spot at a corner of the old 1940s Grandstand, where you could climb in for free!
NORTH GRANDSTAND GATE
SECT 100-1
Though my friend John Morton and me didn't sneak in to the very first Toronto Blue Jays baseball game on April 7, 1977...
If we were going to skip school and sit through a snowstorm, we'd pay $2.00 for a ticket that proved it.
We bore the wintery weather in the far-off bleachers. All the clichés about Canadian climate and the stadium's unsuitable location held true that day.

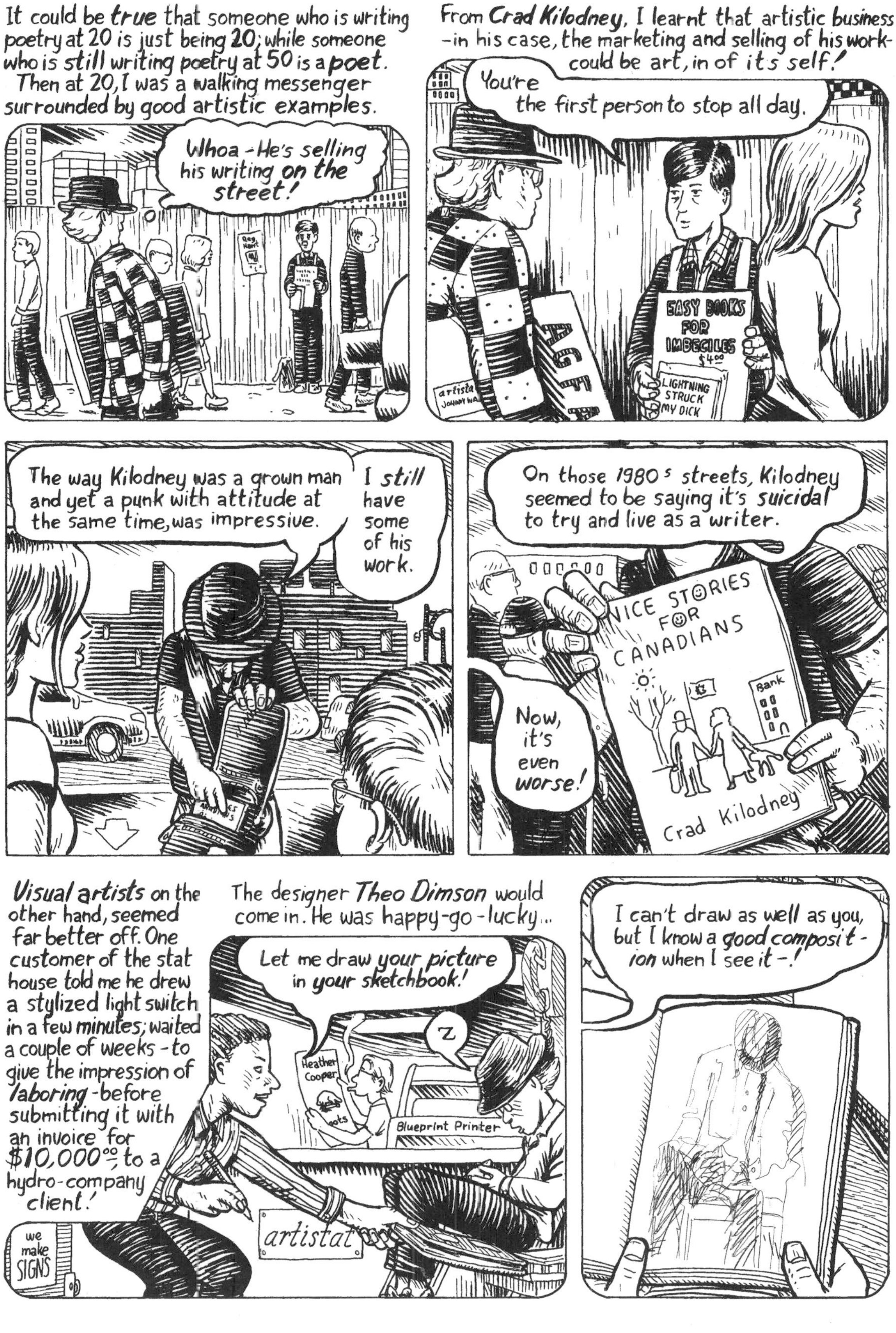
It could be true that someone who is writing poetry at 20 is just being 20; while someone who is still writing poetry at 50 is a poet.
Then at 20, I was a walking messenger surrounded by good artistic examples.
Whoa - He's selling his writing on the street!
From Crad Kilodney, I learnt that artistic business - in his case, the marketing and selling of his work - could be art, in of its self!
You're the first person to stop all day.
EASY BOOKS FOR IMBECILES $4.00
LIGHTNING STRUCK MY DICK
The way Kilodney was a grown man and yet a punk with attitude at the same time, was impressive.
I still have some of his work.
On those 1980s streets, Kilodney seemed to be saying it's suicidal to try and live as a writer.
Now, it's even worse!
NICE STORIES FOR CANADIANS
Bank
Crad Kilodney
Visual artists on the other hand, seemed far better off. One customer of the stat house told me he drew a stylized light switch in a few minutes; waited a couple of weeks - to give the impression of laboring - before submitting it with an invoice for $10,000.00, to a hydro-company client!
The designer Theo Dimson would come in. He was happy-go-lucky...
Let me draw your picture in your sketchbook!
Z
Heather Cooper
Blueprint Printer
artistat
we make SIGNS
I can't draw as well as you, but I know a good composition when I see it -!

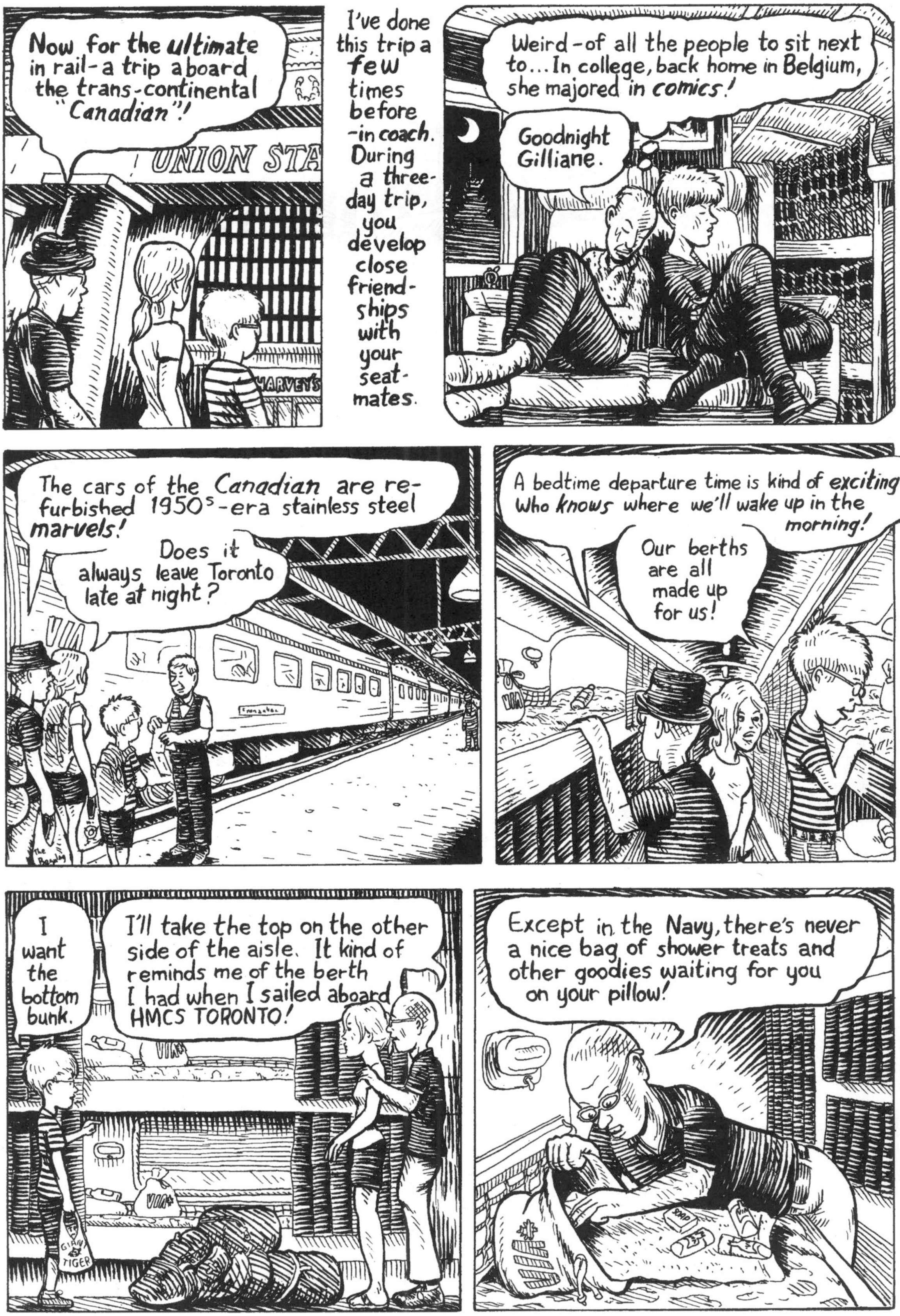
Now for the *ultimate* in rail - a trip aboard the trans-continental "*Canadian*"!
UNION STA
HARVEY'S
I've done this trip a *few* times before - in *coach*. During a three-day trip, you develop close friendships with your seat-mates.
Weird - of all the people to sit next to... In college, back home in Belgium, she majored in *comics*!
Goodnight Gilliane.
The cars of the *Canadian* are refurbished 1950s-era stainless steel *marvels*!
Does it always leave Toronto late at night?
VIA
A bedtime departure time is kind of *exciting* - Who *knows* where we'll wake up in the *morning*!
Our berths are all made up for us!
I want the bottom bunk.
I'll take the top on the other side of the aisle. It kind of reminds me of the berth I had when I sailed aboard HMCS TORONTO!
GIANT TIGER
Except in the Navy, there's never a nice bag of shower treats and other goodies waiting for you on your pillow!

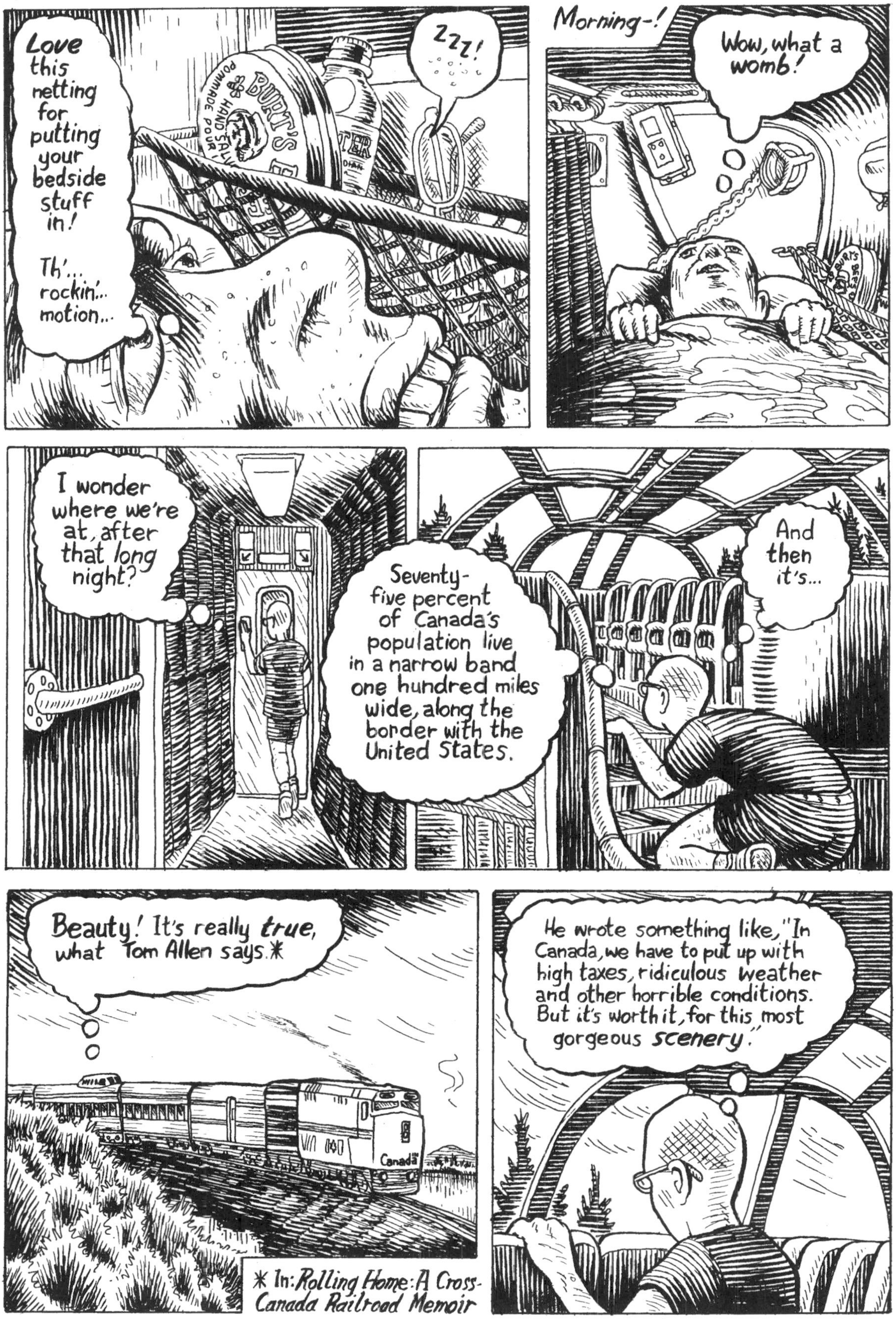
Love this netting for putting your bedside stuff in!
Th'... rockin'... motion...
zzz!
Morning-!
Wow, what a womb!
I wonder where we're at, after that long night?
Seventy-five percent of Canada's population live in a narrow band one hundred miles wide, along the border with the United States.
And then it's...
Beauty! It's really true, what Tom Allen says.*
He wrote something like, "In Canada, we have to put up with high taxes, ridiculous weather and other horrible conditions. But it's worth it, for this most gorgeous scenery."
* In: Rolling Home: A Cross-Canada Railroad Memoir

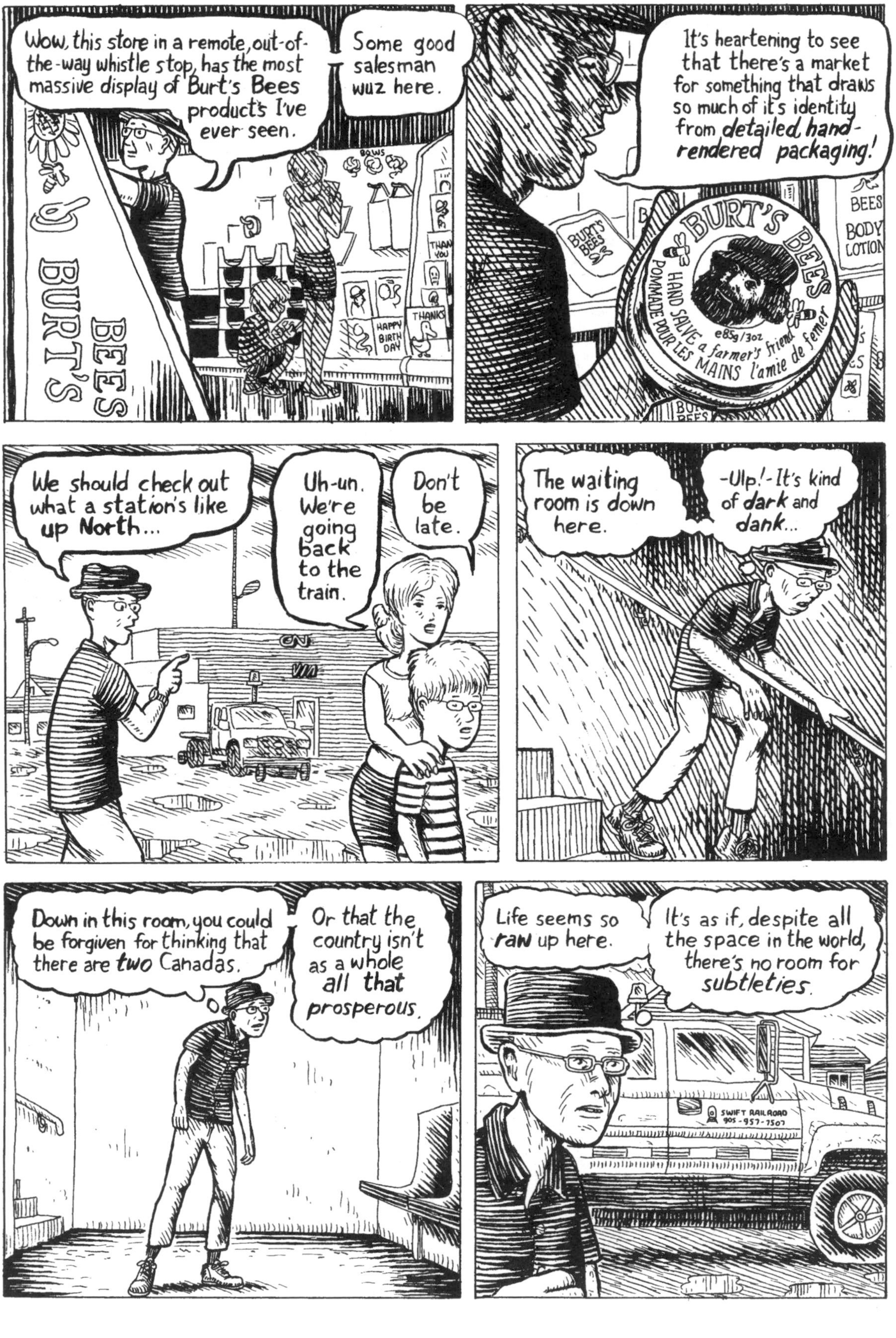
Wow, this store in a remote, out-of-the-way whistle stop, has the most massive display of Burt's Bees product's I've ever seen.
Some good salesman wuz here.
BURT'S BEES
BOWS
THANK YOU
HAPPY BIRTH DAY
THANKS
It's heartening to see that there's a market for something that draws so much of it's identity from **detailed, hand-rendered packaging!**
BURT'S BEES
HAND SALVE a farmer's friend
POMMADE POUR LES MAINS l'amie de femer
e85g/3oz
BEES BODY LOTION
We should check out what a station's like **up North**...
Uh-un. We're going back to the train.
Don't be late.
The waiting room is down here.
-Ulp!- It's kind of **dark** and **dank**...
Down in this room, you could be forgiven for thinking that there are ***two*** Canadas.
Or that the country isn't as a whole **all that prosperous.**
Life seems so ***raw*** up here.
It's as if, despite all the space in the world, there's no room for ***subtleties.***
SWIFT RAILROAD
905-957-7507

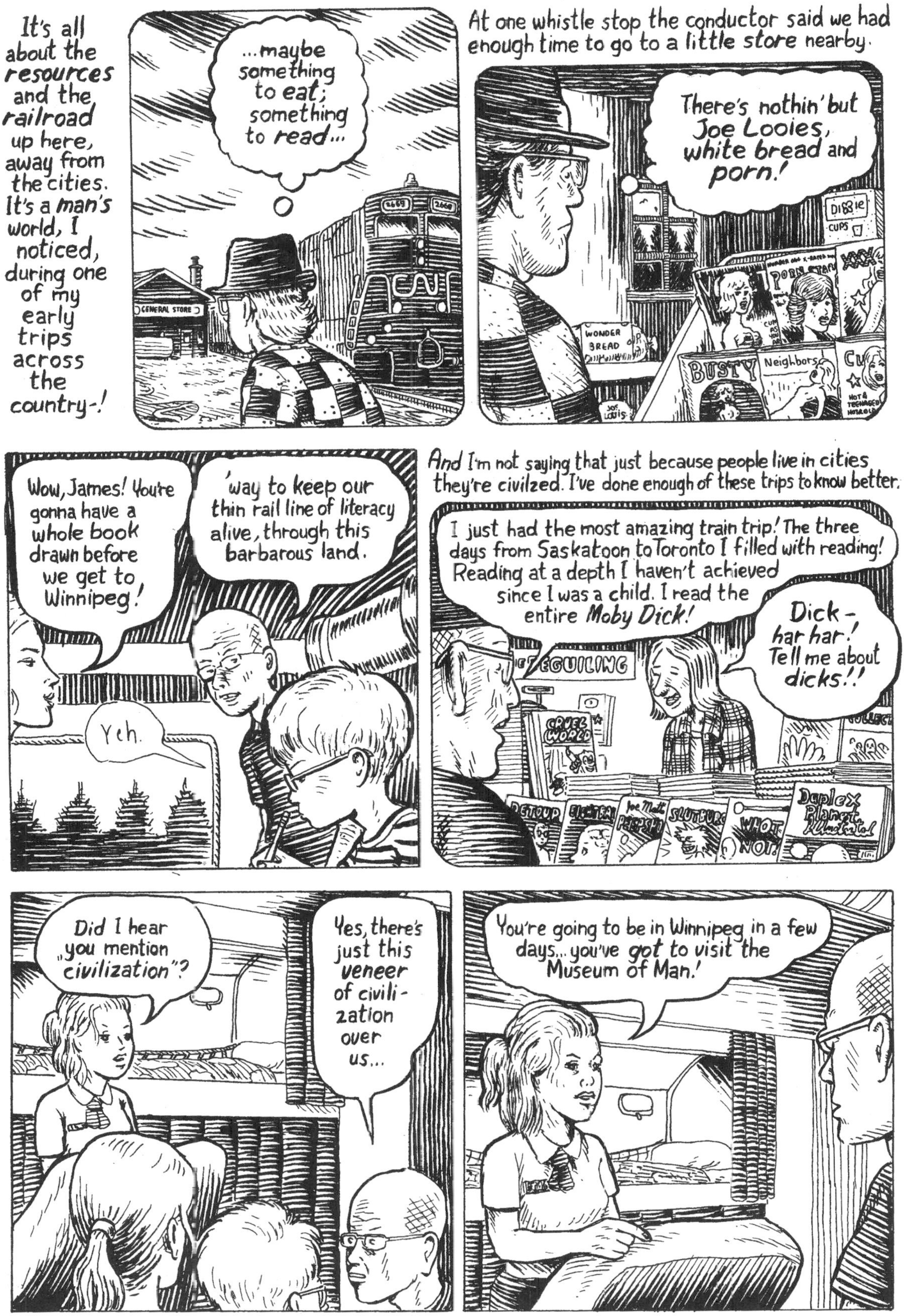
It's all about the resources and the railroad up here, away from the cities. It's a man's world, I noticed, during one of my early trips across the country-!
...maybe something to eat; something to read...
GENERAL STORE
At one whistle stop the conductor said we had enough time to go to a little store nearby.
There's nothin' but Joe Looies, white bread and porn!
DIXIE CUPS
WONDER BREAD
BUSTY
Neighbors
Wow, James! You're gonna have a whole book drawn before we get to Winnipeg!
'way to keep our thin rail line of literacy alive, through this barbarous land.
Yeh.
And I'm not saying that just because people live in cities they're civilzed. I've done enough of these trips to know better.
I just had the most amazing train trip! The three days from Saskatoon to Toronto I filled with reading! Reading at a depth I haven't achieved since I was a child. I read the entire Moby Dick!
Dick - har har! Tell me about dicks!!
CRUEL WORLD
Did I hear you mention "civilization"?
Yes, there's just this veneer of civilization over us...
You're going to be in Winnipeg in a few days... you've got to visit the Museum of Man!

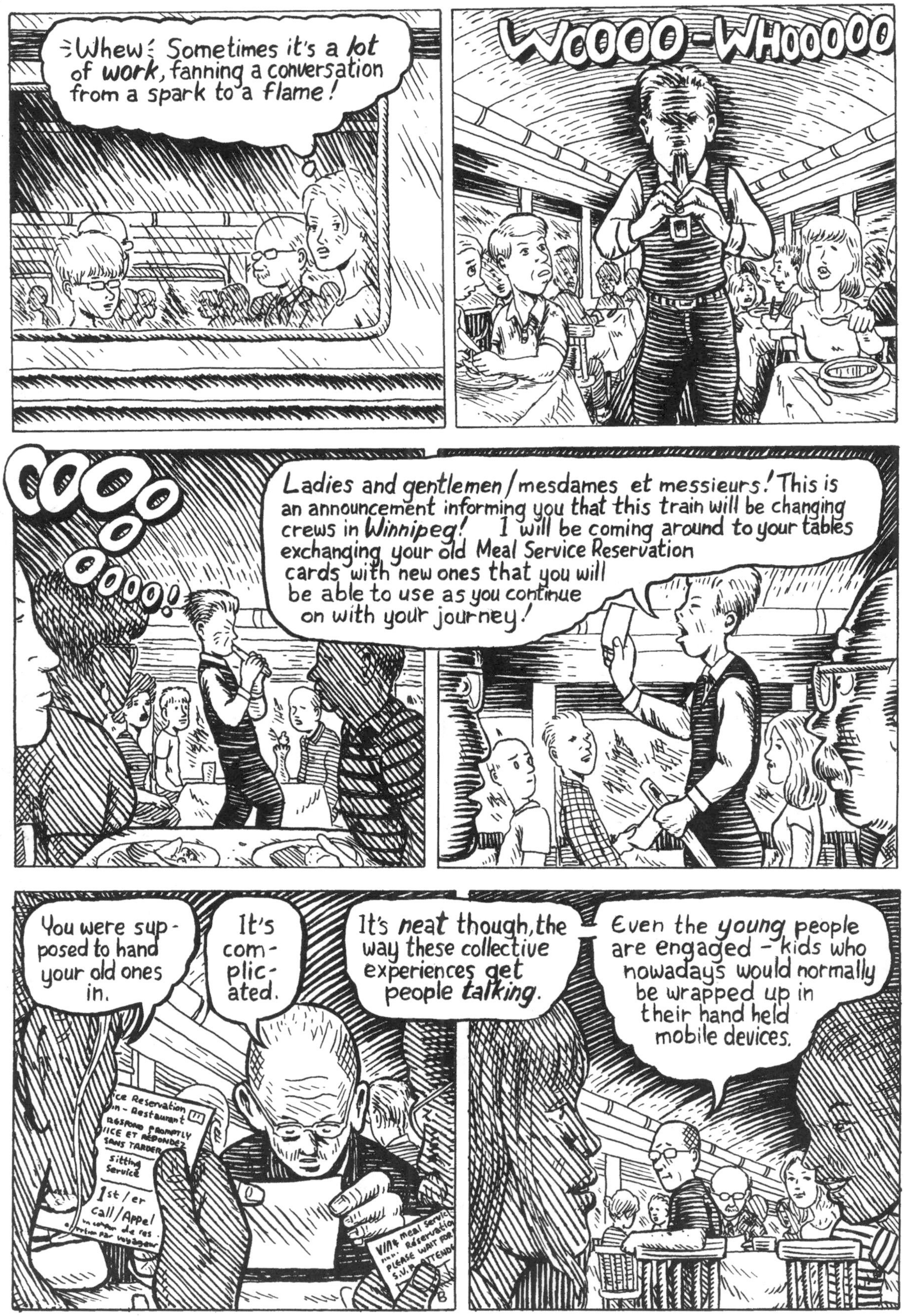
Whew! Sometimes it's a lot of work, fanning a conversation from a spark to a flame!
WOOOO-WHOOOOO
OOOOOOOOOO!
Ladies and gentlemen / mesdames et messieurs! This is an announcement informing you that this train will be changing crews in Winnipeg! I will be coming around to your tables exchanging your old Meal Service Reservation cards with new ones that you will be able to use as you continue on with your journey!
You were supposed to hand your old ones in.
It's complicated.
It's neat though, the way these collective experiences get people talking.
Even the young people are engaged – kids who nowadays would normally be wrapped up in their hand held mobile devices.
Sitting Service
1st/er
Call/Appel!

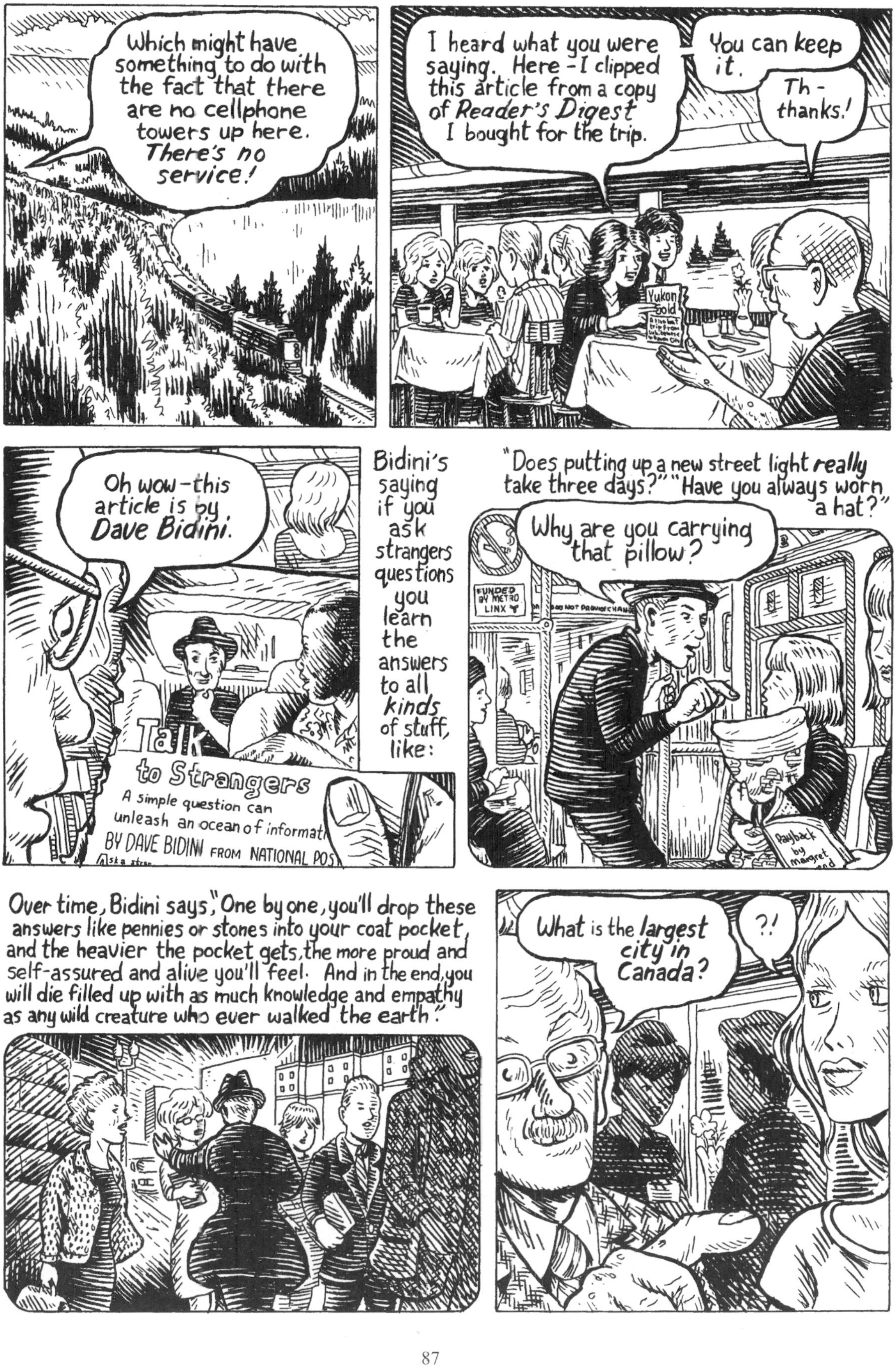

Which might have something to do with the fact that there are no cellphone towers up here. *There's no service!*
I heard what you were saying. Here – I clipped this article from a copy of *Reader's Digest* I bought for the trip.
You can keep it.
Th-thanks!
Yukon Gold
Oh wow – this article is by *Dave Bidini.*
Talk
to Strangers
A simple question can
unleash an ocean of
BY DAVE BIDINI FROM NATIONAL
Bidini's saying if you ask strangers questions you learn the answers to all *kinds* of stuff, like:
"Does putting up a new street light *really* take three days?" "Have you always worn a hat?"
Why are you carrying that pillow?
FUNDED BY METRO LINX
Over time, Bidini says, "One by one, you'll drop these answers like pennies or stones into your coat pocket, and the heavier the pocket gets, the more proud and self-assured and alive you'll feel. And in the end, you will die filled up with as much knowledge and empathy as any wild creature who ever walked the earth."
What is the *largest city in Canada?*
?!

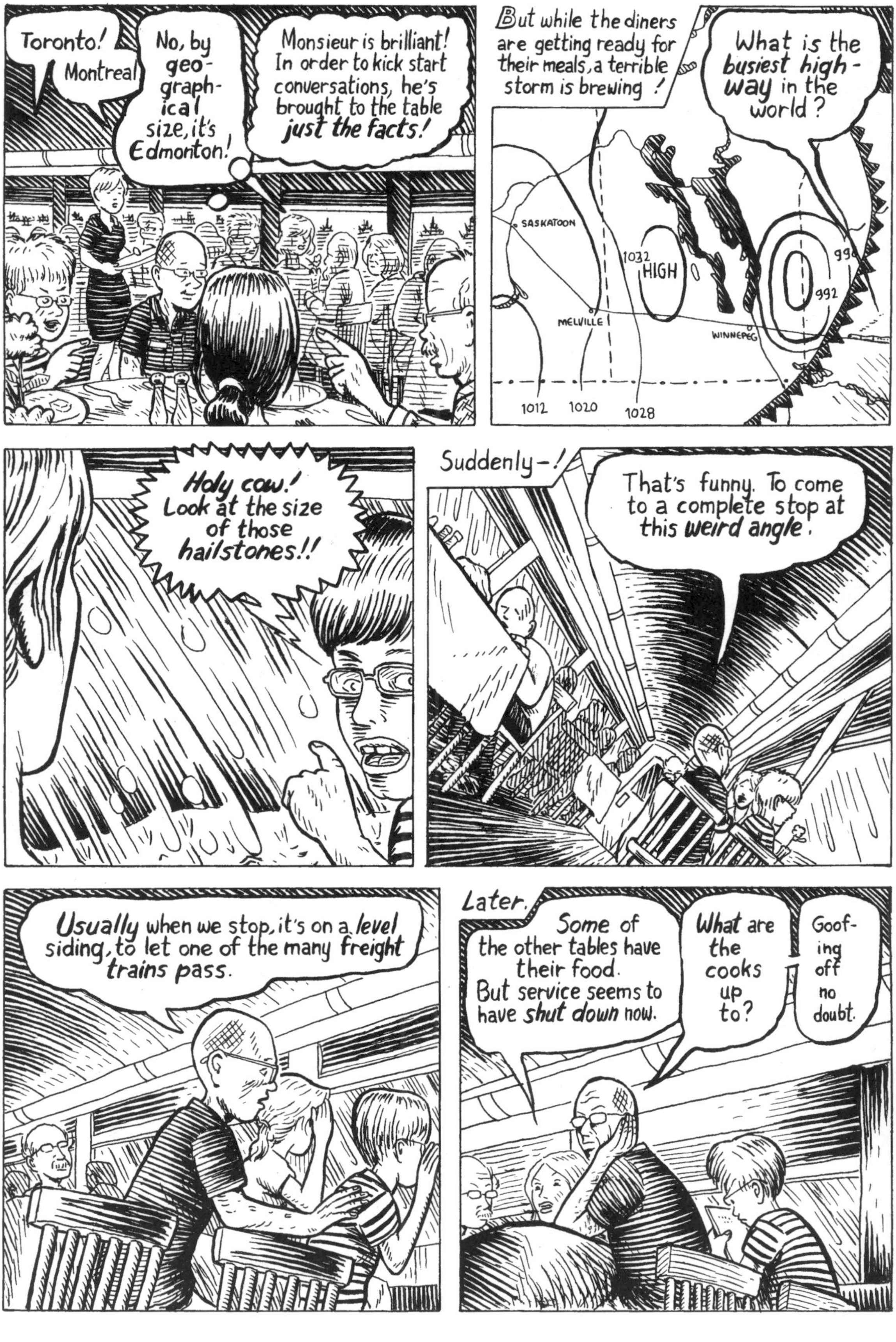
Toronto!
Montreal
No, by geo-graph-ical size, it's Edmonton!
Monsieur is brilliant! In order to kick start conversations, he's brought to the table just the facts!
But while the diners are getting ready for their meals, a terrible storm is brewing!
What is the busiest high-way in the world?
SASKATOON
1032
HIGH
992
MELVILLE
WINNEPEG
1012
1020
1028
Holy cow! Look at the size of those hailstones!!
Suddenly-!
That's funny. To come to a complete stop at this weird angle.
Usually when we stop, it's on a level siding, to let one of the many freight trains pass.
Later.
Some of the other tables have their food. But service seems to have shut down now.
What are the cooks up to?
Goof-ing off no doubt.

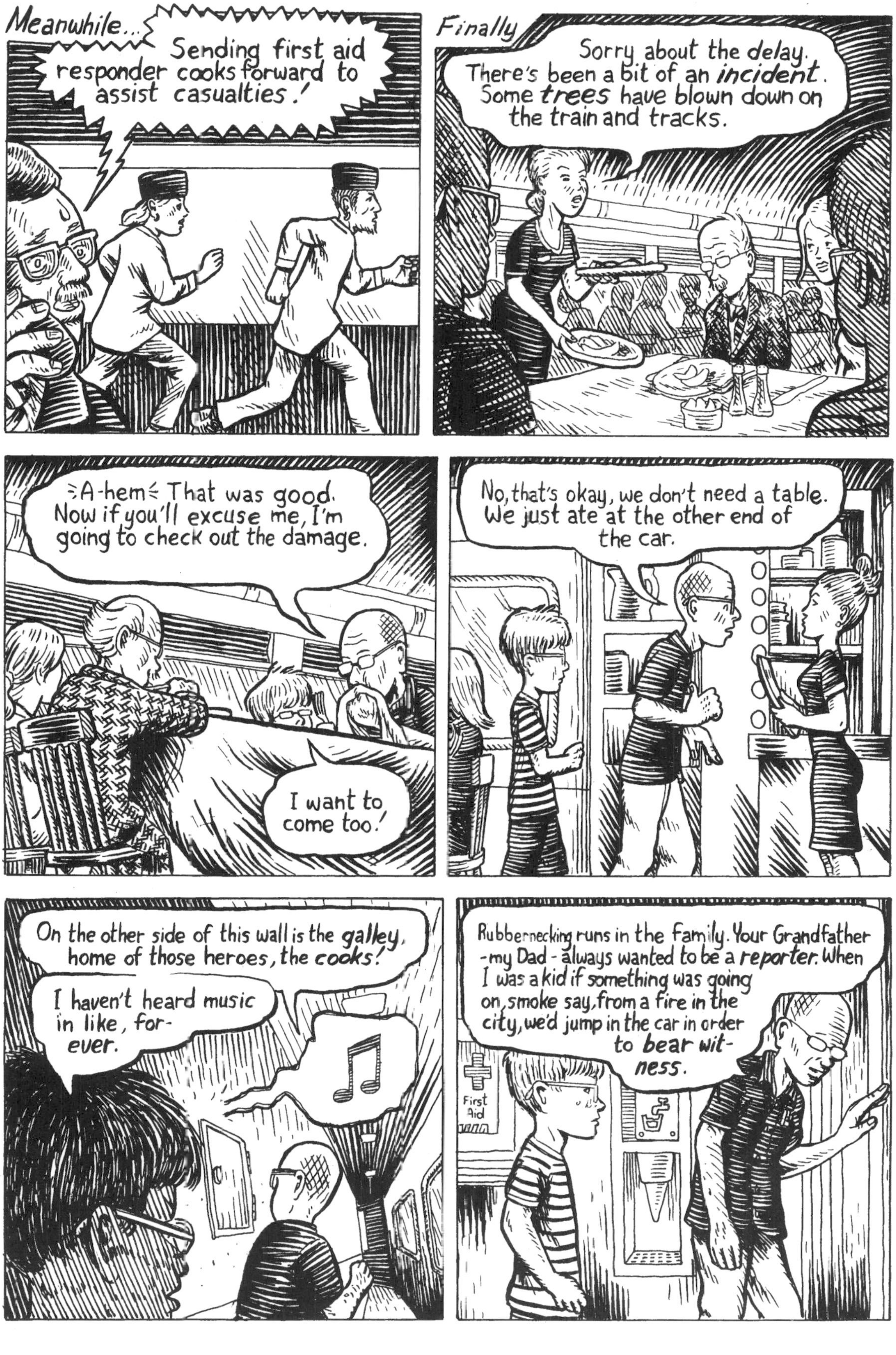
Meanwhile...
Sending first aid responder cooks forward to assist casualties!
Finally
Sorry about the delay. There's been a bit of an incident. Some trees have blown down on the train and tracks.
A-hem That was good. Now if you'll excuse me, I'm going to check out the damage.
I want to come too!
No, that's okay, we don't need a table. We just ate at the other end of the car.
On the other side of this wall is the galley, home of those heroes, the cooks!
I haven't heard music in like, for-ever.
Rubbernecking runs in the family. Your Grandfather -my Dad - always wanted to be a reporter. When I was a kid if something was going on, smoke say, from a fire in the city, we'd jump in the car in order to bear wit-ness.
First Aid

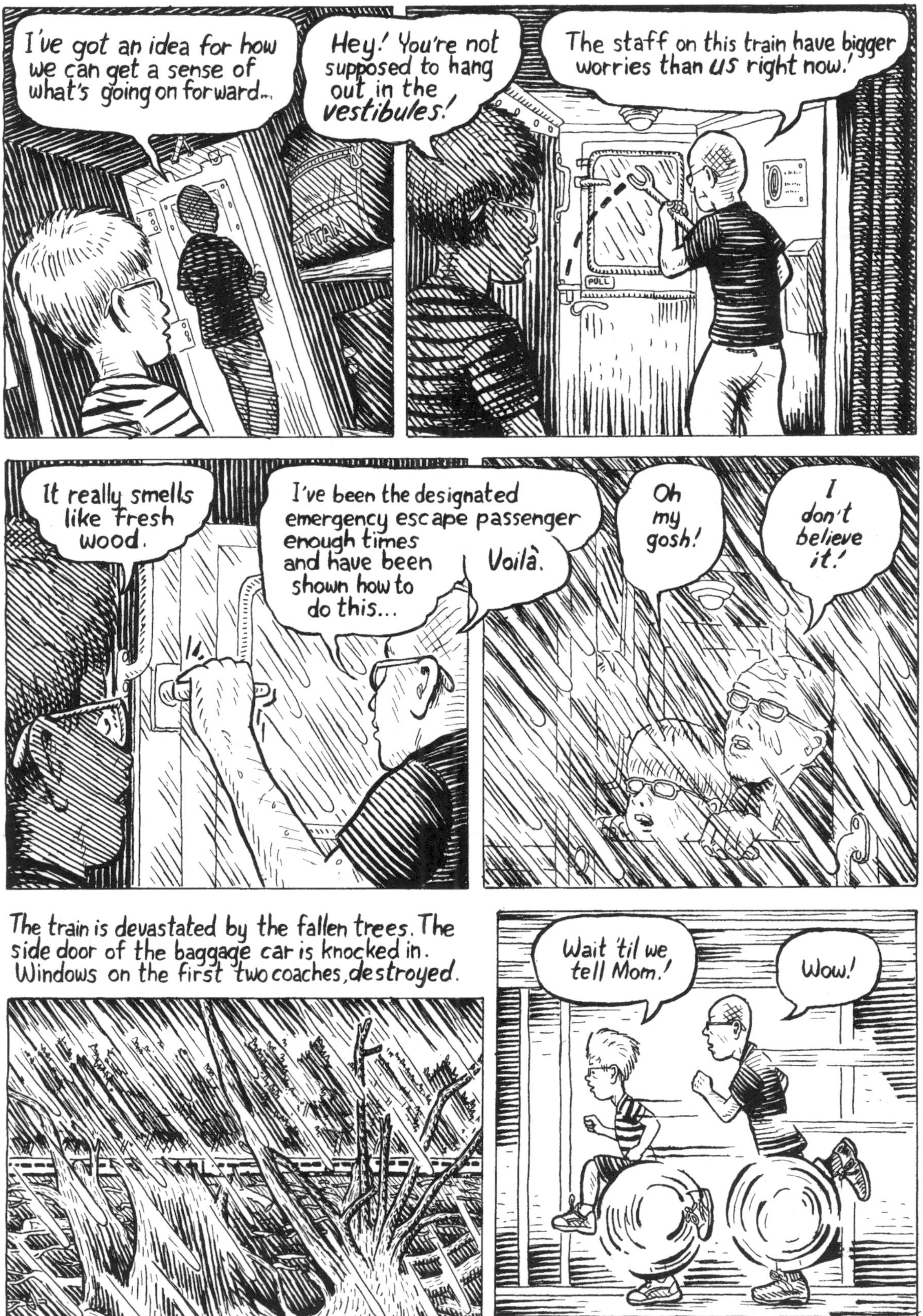
I've got an idea for how we can get a sense of what's going on forward...
Hey! You're not supposed to hang out in the vestibules!
The staff on this train have bigger worries than US right now!
It really smells like fresh wood.
I've been the designated emergency escape passenger enough times and have been shown how to do this...
Voilà.
Oh my gosh!
I don't believe it!
The train is devastated by the fallen trees. The side door of the baggage car is knocked in. Windows on the first two coaches, destroyed.
Wait 'til we tell Mom!
Wow!

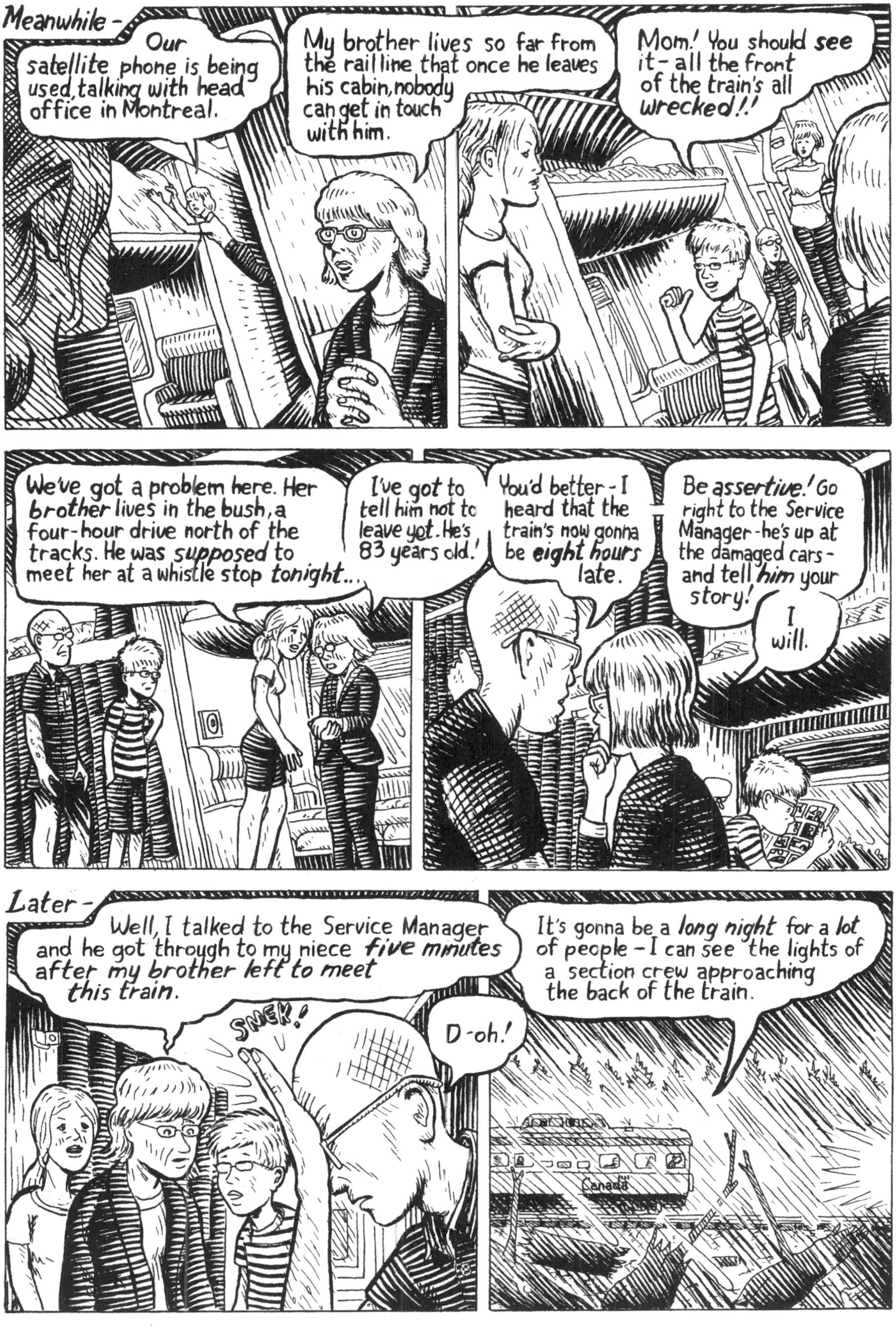
Meanwhile -
Our satellite phone is being used, talking with head office in Montreal.
My brother lives so far from the rail line that once he leaves his cabin, nobody can get in touch with him.
Mom! You should see it - all the front of the train's all wrecked!!
We've got a problem here. Her brother lives in the bush, a four-hour drive north of the tracks. He was supposed to meet her at a whistle stop tonight...
I've got to tell him not to leave yet. He's 83 years old!
You'd better - I heard that the train's now gonna be eight hours late.
Be assertive! Go right to the Service Manager - he's up at the damaged cars - and tell him your story!
I will.
Later -
Well, I talked to the Service Manager and he got through to my niece five minutes after my brother left to meet this train.
SMEK!
D-oh!
It's gonna be a long night for a lot of people - I can see the lights of a section crew approaching the back of the train.
Canada

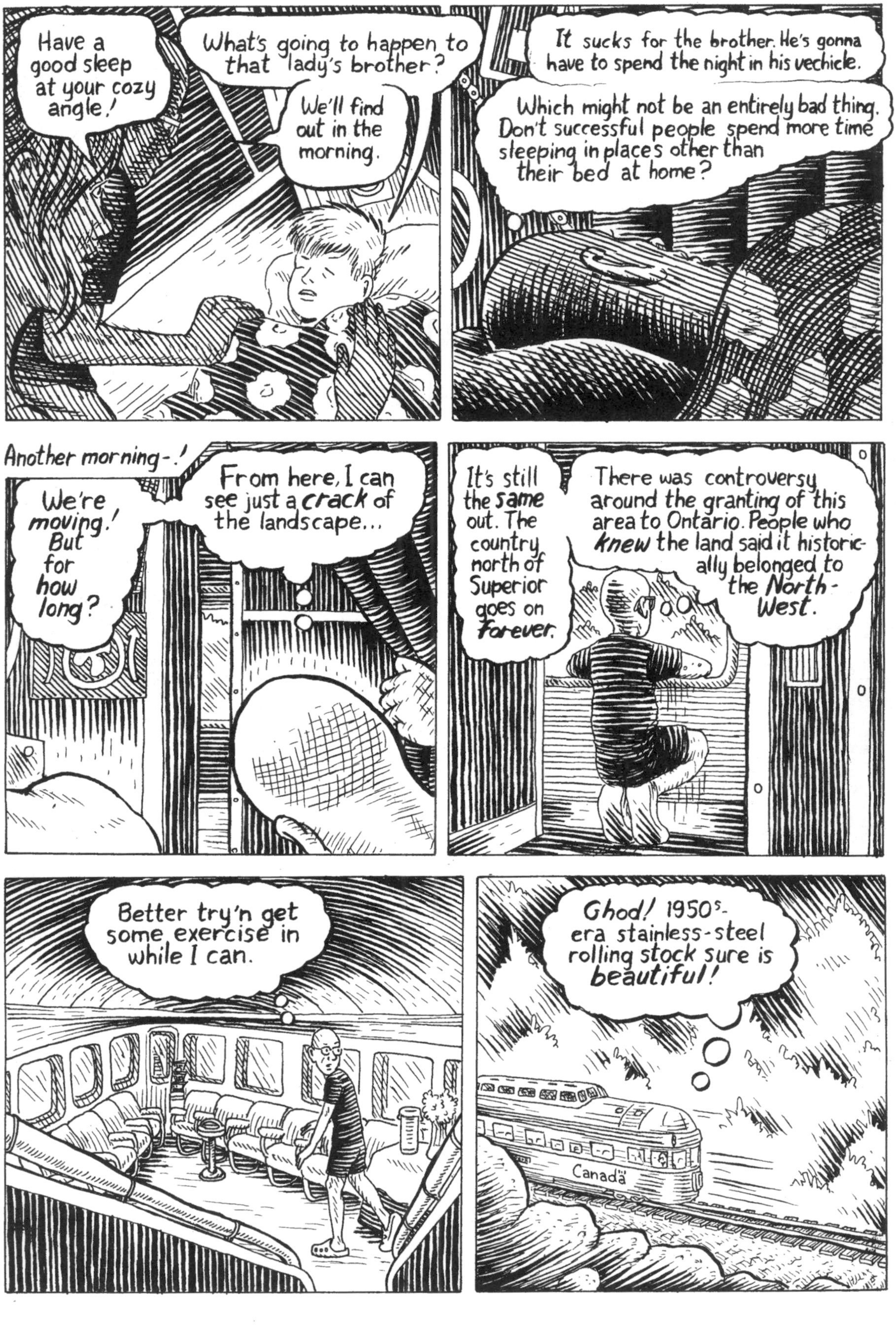
Have a good sleep at your cozy angle!
What's going to happen to that lady's brother?
We'll find out in the morning.
It sucks for the brother. He's gonna have to spend the night in his vechicle.
Which might not be an entirely bad thing. Don't successful people spend more time sleeping in places other than their bed at home?
Another morning-!
We're moving! But for how long?
From here, I can see just a crack of the landscape...
It's still the same out. The country north of Superior goes on forever.
There was controversy around the granting of this area to Ontario. People who knew the land said it historically belonged to the North-West.
Better try'n get some exercise in while I can.
Ghod! 1950s-era stainless-steel rolling stock sure is beautiful!
Canadä

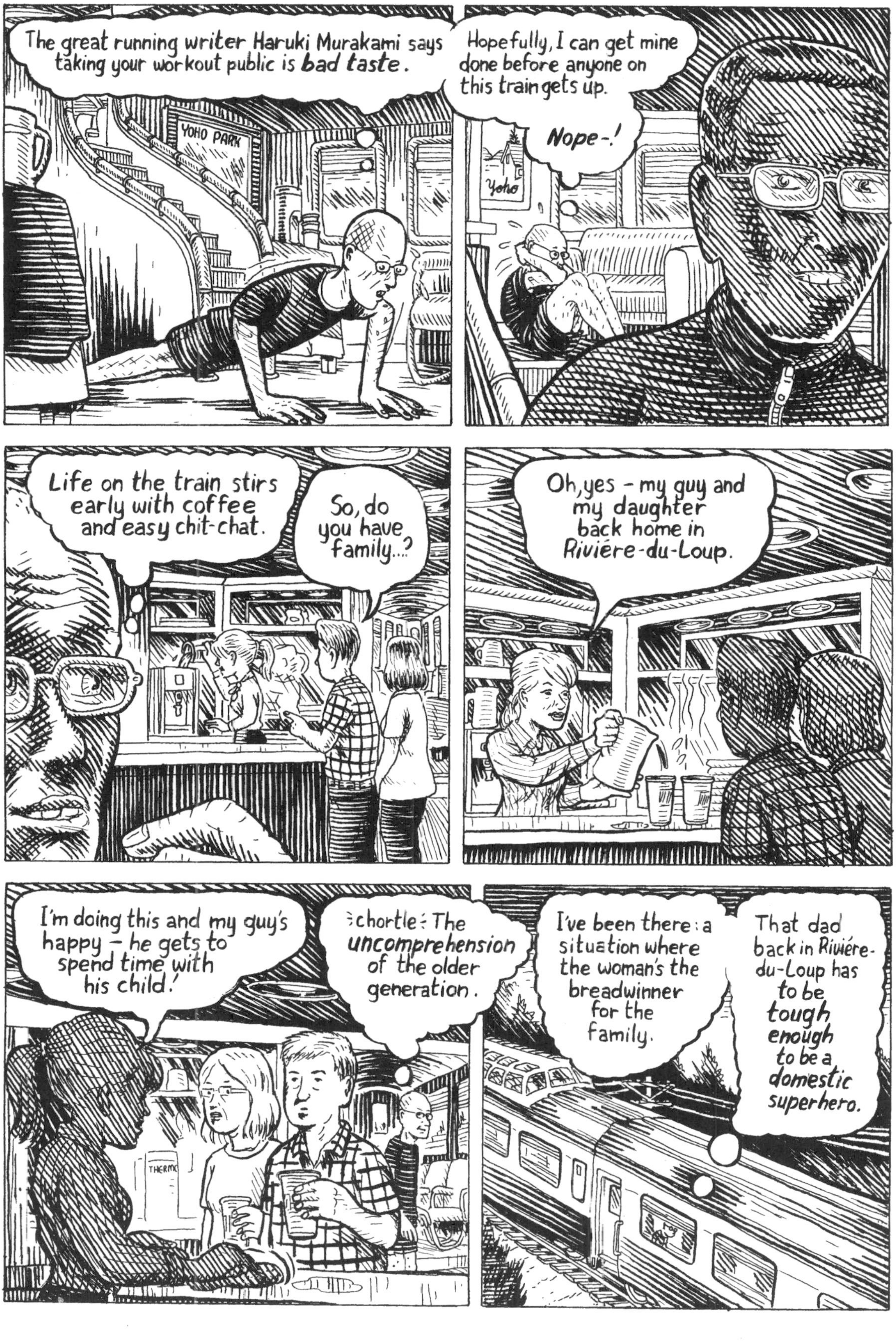
The great running writer Haruki Murakami says taking your workout public is **bad taste**.
YOHO PARK
Hopefully, I can get mine done before anyone on this train gets up.
Nope-!
Yoho
Life on the train stirs early with coffee and easy chit-chat.
So, do you have family...?
Oh, yes - my guy and my daughter back home in Riviére-du-Loup.
I'm doing this and my guy's happy - he gets to spend time with his child!
:chortle: The *uncomprehension* of the older generation.
THERMO
I've been there: a situation where the woman's the breadwinner for the family.
That dad back in Riviére-du-Loup has to be **tough enough** to be a **domestic superhero**.

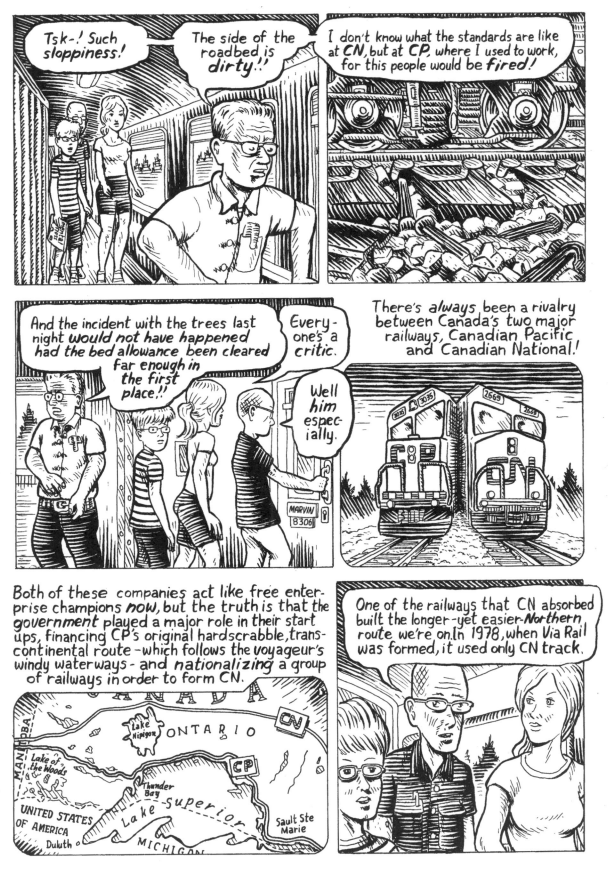

Tsk-! Such sloppiness!

The side of the roadbed is *dirty!!*

I don't know what the standards are like at *CN,* but at *CP,* where I used to work, for this people would be *fired!*

And the incident with the trees last night *would not have happened* had the bed allowance been cleared far enough in the first place!!

Everyone's a critic.

Well him especially.

MARVIN 8306

There's *always* been a rivalry between Canada's two major railways, Canadian Pacific and Canadian National!

3035 2669

Both of these companies act like free enter-prise champions *now,* but the truth is that the *government* played a major role in their start ups, financing CP's original hardscrabble, trans-continental route – which follows the *voyageur's* windy waterways – and *nationalizing* a group of railways in order to form CN.

CANADA

MANITOBA

Lake of the Woods

Lake Nipigon

ONTARIO

CN

CP

Thunder Bay

UNITED STATES OF AMERICA

Duluth

Lake Superior

Sault Ste Marie

MICHIGAN

One of the railways that CN absorbed built the longer-yet easier-*Northern* route we're on. In 1978, when Via Rail was formed, it used only CN track.

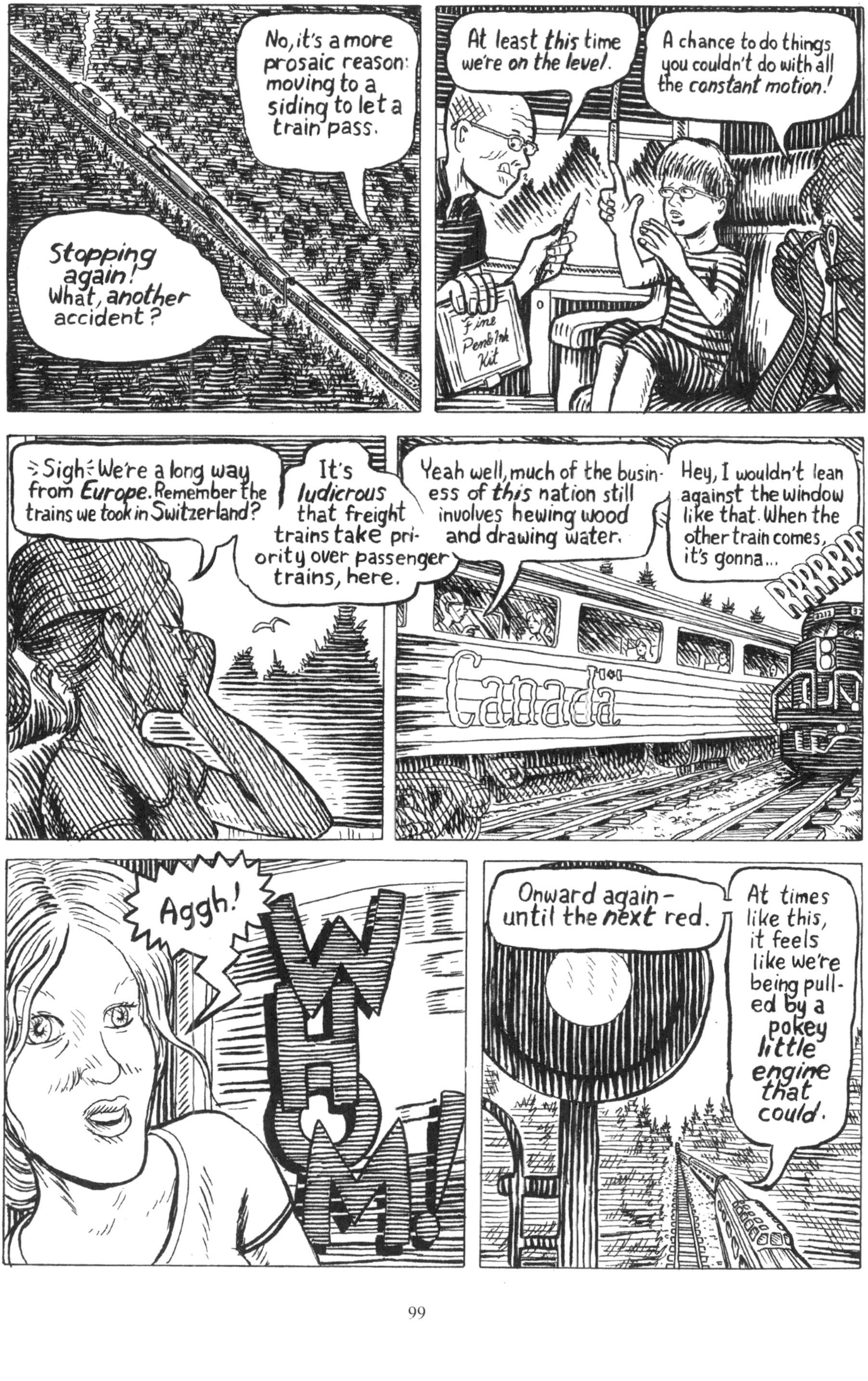
Stopping again! What, *another* accident?
No, it's a more prosaic reason: moving to a siding to let a train pass.
At least *this* time we're *on the level*.
A chance to do things you couldn't do with all the *constant motion*!
Fine Pen & Ink Kit
~Sigh~ We're a long way from *Europe*. Remember the trains we took in Switzerland?
It's *ludicrous* that freight trains take priority over passenger trains, here.
Yeah well, much of the business of *this* nation still involves hewing wood and drawing water.
Hey, I wouldn't lean against the window like that. When the other train comes, it's gonna...
RRRRRR
Canada
Aggh!
WHOOM!
Onward again – until the *next* red.
At times like this, it feels like we're being pulled by a pokey *little engine that could*.

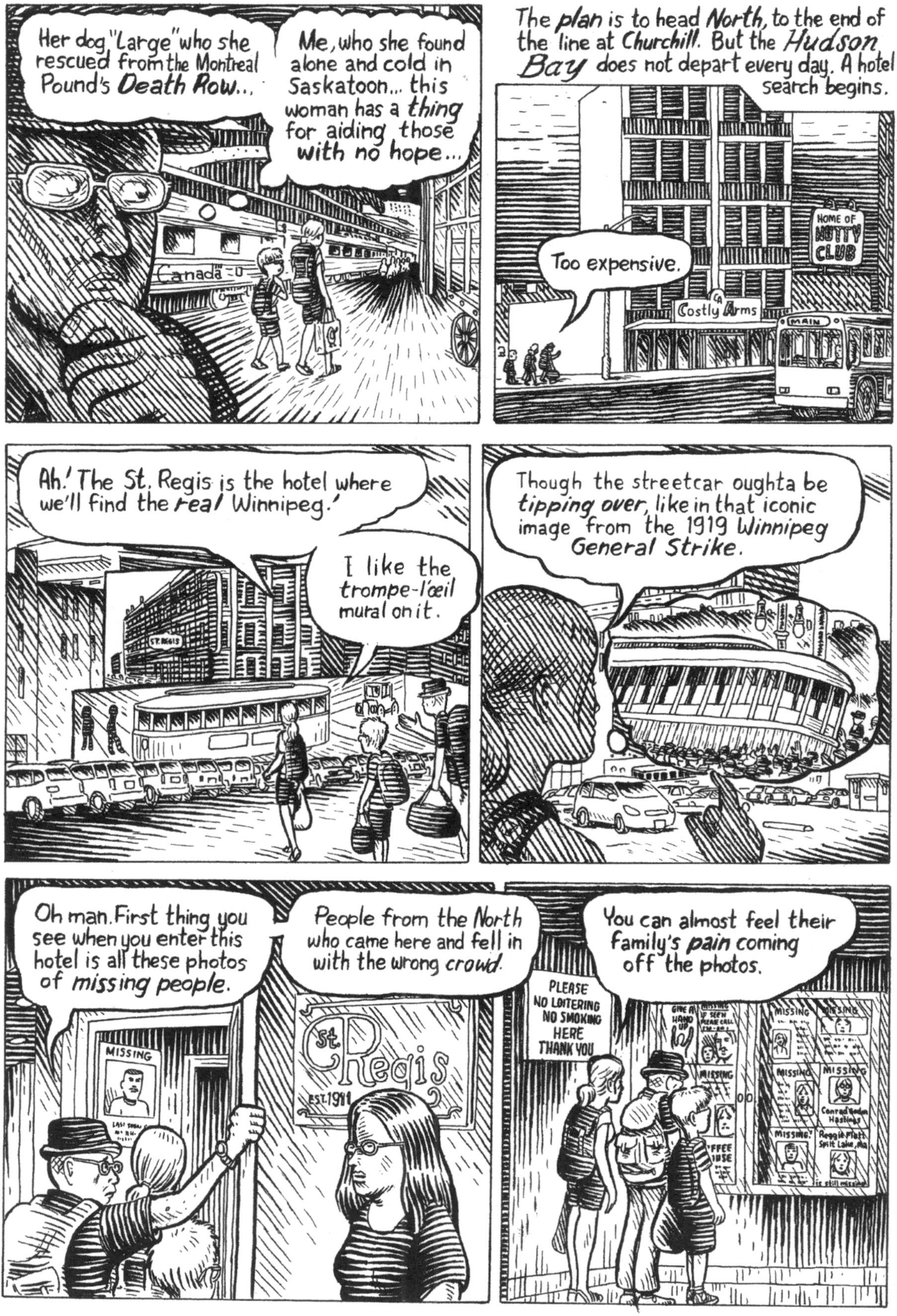

Her dog "Large" who she rescued from the Montreal Pound's Death Row...
Me, who she found alone and cold in Saskatoon... this woman has a thing for aiding those with no hope...
Canada
The plan is to head North, to the end of the line at Churchill. But the Hudson Bay does not depart every day. A hotel search begins.
HOME OF NUTTY CLUB
Too expensive.
Costly Arms
MAIN
Ah! The St. Regis is the hotel where we'll find the real Winnipeg!
I like the trompe-l'œil mural on it.
Though the streetcar oughta be tipping over, like in that iconic image from the 1919 Winnipeg General Strike.
Oh man. First thing you see when you enter this hotel is all these photos of missing people.
MISSING
People from the North who came here and fell in with the wrong crowd.
St. Regis
You can almost feel their family's pain coming off the photos.
PLEASE NO LOITERING NO SMOKING HERE THANK YOU
MISSING
MISSING
MISSING
MISSING
MISSING

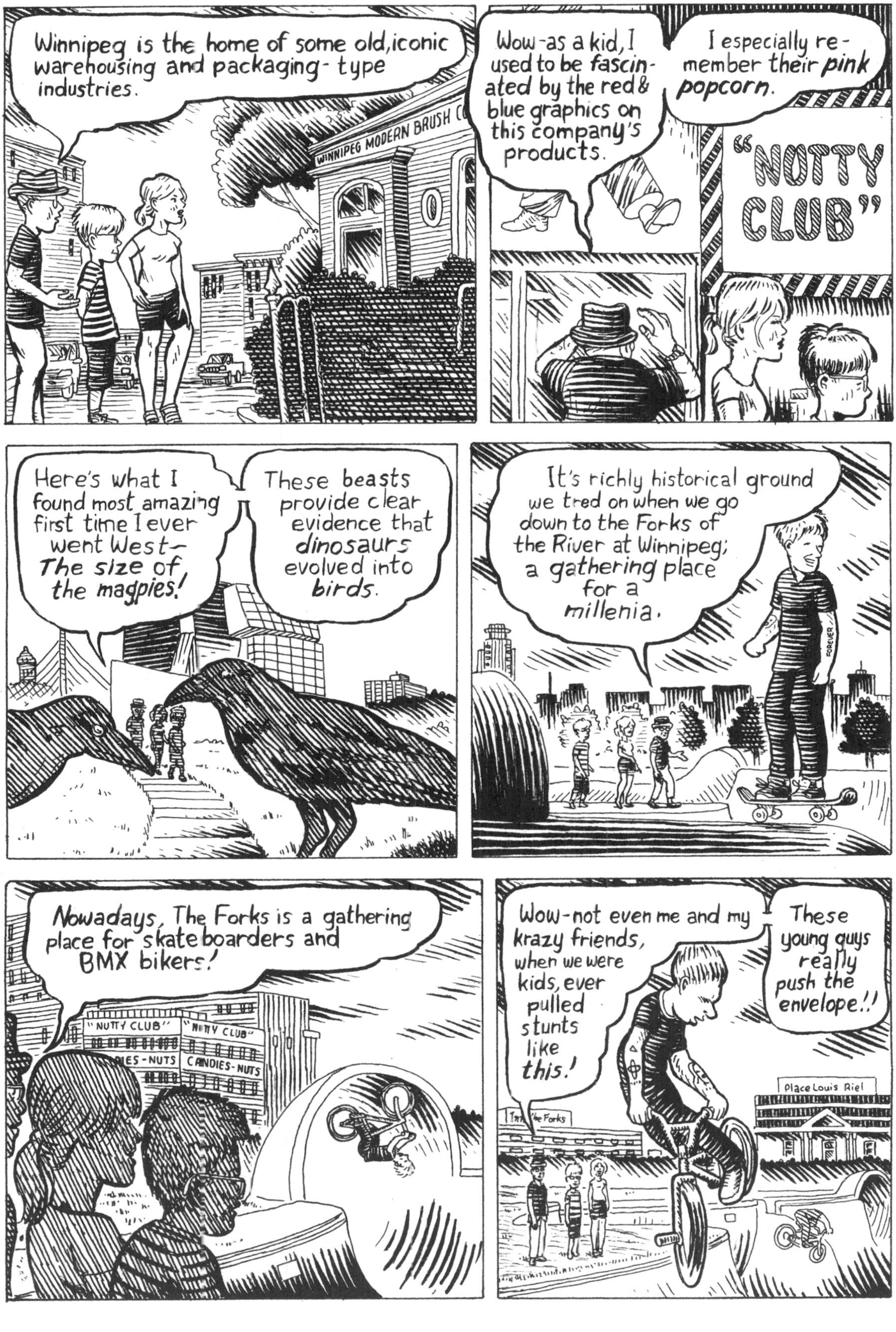
Winnipeg is the home of some old, iconic warehousing and packaging-type industries.
WINNIPEG MODERN BRUSH CO
Wow-as a kid, I used to be fascinated by the red & blue graphics on this company's products.
I especially remember their pink popcorn.
"NOTTY CLUB"
Here's what I found most amazing first time I ever went West- The size of the magpies!
These beasts provide clear evidence that dinosaurs evolved into birds.
It's richly historical ground we tred on when we go down to the Forks of the River at Winnipeg; a gathering place for a millenia.
FOREVER
Nowadays, The Forks is a gathering place for skateboarders and BMX bikers!
"NUTTY CLUB"
"NUTTY CLUB"
CANDIES-NUTS
Wow-not even me and my krazy friends, when we were kids, ever pulled stunts like this!
These young guys really push the envelope!!
Place Louis Riel

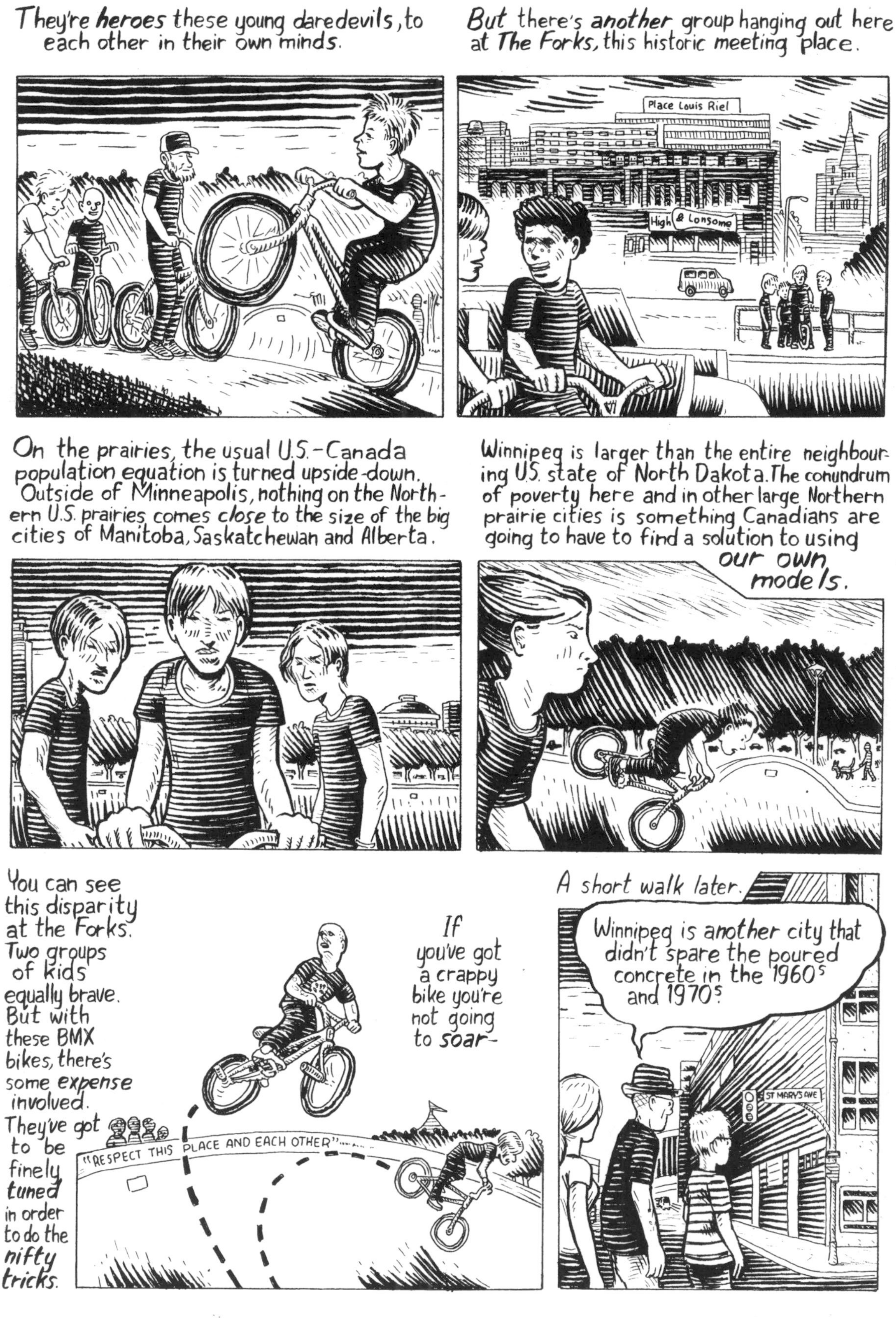
They're heroes these young daredevils, to each other in their own minds.
But there's another group hanging out here at The Forks, this historic meeting place.
Place Louis Riel
High & Lonsome
On the prairies, the usual U.S.-Canada population equation is turned upside-down. Outside of Minneapolis, nothing on the Northern U.S. prairies comes close to the size of the big cities of Manitoba, Saskatchewan and Alberta.
Winnipeg is larger than the entire neighbouring U.S. state of North Dakota. The conundrum of poverty here and in other large Northern prairie cities is something Canadians are going to have to find a solution to using our own models.
You can see this disparity at the Forks. Two groups of kids equally brave. But with these BMX bikes, there's some expense involved. They've got to be finely tuned in order to do the nifty tricks.
If you've got a crappy bike you're not going to soar-
"RESPECT THIS PLACE AND EACH OTHER"
A short walk later.
Winnipeg is another city that didn't spare the poured concrete in the 1960s and 1970s.
ST MARY'S AVE

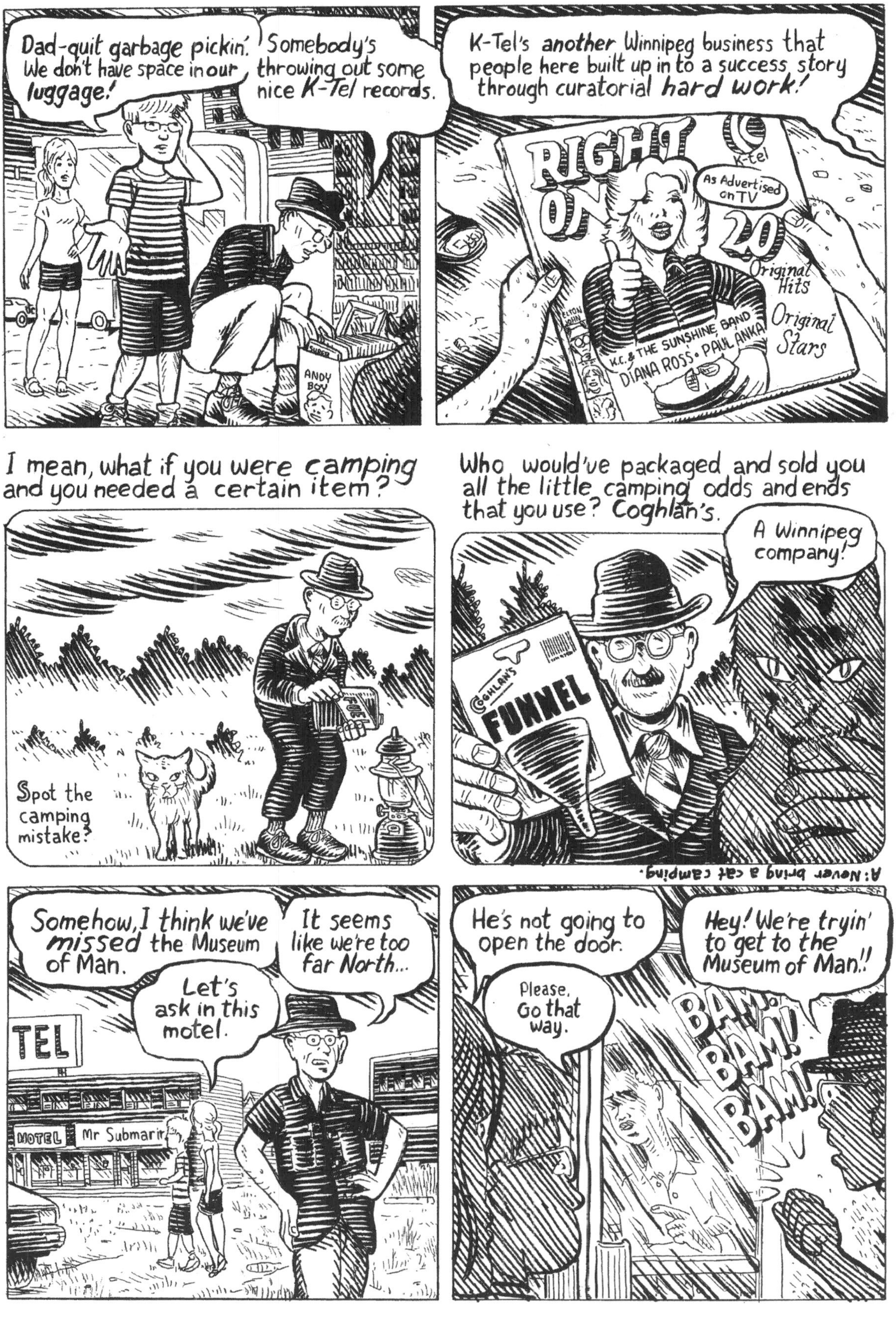
Dad-quit garbage pickin'. We don't have space in our luggage!
Somebody's throwing out some nice K-Tel records.
ANDY BOY
K-Tel's another Winnipeg business that people here built up in to a success story through curatorial hard work!
RIGHT ON
K-tel
As Advertised on TV
20 Original Hits
Original Stars
ELTON JOHN
K.C. & THE SUNSHINE BAND
DIANA ROSS • PAUL ANKA
I mean, what if you were camping and you needed a certain item?
Spot the camping mistake?
FUEL
Who would've packaged and sold you all the little camping odds and ends that you use? Coghlan's.
A Winnipeg company!
COGHLAN'S
FUNNEL
A: Never bring a cat camping.
Somehow, I think we've missed the Museum of Man.
It seems like we're too far North...
Let's ask in this motel.
TEL
MOTEL
Mr Submarin
He's not going to open the door.
Hey! We're tryin' to get to the Museum of Man!!
Please, Go that way.
BAM! BAM! BAM! BAM!

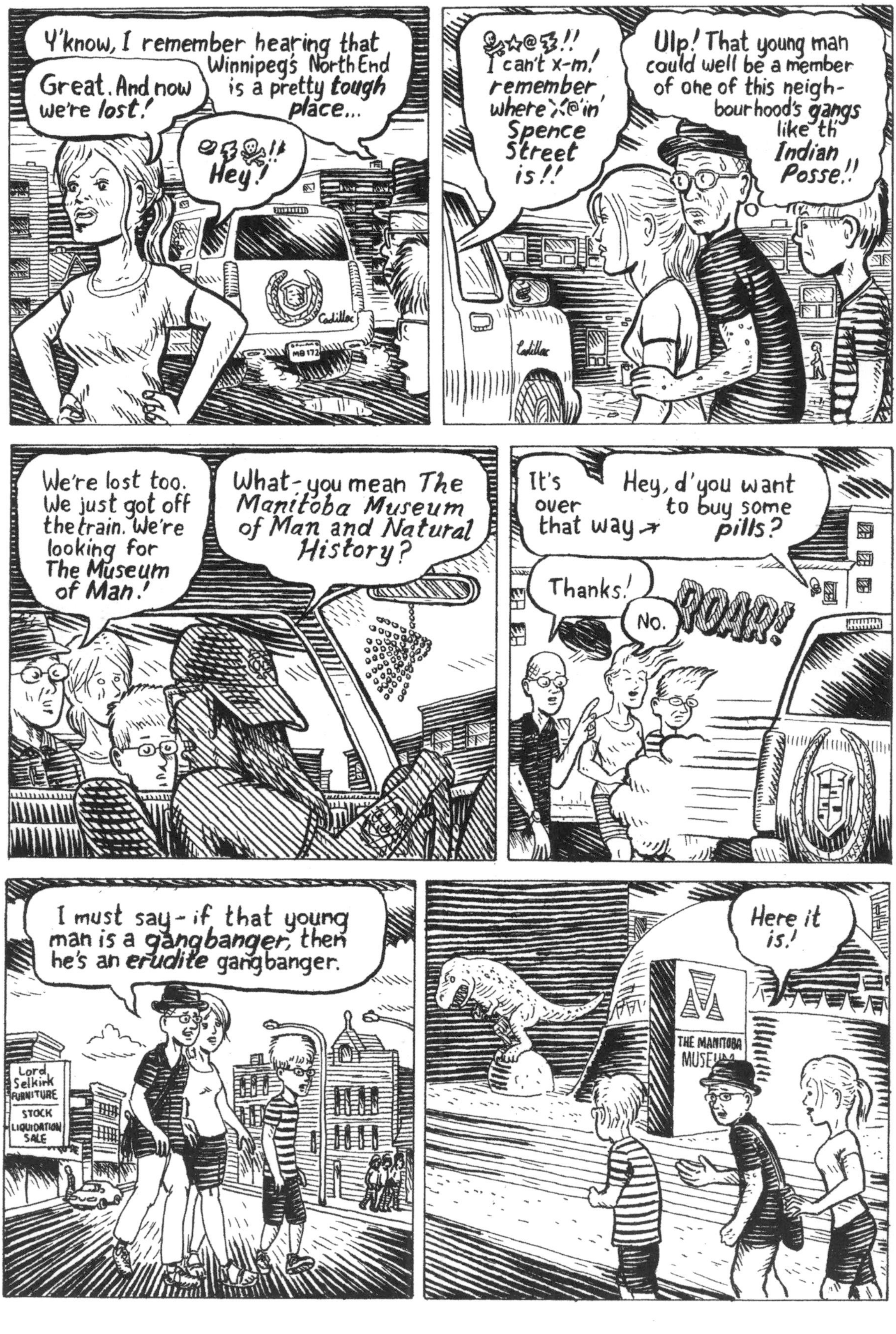

Y'know, I remember hearing that Winnipeg's North End is a pretty *tough* place...
Great. And now we're *lost!*
Hey!
Cadillac
I can't x-m! *remember*, where 'in' Spence Street is!!
Ulp! That young man could well be a member of one of this neighbourhood's *gangs* like th' *Indian Posse!!*
Cadillac
We're lost too. We just got off the train. We're looking for The *Museum* of *Man!*
What- you mean *The Manitoba Museum of Man and Natural History?*
It's over that way →
Hey, d'you want to buy some *pills?*
Thanks!
No.
ROAR!
I must say- if that young man is a *gangbanger*, then he's an *erudite* gangbanger.
Lord Selkirk FURNITURE
STOCK LIQUIDATION SALE
Here it is!
THE MANITOBA

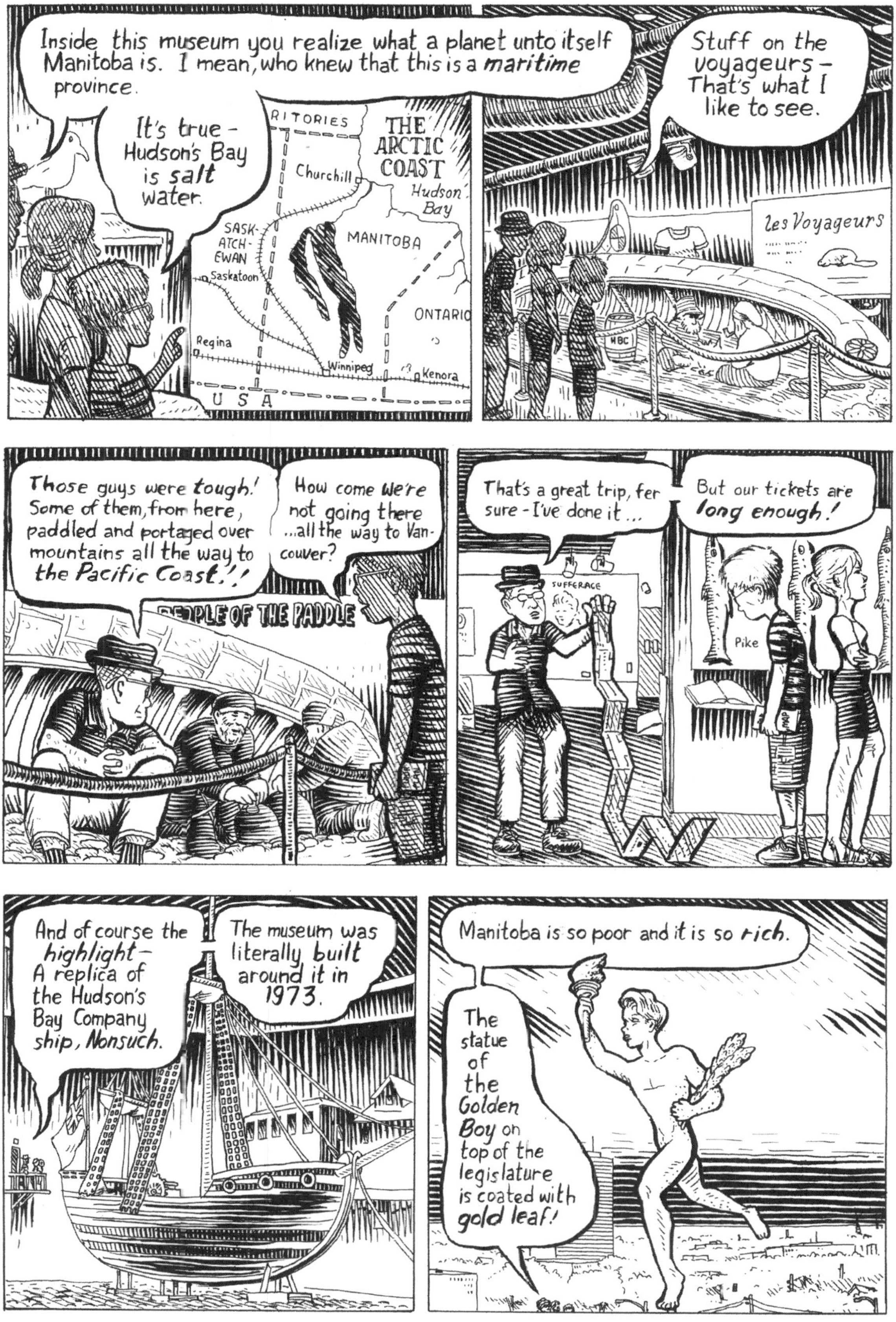
Inside this museum you realize what a planet unto itself Manitoba is. I mean, who knew that this is a *maritime* province.
It's true - Hudson's Bay is *salt* water.
RITORIES
THE ARCTIC COAST
Churchill
Hudson Bay
MANITOBA
SASK-ATCH-EWAN
Saskatoon
Regina
Winnipeg
Kenora
ONTARIO
U S A
Stuff on the voyageurs - That's what I like to see.
les Voyageurs
HBC
Those guys were *tough!* Some of them, from here, paddled and portaged over mountains all the way to *the Pacific Coast!!*
How come *we're* not going there ...all the way to Vancouver?
PEOPLE OF THE PADDLE
That's a great trip, fer sure - I've done it ...
But our tickets are *long enough!*
SUFFERAGE
Pike
And of course the *highlight* - A replica of the Hudson's Bay Company ship, *Nonsuch*.
The museum was literally *built* around it in 1973.
Manitoba is so poor and it is so *rich*.
The statue of the Golden Boy on top of the legislature is coated with *gold leaf!*

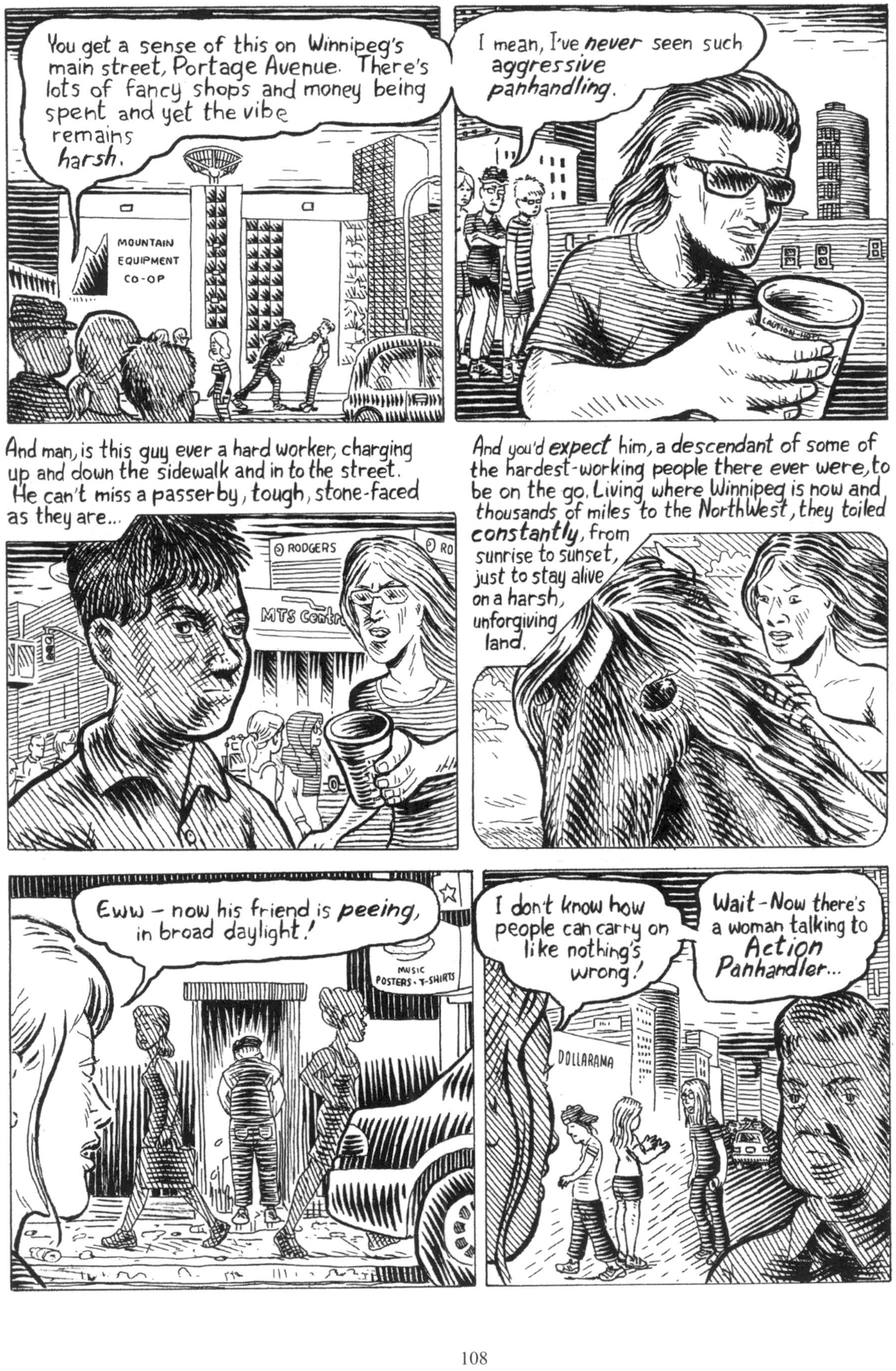
You get a sense of this on Winnipeg's main street, Portage Avenue. There's lots of fancy shops and money being spent and yet the vibe remains harsh.
MOUNTAIN EQUIPMENT CO-OP
I mean, I've never seen such aggressive panhandling.
CAUTION-HOT
And man, is this guy ever a hard worker, charging up and down the sidewalk and in to the street. He can't miss a passerby, tough, stone-faced as they are...
RODGERS
MTS Centr
And you'd expect him, a descendant of some of the hardest-working people there ever were, to be on the go. Living where Winnipeg is now and thousands of miles to the NorthWest, they toiled constantly, from sunrise to sunset, just to stay alive on a harsh, unforgiving land.
Eww – now his friend is peeing, in broad daylight!
MUSIC POSTERS • T-SHIRTS
I don't know how people can carry on like nothing's wrong!
Wait – Now there's a woman talking to Action Panhandler...
DOLLARAMA

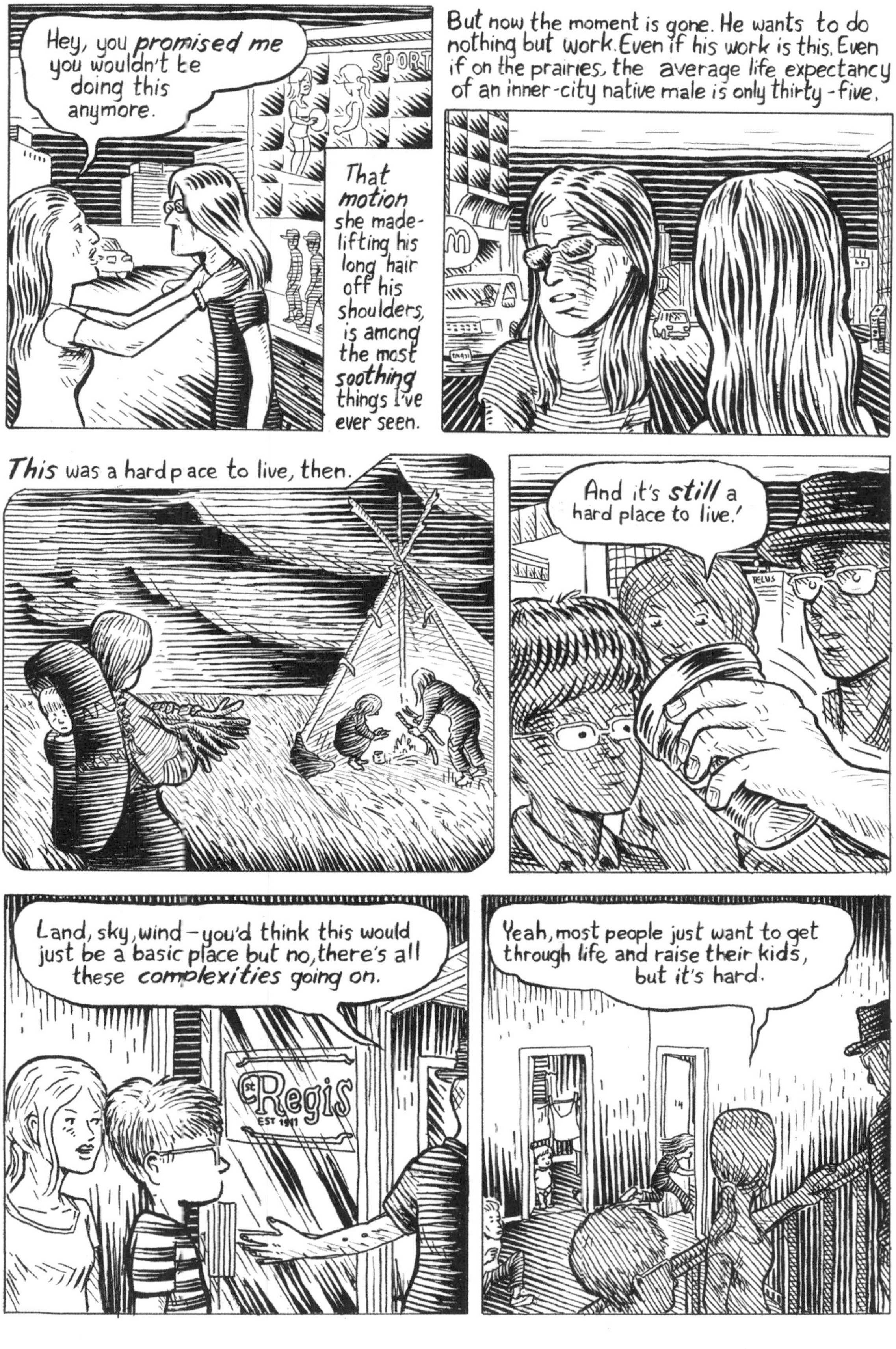
Hey, you promised me you wouldn't be doing this anymore.
That motion she made - lifting his long hair off his shoulders, is among the most soothing things I've ever seen.
But now the moment is gone. He wants to do nothing but work. Even if his work is this. Even if on the prairies, the average life expectancy of an inner-city native male is only thirty-five.
SPORT
This was a hard place to live, then.
And it's still a hard place to live.
TELUS
Land, sky, wind - you'd think this would just be a basic place but no, there's all these complexities going on.
St Regis
EST 1911
Yeah, most people just want to get through life and raise their kids, but it's hard.

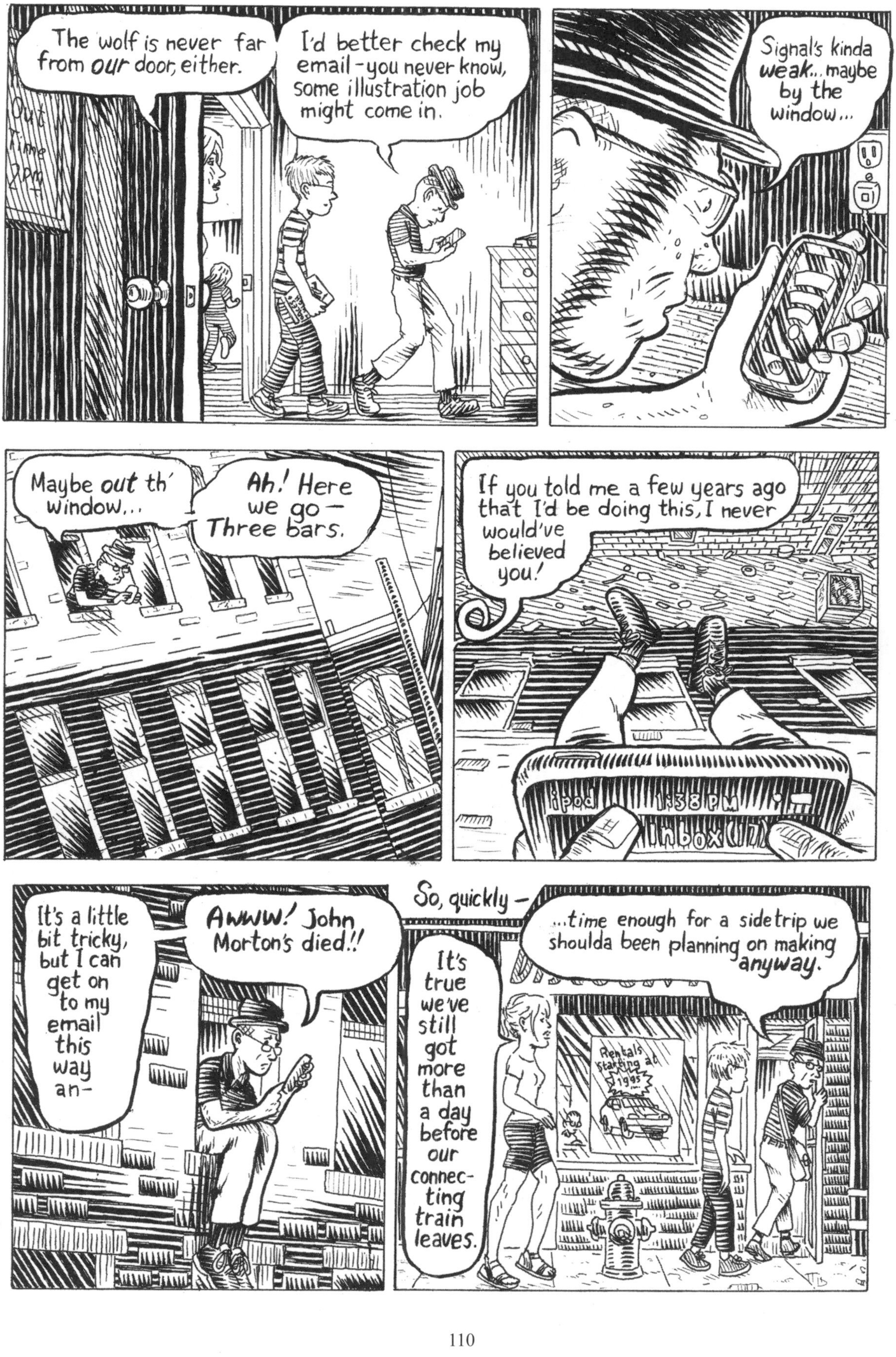
Out Time 2pm
The wolf is never far from *our* door, either.
I'd better check my email - you never know, some illustration job might come in.
Signal's kinda *weak*... maybe by the window...
Maybe *out* th' window...
Ah! Here we go — Three bars.
If you told me a few years ago that I'd be doing this, I never would've believed you!
ipod 1:38 PM
inbox(17)
It's a little bit tricky, but I can get on to my email this way an-
AWWW! John Morton's died!!
So, quickly —
It's true we've still got more than a day before our connecting train leaves.
...time enough for a side trip we shoulda been planning on making *anyway*.
Rentals starting at 1995

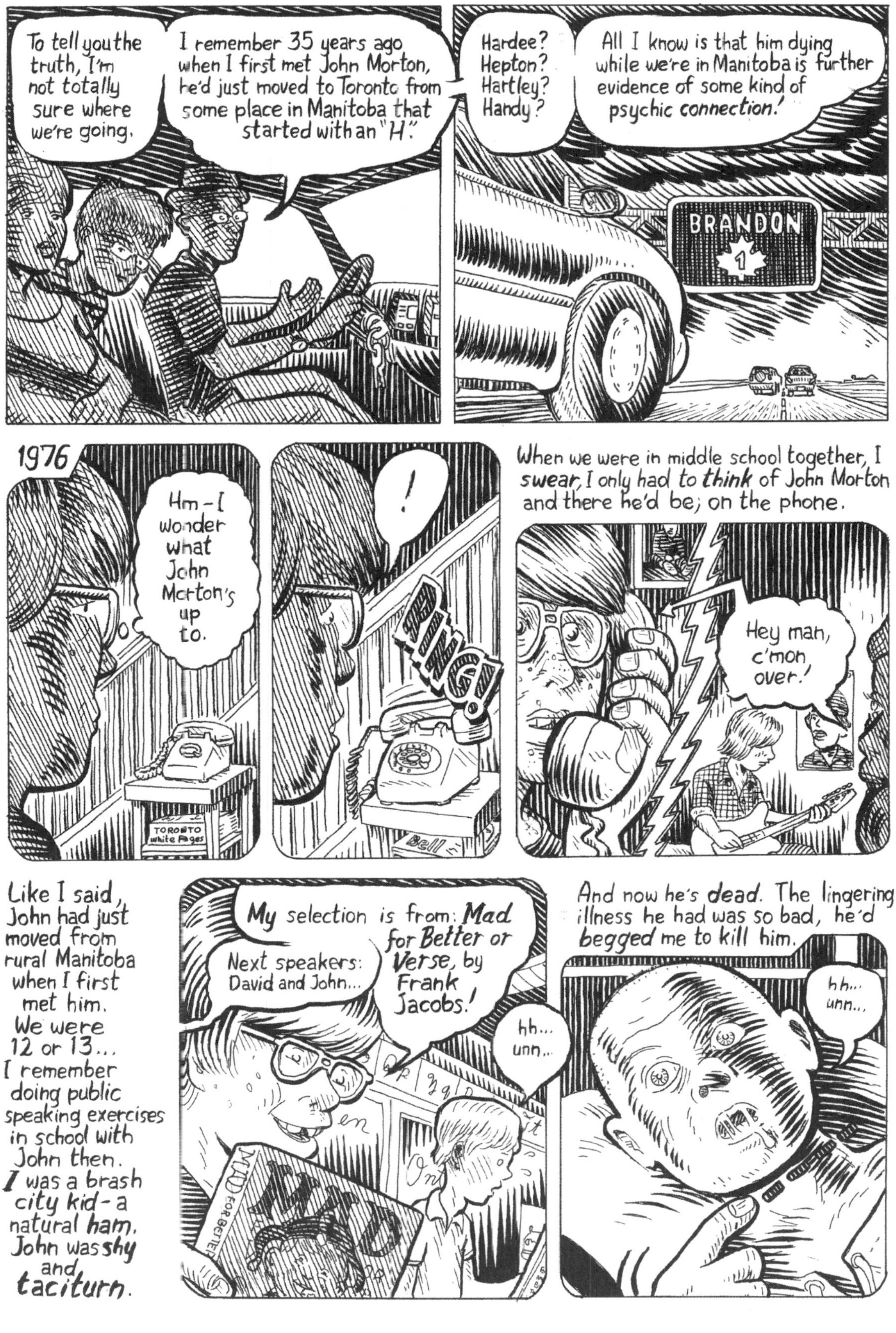

To tell you the truth, I'm not totally sure where we're going.
I remember 35 years ago when I first met John Morton, he'd just moved to Toronto from some place in Manitoba that started with an "H."
Hardee? Hepton? Hartley? Handy?
All I know is that him dying while we're in Manitoba is further evidence of some kind of psychic connection!
BRANDON
1
1976
Hm - I wonder what John Morton's up to.
TORONTO white Pages
!
RING!
Bell
When we were in middle school together, I swear, I only had to think of John Morton and there he'd be, on the phone.
Hey man, c'mon over!
Like I said, John had just moved from rural Manitoba when I first met him. We were 12 or 13... I remember doing public speaking exercises in school with John then. I was a brash city kid - a natural ham. John was shy and taciturn.
Next speakers: David and John...
My selection is from: Mad for Better or Verse, by Frank Jacobs!
hh... unn...
MAD
And now he's dead. The lingering illness he had was so bad, he'd begged me to kill him.
hh... unn...

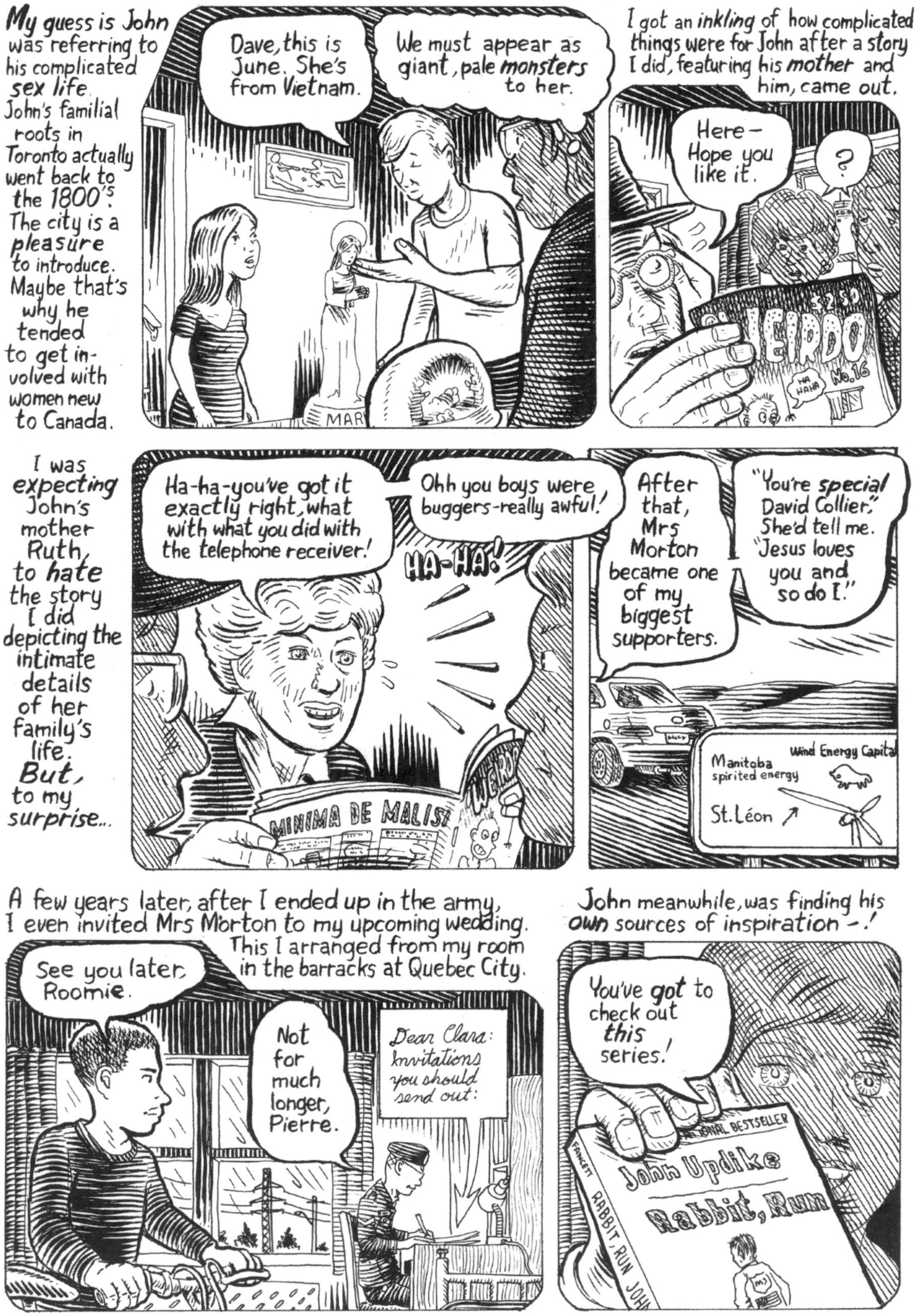
My guess is John was referring to his complicated sex life. John's familial roots in Toronto actually went back to the 1800's. The city is a pleasure to introduce. Maybe that's why he tended to get involved with women new to Canada.
Dave, this is June. She's from Vietnam.
We must appear as giant, pale monsters to her.
I got an inkling of how complicated things were for John after a story I did, featuring his mother and him, came out.
Here – Hope you like it.
?
WEIRDO
No. 16
HA HAHA
I was expecting John's mother Ruth, to hate the story I did depicting the intimate details of her family's life. But, to my surprise...
Ha-ha-you've got it exactly right, what with what you did with the telephone receiver!
Ohh you boys were buggers-really awful!
HA-HA!
MINIMA DE MALIS!
After that, Mrs Morton became one of my biggest supporters.
"You're special David Collier." She'd tell me. "Jesus loves you and so do I."
Manitoba spirited energy
Wind Energy Capital
St. Léon
A few years later, after I ended up in the army, I even invited Mrs Morton to my upcoming wedding. This I arranged from my room in the barracks at Quebec City.
See you later, Roomie.
Not for much longer, Pierre.
Dear Clara: Invitations you should send out:
John meanwhile, was finding his own sources of inspiration –!
You've got to check out this series!
NATIONAL BESTSELLER
John Updike
Rabbit, Run
FAWCETT
RABBIT, RUN

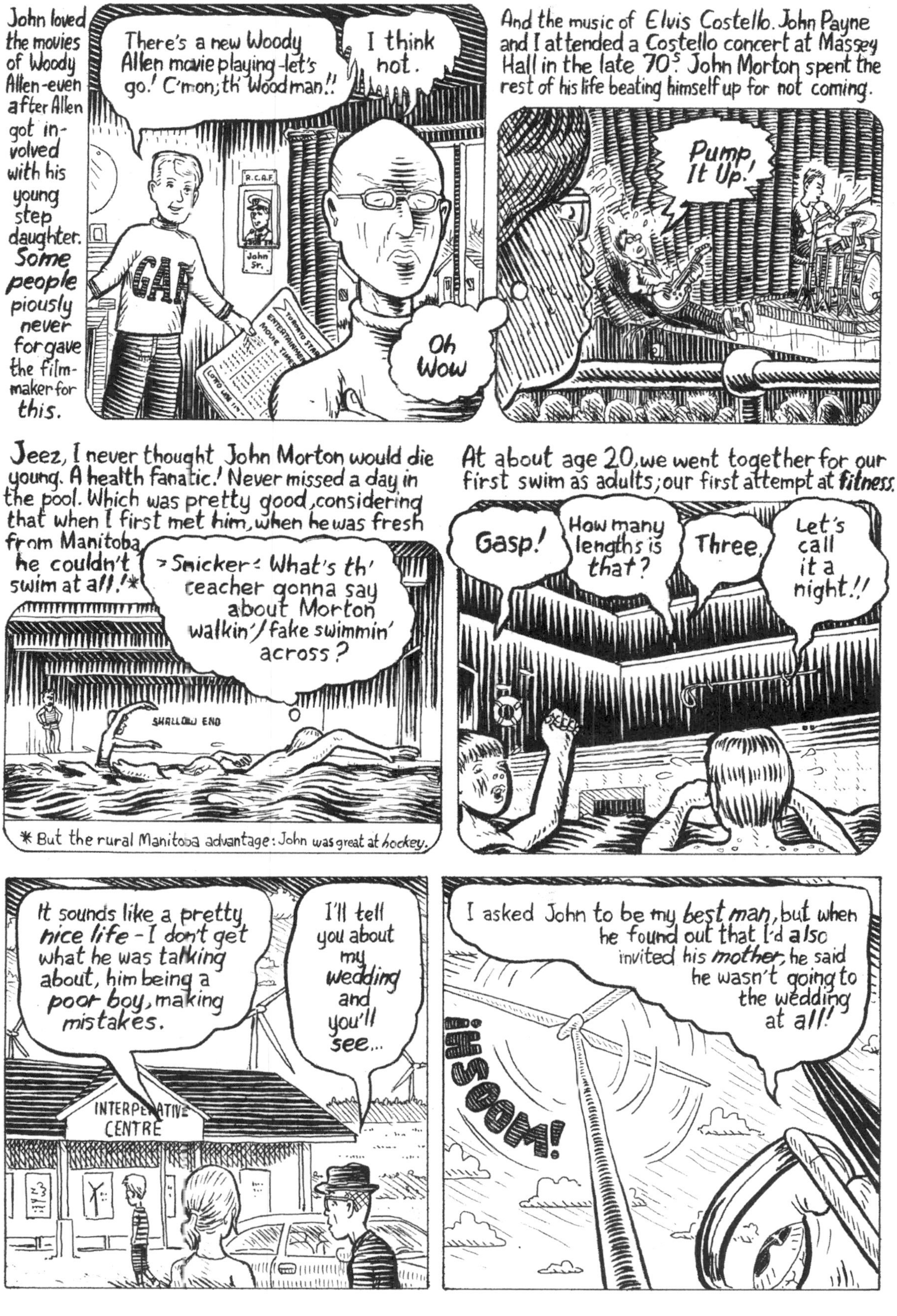

John loved the movies of Woody Allen–even after Allen got involved with his young step daughter. Some people piously never forgave the filmmaker for this.
There's a new Woody Allen movie playing–let's go! C'mon, th' Woodman!!
I think not.
Oh Wow
R.C.A.F.
John Sr.
GAP
TORONTO STAR ENTERTAINMENT MOVIE TIMES
And the music of Elvis Costello. John Payne and I attended a Costello concert at Massey Hall in the late 70s. John Morton spent the rest of his life beating himself up for not coming.
Pump It Up!
Jeez, I never thought John Morton would die young. A health fanatic! Never missed a day in the pool. Which was pretty good, considering that when I first met him, when he was fresh from Manitoba, he couldn't swim at all!*
> Snicker < What's th' teacher gonna say about Morton walkin'/fake swimmin' across?
SHALLOW END
* But the rural Manitoba advantage: John was great at hockey.
At about age 20, we went together for our first swim as adults; our first attempt at fitness.
Gasp!
How many lengths is that?
Three.
Let's call it a night!!
It sounds like a pretty nice life–I don't get what he was talking about, him being a poor boy, making mistakes.
I'll tell you about my wedding and you'll see...
INTERPRETATIVE CENTRE
I asked John to be my best man, but when he found out that I'd also invited his mother, he said he wasn't going to the wedding at all!
WHOOSH!

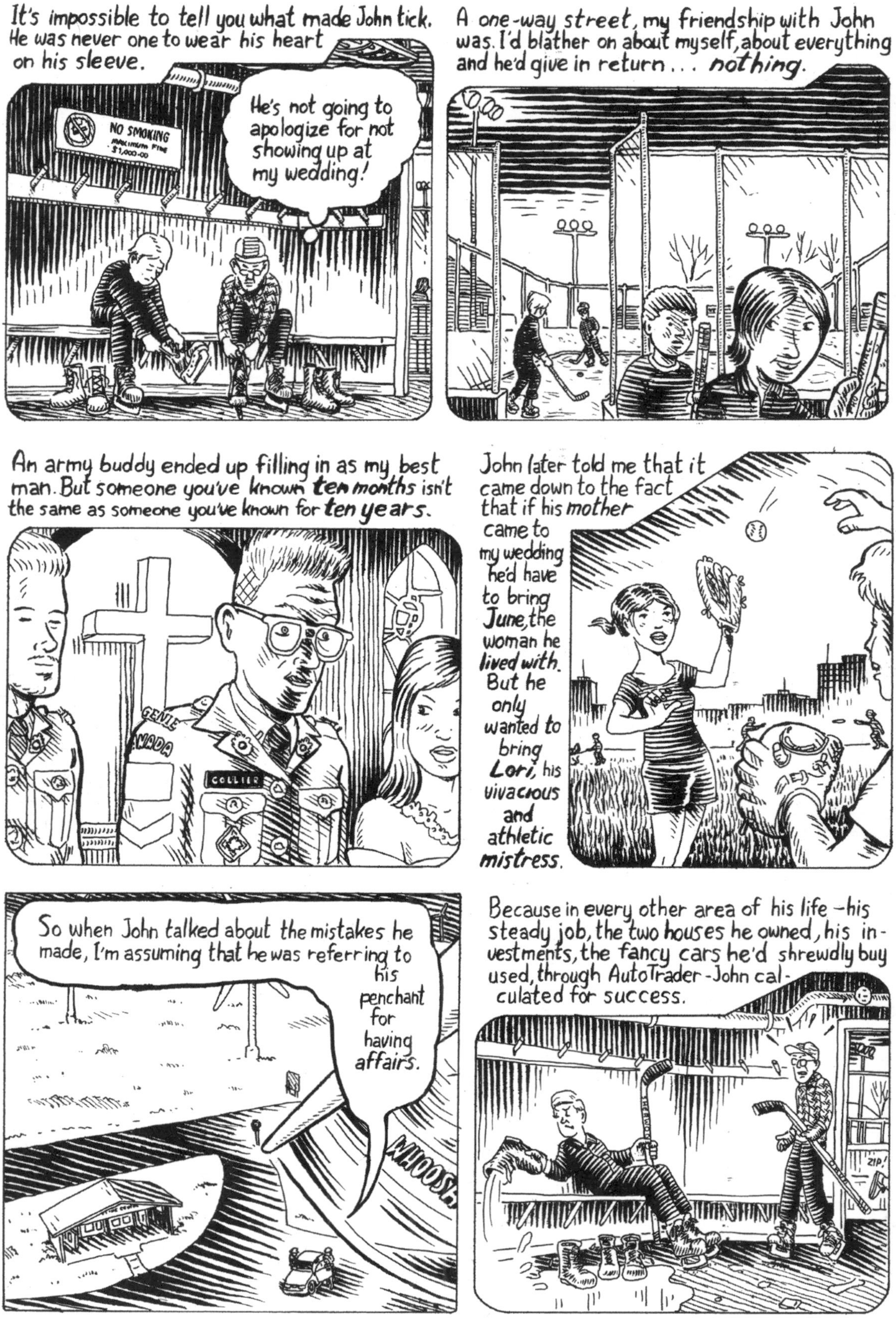
It's impossible to tell you what made John tick. He was never one to wear his heart on his sleeve.
NO SMOKING
MAXIMUM FINE $1,000.00
He's not going to apologize for not showing up at my wedding!
A one-way *street*, my friendship with John was. I'd blather on about myself, about everything and he'd give in return . . . ***nothing***.
An army buddy ended up filling in as my best man. But someone you've known **ten months** isn't the same as someone you've known for **ten years**.
COLLIER
John later told me that it came down to the fact that if his *mother* came to my wedding he'd have to bring **June**, the woman he *lived with*. But he only wanted to bring ***Lori***, his *vivacious* **and** *athletic* ***mistress***.
So when John talked about the mistakes he made, I'm assuming that he was referring to his penchant for having *affairs*.
Because in every other area of his life - his steady job, the two houses he owned, his investments, the fancy cars he'd shrewdly buy used, through AutoTrader - John calculated for success.
ZIP!

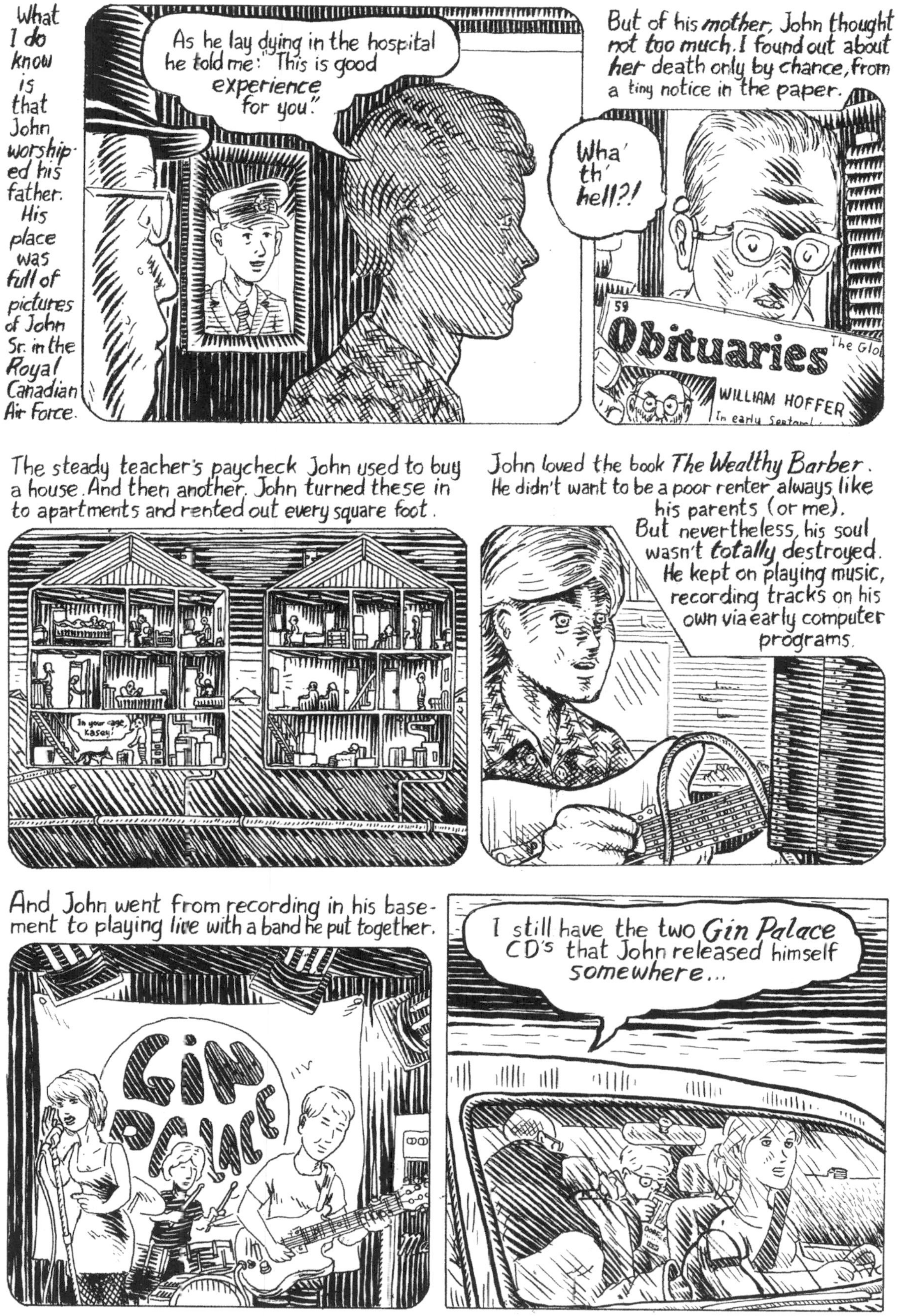
What I do know is that John worshiped his father. His place was full of pictures of John Sr. in the Royal Canadian Air Force.
As he lay dying in the hospital he told me: "This is good experience for you."
But of his mother, John thought not too much. I found out about her death only by chance, from a tiny notice in the paper.
Wha' th' hell?!
59
Obituaries
The Glo
WILLIAM HOFFER
The steady teacher's paycheck John used to buy a house. And then another. John turned these in to apartments and rented out every square foot.
In your cage, Kasey!
John loved the book The Wealthy Barber. He didn't want to be a poor renter always like his parents (or me).
But nevertheless, his soul wasn't totally destroyed. He kept on playing music, recording tracks on his own via early computer programs.
And John went from recording in his basement to playing live with a band he put together.
GIN PALACE
I still have the two Gin Palace CD's that John released himself somewhere...

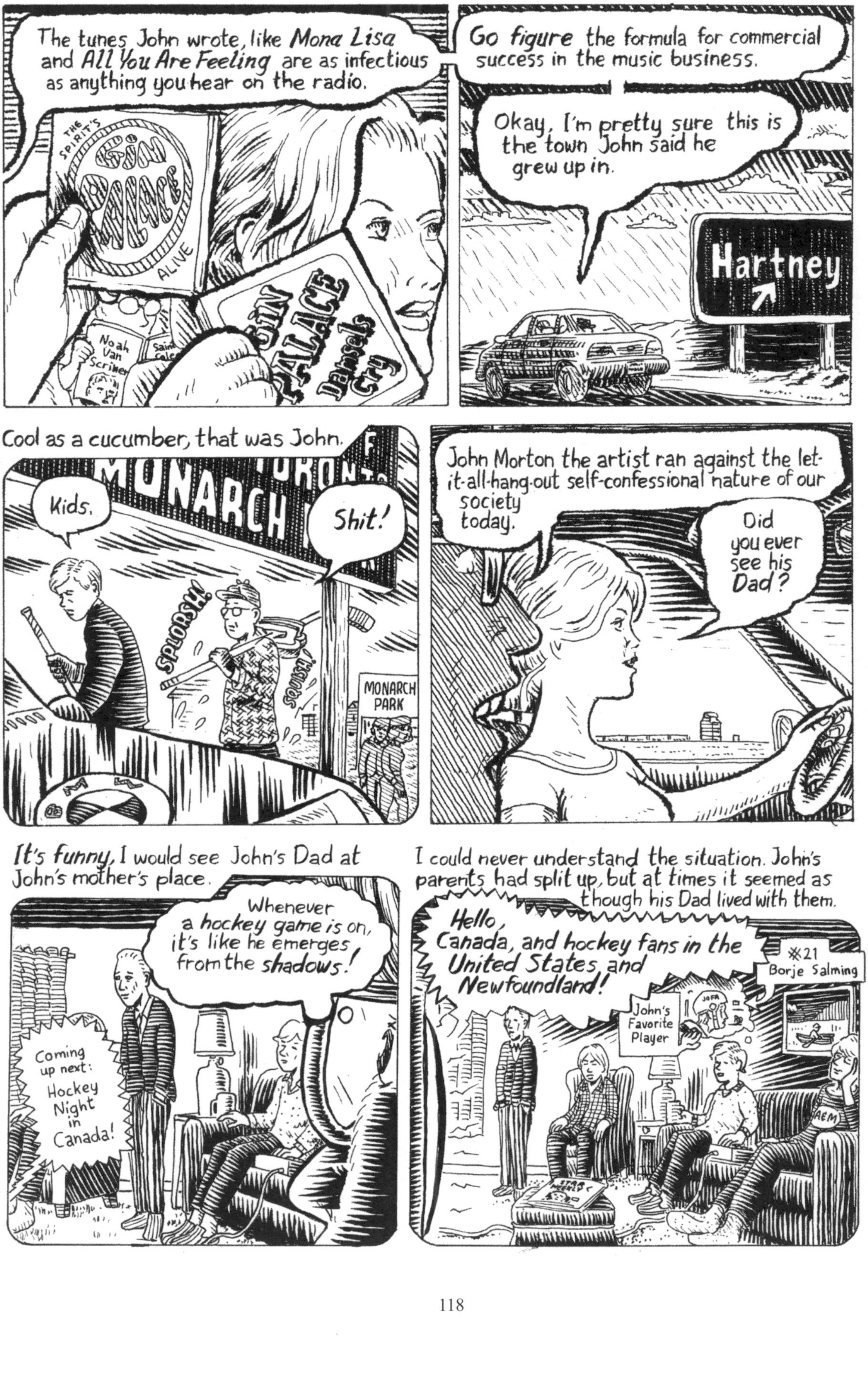
The tunes John wrote, like *Mona Lisa* and *All You Are Feeling* are as infectious as anything you hear on the radio.
THE SPIRIT'S GIN PALACE ALIVE
GIN PALACE Damsels Cry
Noah Van Scriber
Go *figure* the formula for commercial success in the music business.
Okay, I'm pretty sure this is the town John said he grew up in.
Hartney
Cool as a cucumber, that was John.
MONARCH
Kids.
Shit!
SPLORSH!
SQUISH!
MONARCH PARK
John Morton the artist ran against the let-it-all-hang-out self-confessional nature of our society today.
Did you ever see his *Dad*?
It's funny, I would see John's Dad at John's mother's place.
Whenever a *hockey game* is on, it's like he emerges from the *shadows!*
Coming up next: Hockey Night in Canada!
I could never understand the situation. John's parents had split up, but at times it seemed as though his Dad lived with them.
Hello, Canada, and hockey fans in the United States and Newfoundland!
※21 Borje Salming
John's Favorite Player
JOFA
AEM

John went to Radio & Television College. And after, he got a job in a high-pressure TV newsroom. He didn't last a day.

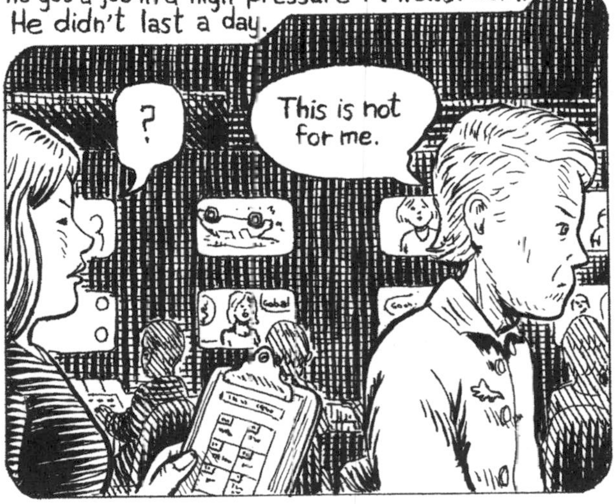
?
This is not for me.

So John went to Teacher's College and got a job with the Toronto District School Board. Working with kindergarten kids was more his speed. John was known as The Singing Teacher.

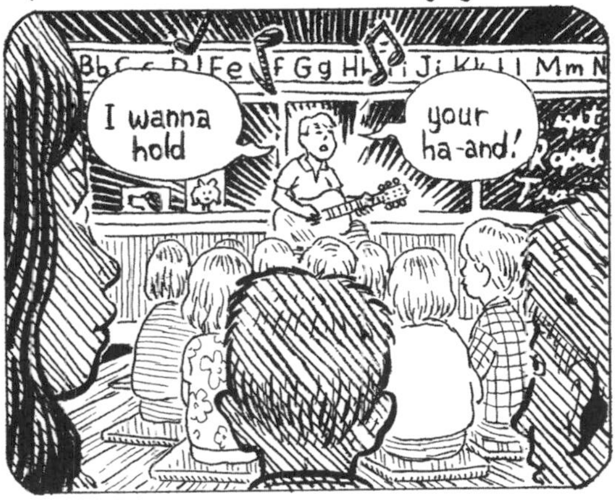
I wanna hold
your ha-and!

John loved the steady pay check of a teacher's job. But he felt **constrained** being in the community-level **public eye**.

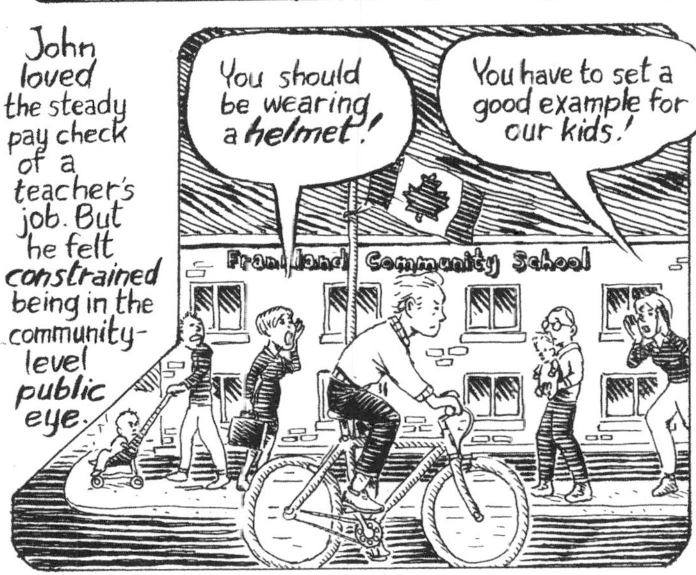
You should be wearing a *helmet*!
You have to set a good example for our kids!
Frankland Community School

John incidently, is the one who got me back to biking as an adult. He pointed out: a **bike** is the perfect device for scoping out chicks.

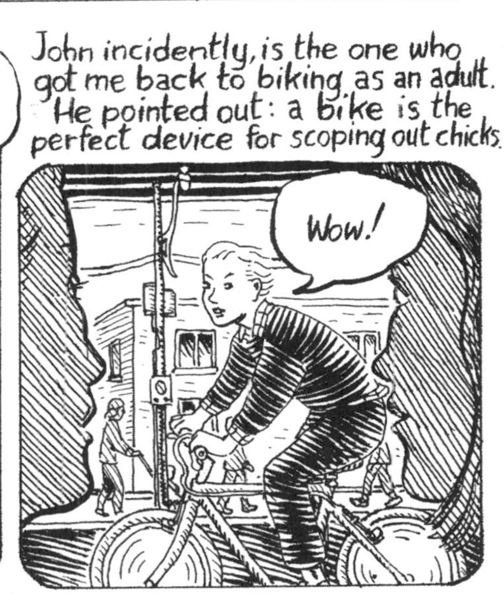
Wow!

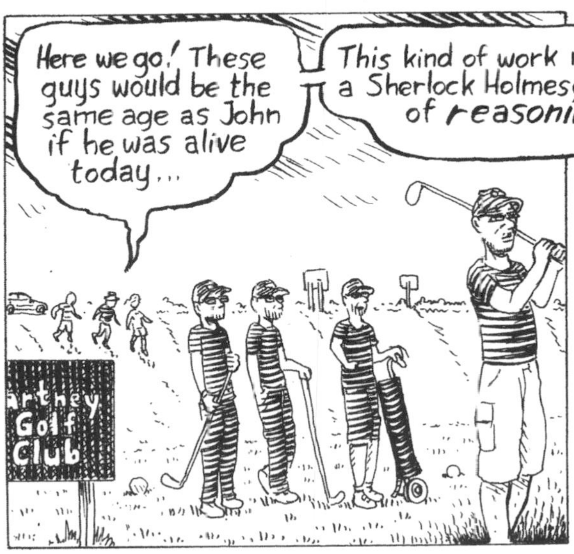
Here we go! These guys would be the same age as John if he was alive today...
This kind of work requires a Sherlock Holmesque-sense of **reasoning**!
Golf Club

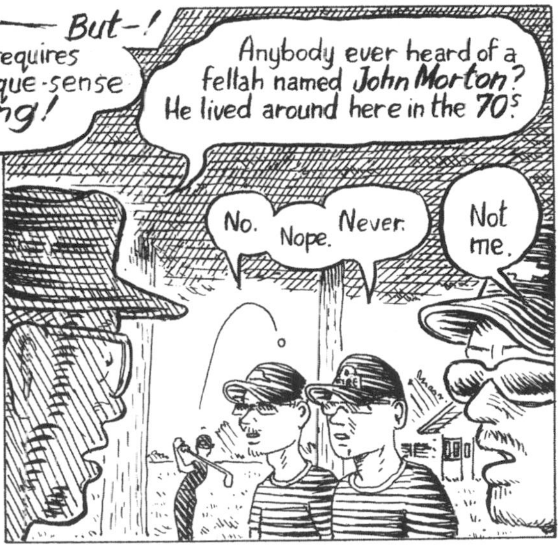
But-!
Anybody ever heard of a fellah named *John Morton*? He lived around here in the 70s
No.
Nope.
Never.
Not me.

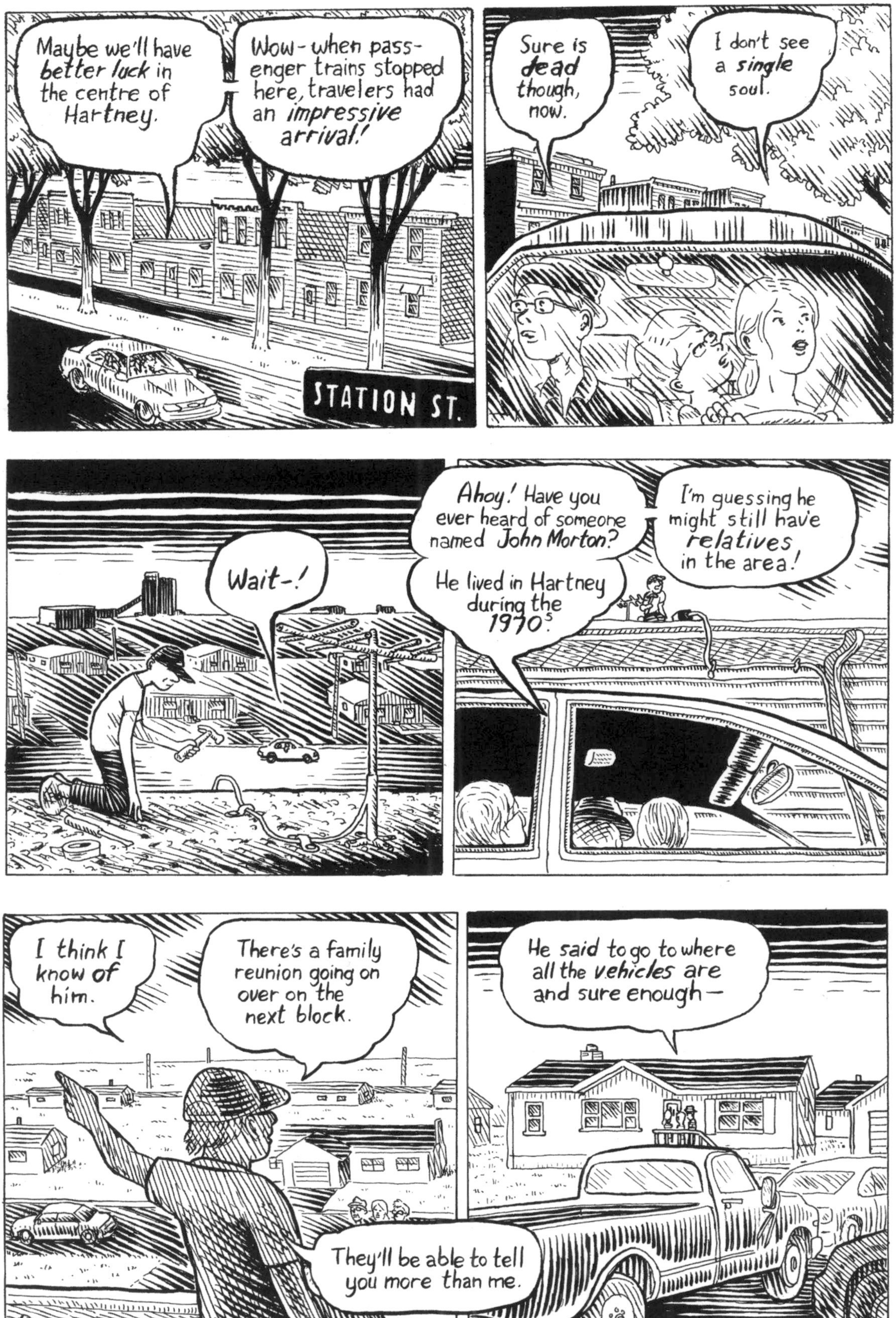
Maybe we'll have better luck in the centre of Hartney.
Wow - when passenger trains stopped here, travelers had an impressive arrival!
STATION ST.
Sure is dead though, now.
I don't see a single soul.
Wait-!
Ahoy! Have you ever heard of someone named John Morton?
He lived in Hartney during the 1970s.
I'm guessing he might still have relatives in the area!
I think I know of him.
There's a family reunion going on over on the next block.
They'll be able to tell you more than me.
He said to go to where all the vehicles are and sure enough—

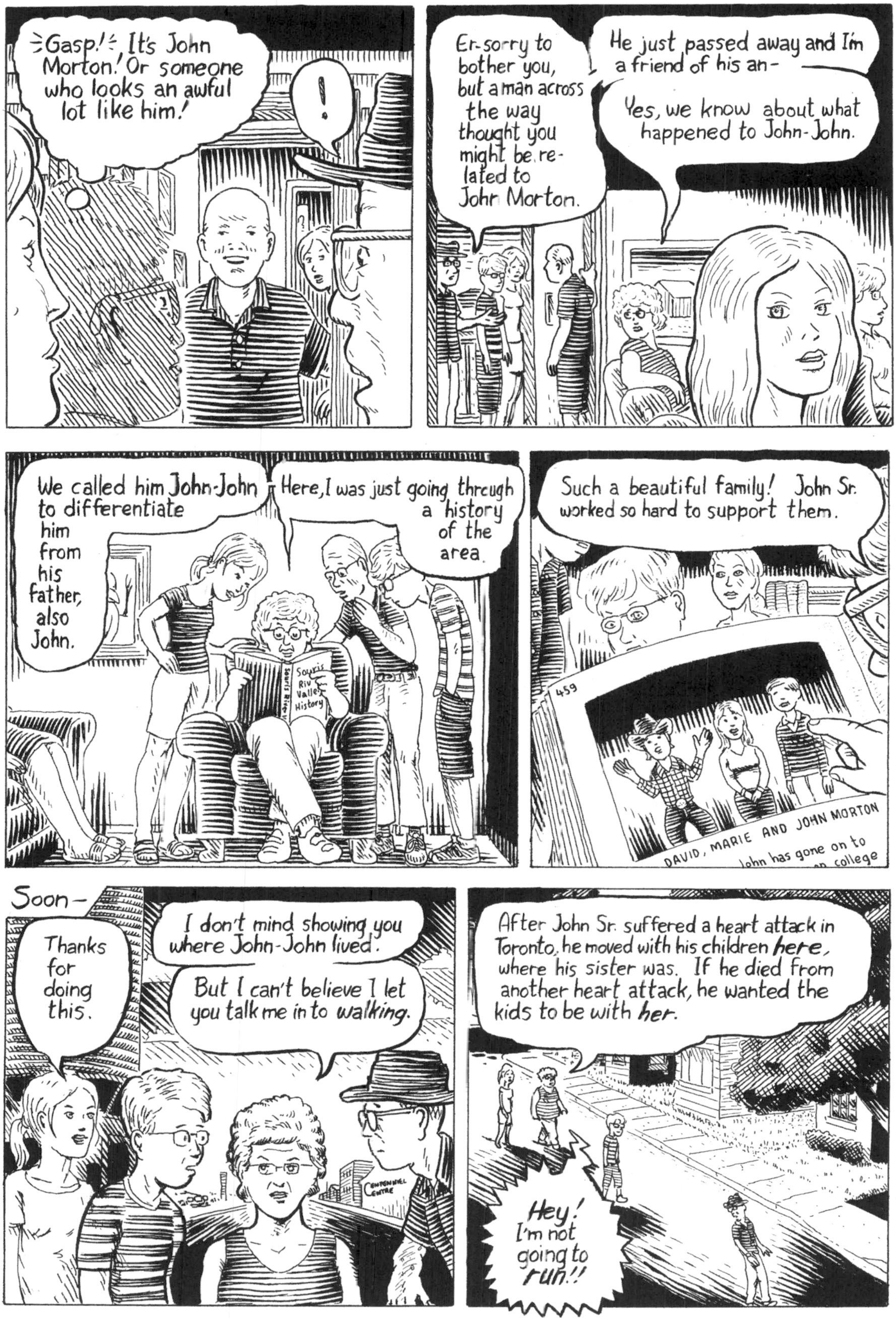
Gasp! It's John Morton! Or someone who looks an awful lot like him!
!
Er-sorry to bother you, but a man across the way thought you might be related to John Morton.
He just passed away and I'm a friend of his an-
Yes, we know about what happened to John-John.
We called him John-John to differentiate him from his father, also John.
Here, I was just going through a history of the area.
Souris River Valley History
Such a beautiful family! John Sr. worked so hard to support them.
459
DAVID, MARIE AND JOHN MORTON
John has gone on to
college
Soon-
Thanks for doing this.
I don't mind showing you where John-John lived.
But I can't believe I let you talk me in to walking.
CENTENNIAL CENTRE
After John Sr. suffered a heart attack in Toronto, he moved with his children here, where his sister was. If he died from another heart attack, he wanted the kids to be with her.
Hey! I'm not going to run!!

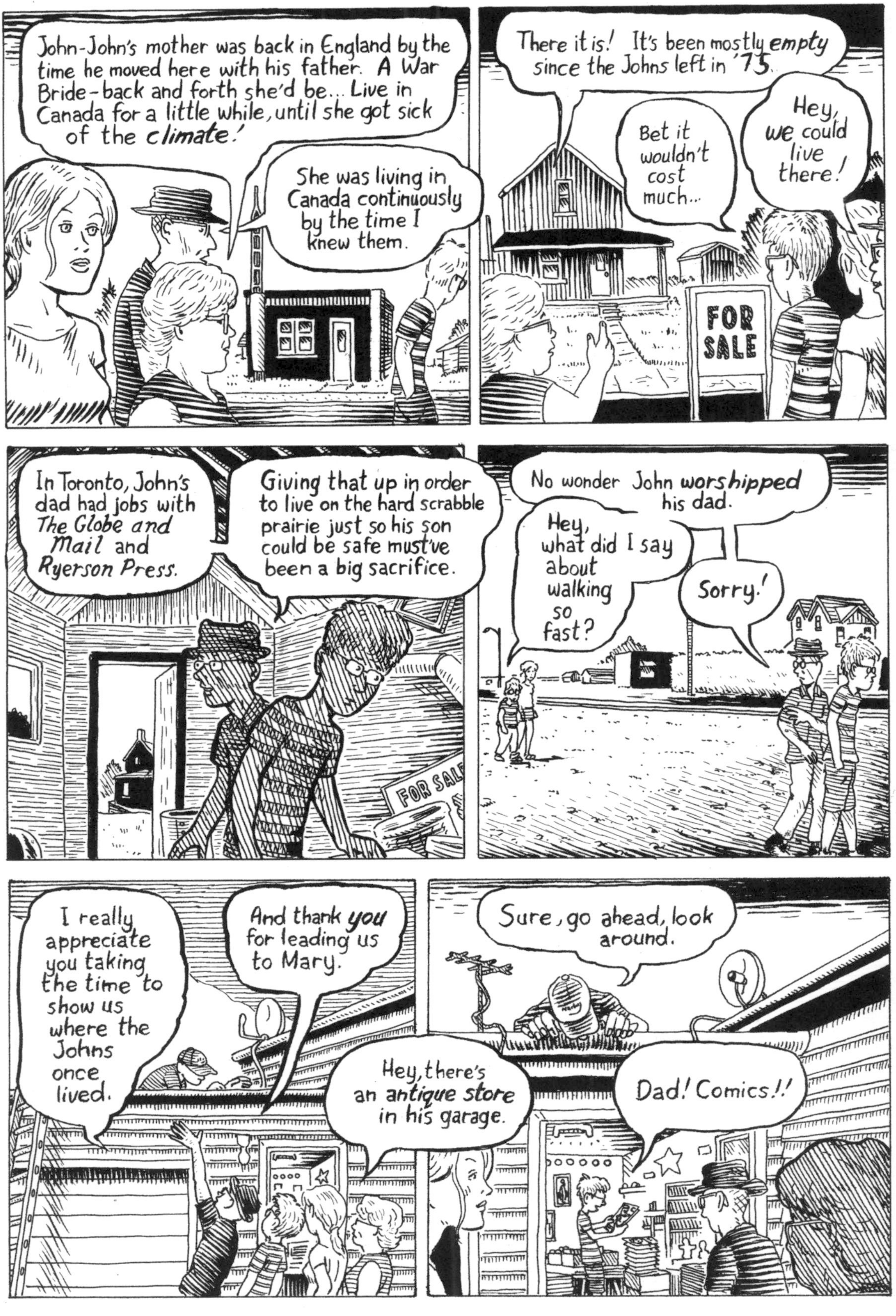
John-John's mother was back in England by the time he moved here with his father. A War Bride - back and forth she'd be... Live in Canada for a little while, until she got sick of the climate!
She was living in Canada continuously by the time I knew them.
There it is! It's been mostly empty since the Johns left in '75.
Bet it wouldn't cost much...
Hey, we could live there!
FOR SALE
In Toronto, John's dad had jobs with The Globe and Mail and Ryerson Press.
Giving that up in order to live on the hard scrabble prairie just so his son could be safe must've been a big sacrifice.
FOR SALE
No wonder John worshipped his dad.
Hey, what did I say about walking so fast?
Sorry!
I really appreciate you taking the time to show us where the Johns once lived.
And thank you for leading us to Mary.
Hey, there's an antique store in his garage.
Sure, go ahead, look around.
Dad! Comics!!

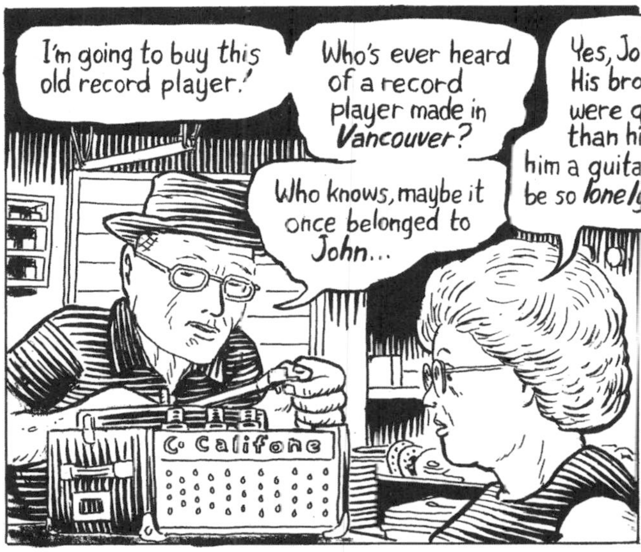
I'm going to buy this old record player!
Who's ever heard of a record player made in *Vancouver*?
Who knows, maybe it once belonged to John...
Califone
Yes, John *loved music*. His brother and sister were quite a bit older than him, so we bought him a guitar so he wouldn't be so *lonely*.

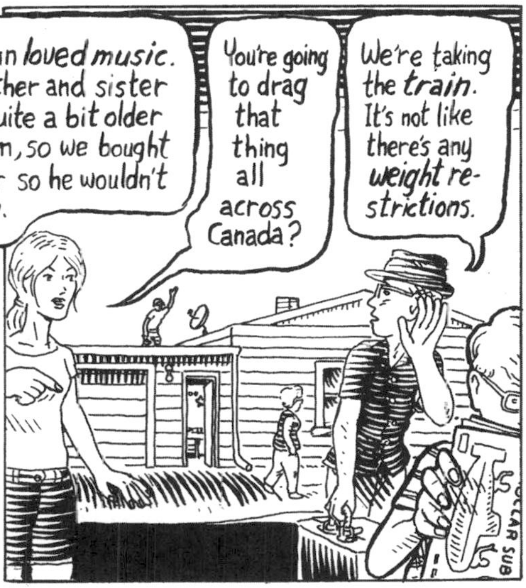
You're going to drag that thing all across Canada?
We're taking the *train*. It's not like there's any *weight* restrictions.

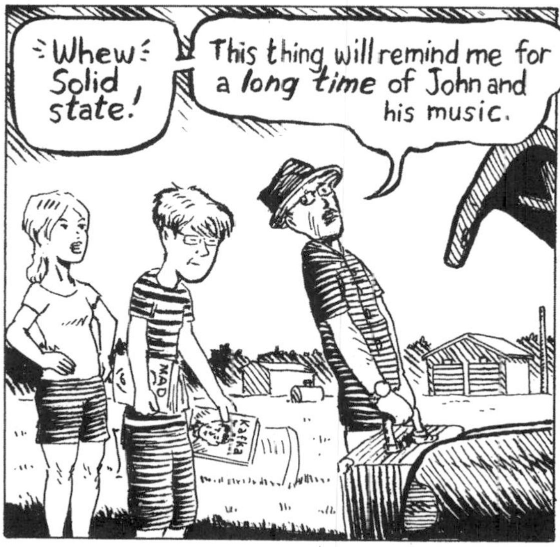
Whew Solid state!
This thing will remind me for a *long time* of John and his music.
MAD

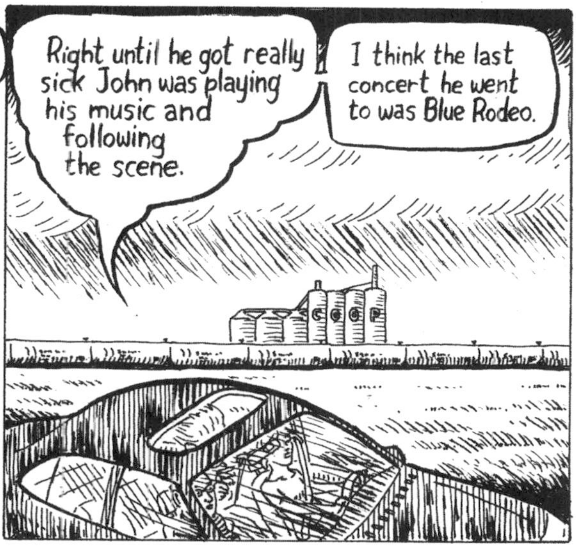
Right until he got really sick John was playing his music and following the scene.
I think the last concert he went to was Blue Rodeo.

See, what you've got to realize about John Morton is that he was a bit of a rock star. In the end, he even got into *sports cars!*

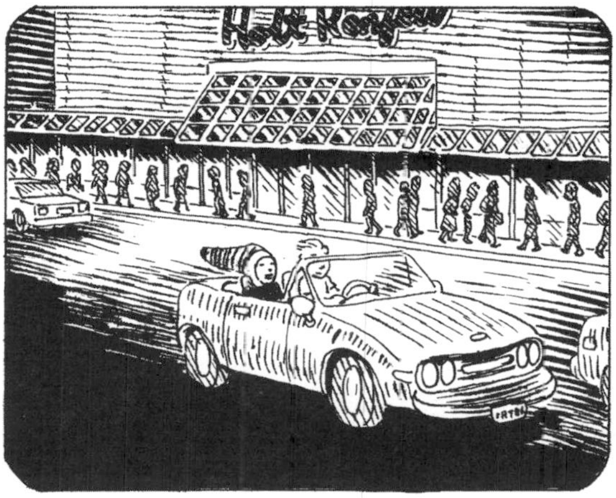

The old cars gave him a lot of *headaches*, though. The last time John visited me in Hamilton, his little *Aston Martin Spider* broke down on a narrow ramp that leads to the highway here. The experience left him *extremely agitated*.

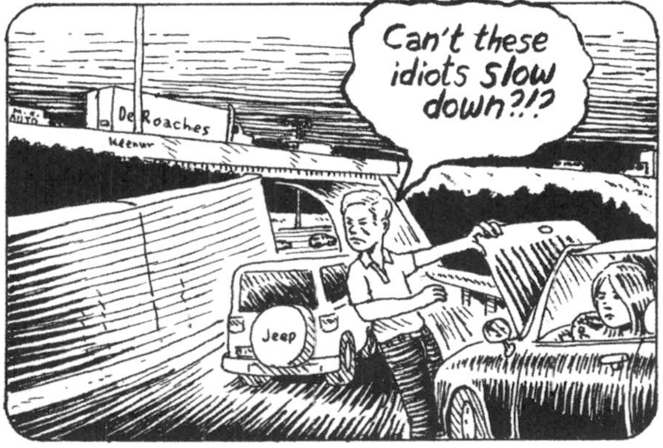
Can't these idiots *slow* down?!?
Jeep

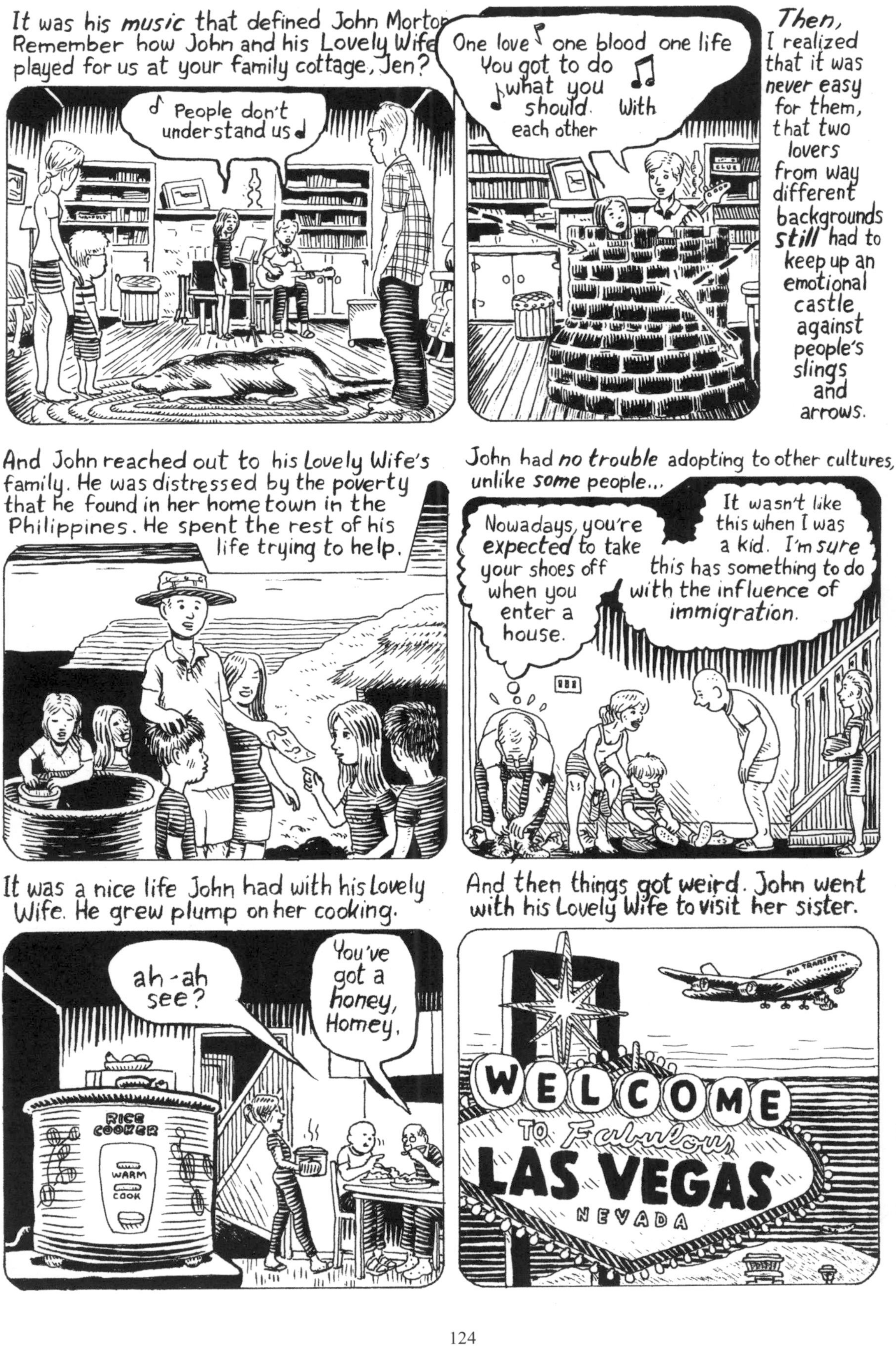
It was his music that defined John Morto
Remember how John and his Lovely Wife played for us at your family cottage, Jen?
People don't understand us
One love one blood one life You got to do what you should. With each other
Then, I realized that it was never easy for them, that two lovers from way different backgrounds still had to keep up an emotional castle against people's slings and arrows.
And John reached out to his Lovely Wife's family. He was distressed by the poverty that he found in her home town in the Philippines. He spent the rest of his life trying to help.
John had no trouble adopting to other cultures, unlike some people...
Nowadays, you're expected to take your shoes off when you enter a house.
It wasn't like this when I was a kid. I'm sure this has something to do with the influence of immigration.
It was a nice life John had with his Lovely Wife. He grew plump on her cooking.
ah-ah see?
You've got a honey, Homey.
RICE COOKER
WARM
COOK
And then things got weird. John went with his Lovely Wife to visit her sister.
WELCOME TO Fabulous LAS VEGAS NEVADA

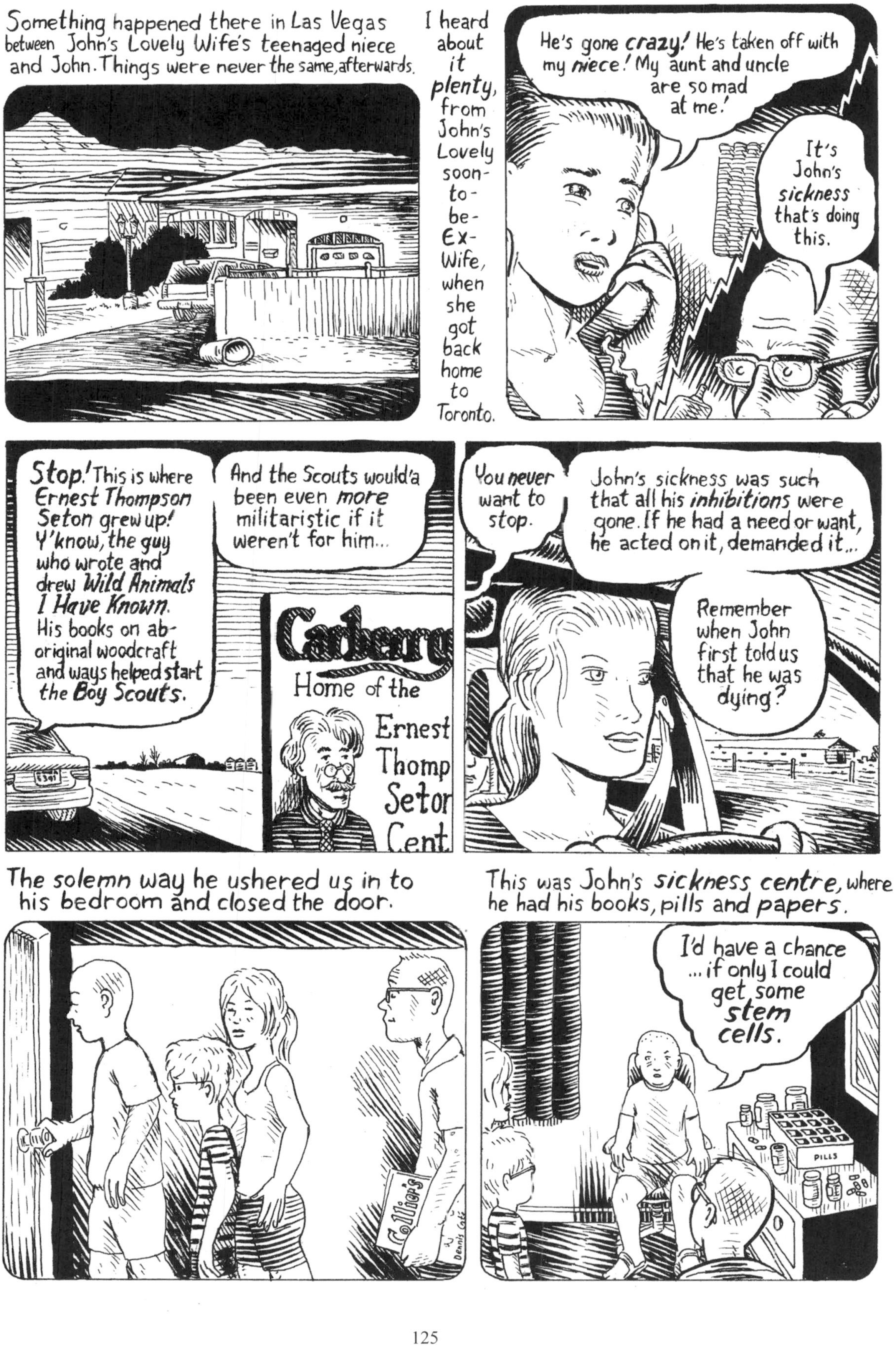
Something happened there in Las Vegas between John's Lovely Wife's teenaged niece and John. Things were never the same, afterwards.
I heard about *it* *plenty*, from John's Lovely soon-to-be-Ex-Wife, when she got back home to Toronto.
He's gone *crazy!* He's taken off with my *niece!* My aunt and uncle are so mad at me!
It's John's *sickness* that's doing this.
Stop! This is where Ernest Thompson Seton grew up! Y'know, the guy who wrote and drew *Wild Animals I Have Known*. His books on aboriginal woodcraft and ways helped start *the Boy Scouts*.
And the Scouts would'a been even *more* militaristic if it weren't for him...
Home of the
Ernest
Thomp
Seton
Cent
You *never* want to stop.
John's sickness was such that all his *inhibitions* were gone. If he had a need or want, he acted on it, demanded it...
Remember when John first told us that he was dying?
The solemn way he ushered us in to his bedroom and closed the door.
Collier's
This was John's *sickness centre*, where he had his books, pills and *papers*.
I'd have a chance ...if only I could get some **stem cells**.
PILLS

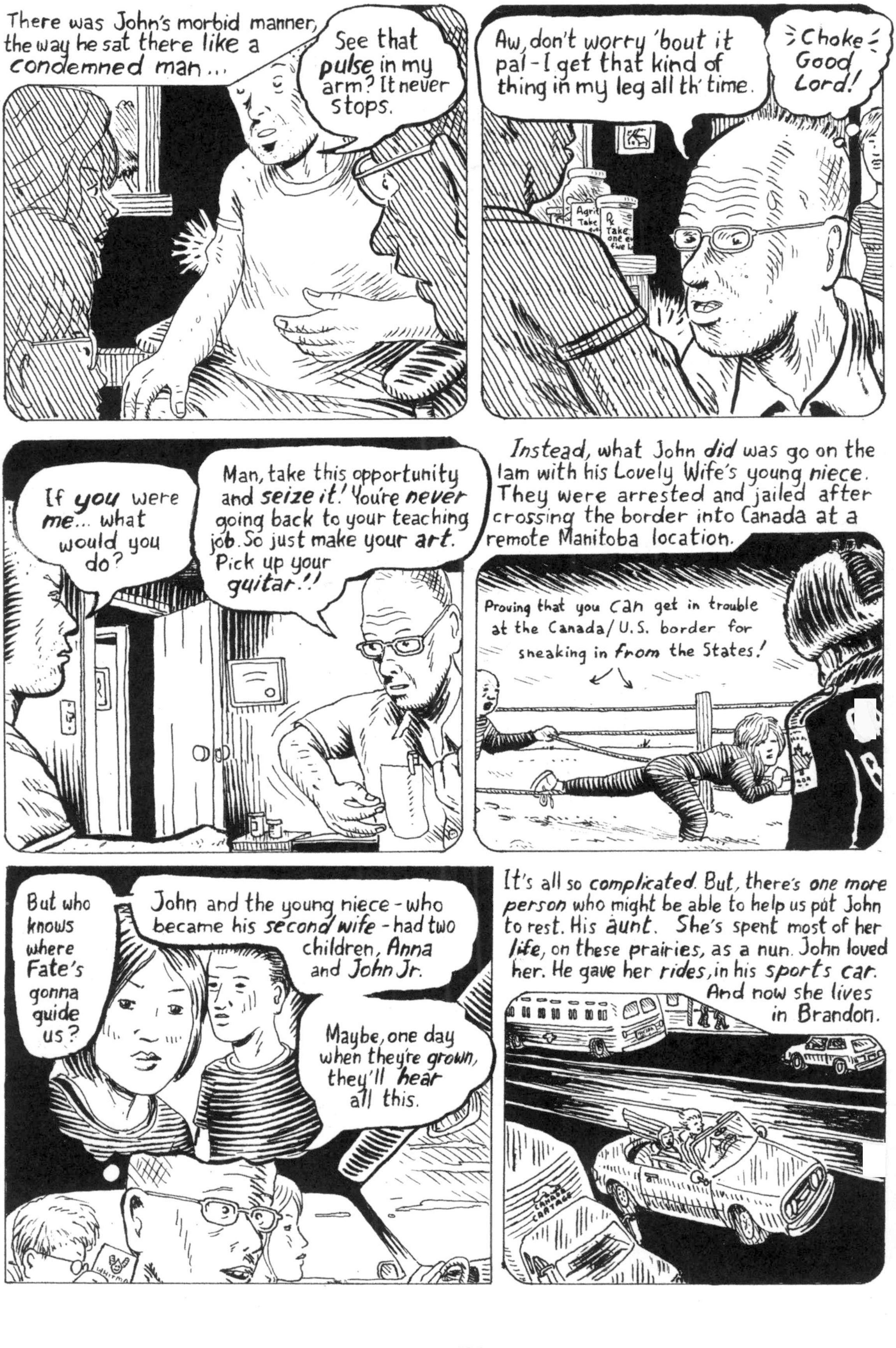

There was John's morbid manner, the way he sat there like a condemned man...
See that pulse in my arm? It never stops.
Aw, don't worry 'bout it pal - I get that kind of thing in my leg all th' time.
Choke Good Lord!
If you were me... what would you do?
Man, take this opportunity and seize it! You're never going back to your teaching job. So just make your art. Pick up your guitar!!
Instead, what John did was go on the lam with his Lovely Wife's young niece. They were arrested and jailed after crossing the border into Canada at a remote Manitoba location.
Proving that you can get in trouble at the Canada/U.S. border for sneaking in from the States!
But who knows where Fate's gonna guide us?
John and the young niece - who became his second wife - had two children, Anna and John Jr.
Maybe, one day when they're grown, they'll hear all this.
It's all so complicated. But, there's one more person who might be able to help us put John to rest. His aunt. She's spent most of her life, on these prairies, as a nun. John loved her. He gave her rides, in his sports car. And now she lives in Brandon.

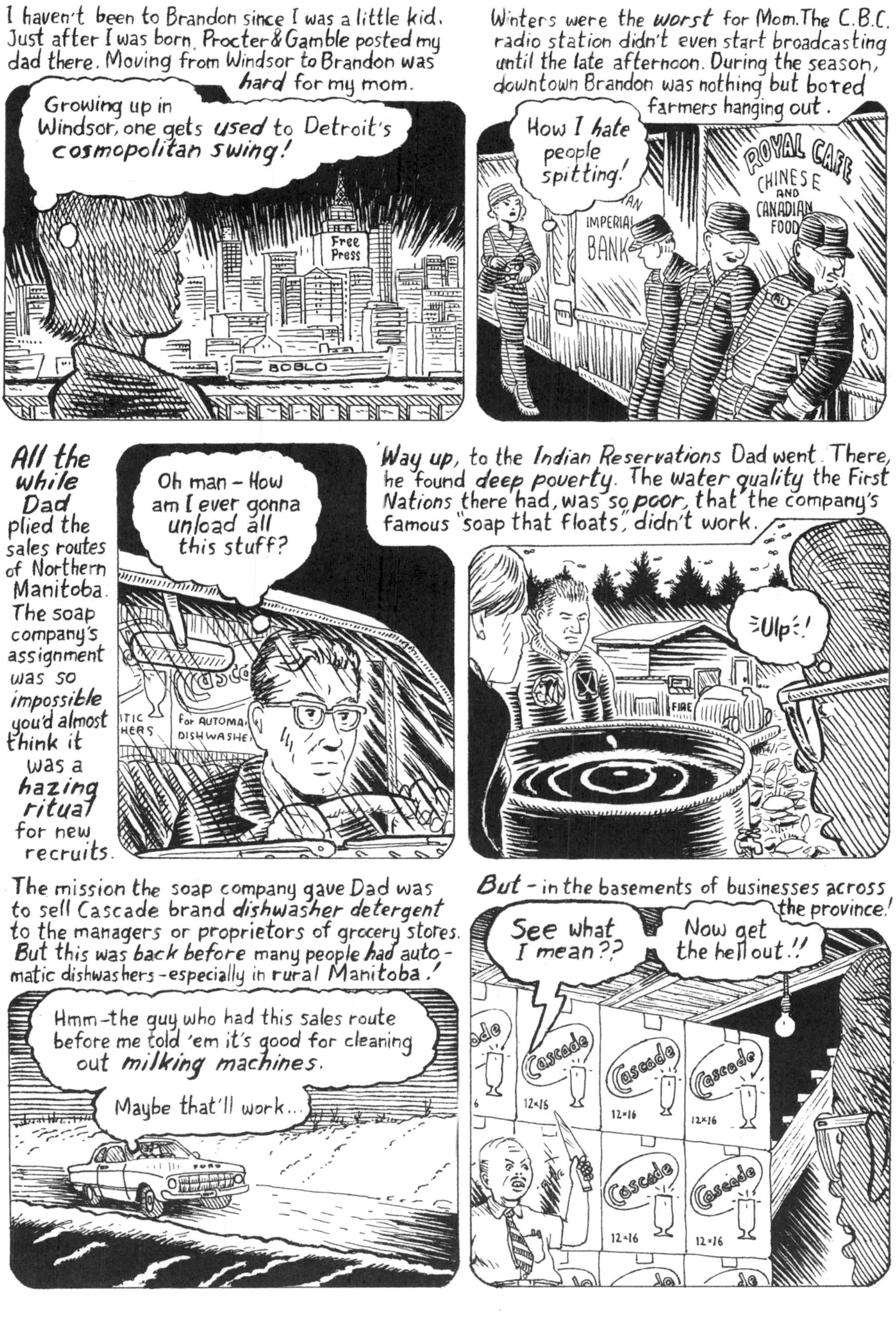
I haven't been to Brandon since I was a little kid. Just after I was born, Procter & Gamble posted my dad there. Moving from Windsor to Brandon was *hard* for my mom.
Growing up in Windsor, one gets *used* to Detroit's *cosmopolitan swing!*
Free Press
BOBLO
Winters were the *worst* for Mom. The C.B.C. radio station didn't even start broadcasting until the late afternoon. During the season, downtown Brandon was nothing but bored farmers hanging out.
How I *hate* people spitting!
IMPERIAL BANK
ROYAL CAFE CHINESE AND CANADIAN FOOD
AL
All the while Dad plied the sales routes of Northern Manitoba. The soap company's assignment was so *impossible* you'd almost *think it* was a *hazing ritual* for new recruits.
Oh man - How am I ever gonna *unload* all this stuff?
'*Way up*, to the *Indian Reservations* Dad went. There, he found *deep poverty*. The *water quality* the First Nations there had, was so *poor*, that the company's famous "soap that floats", didn't work.
Ulp!
FIRE
The mission the soap company gave Dad was to sell Cascade brand *dishwasher detergent* to the managers or proprietors of grocery stores. *But this was back before* many people *had* automatic dishwashers - especially in *rural* Manitoba!
Hmm - the guy who had this sales route before me told 'em it's good for cleaning out *milking machines*.
Maybe that'll work...
FORD
But - in the basements of businesses across the province!
See what I mean??
Now get the hell out!!
Cascade 12×16
Cascade 12×16
Cascade 12×16
Cascade 12×16
Cascade 12×16

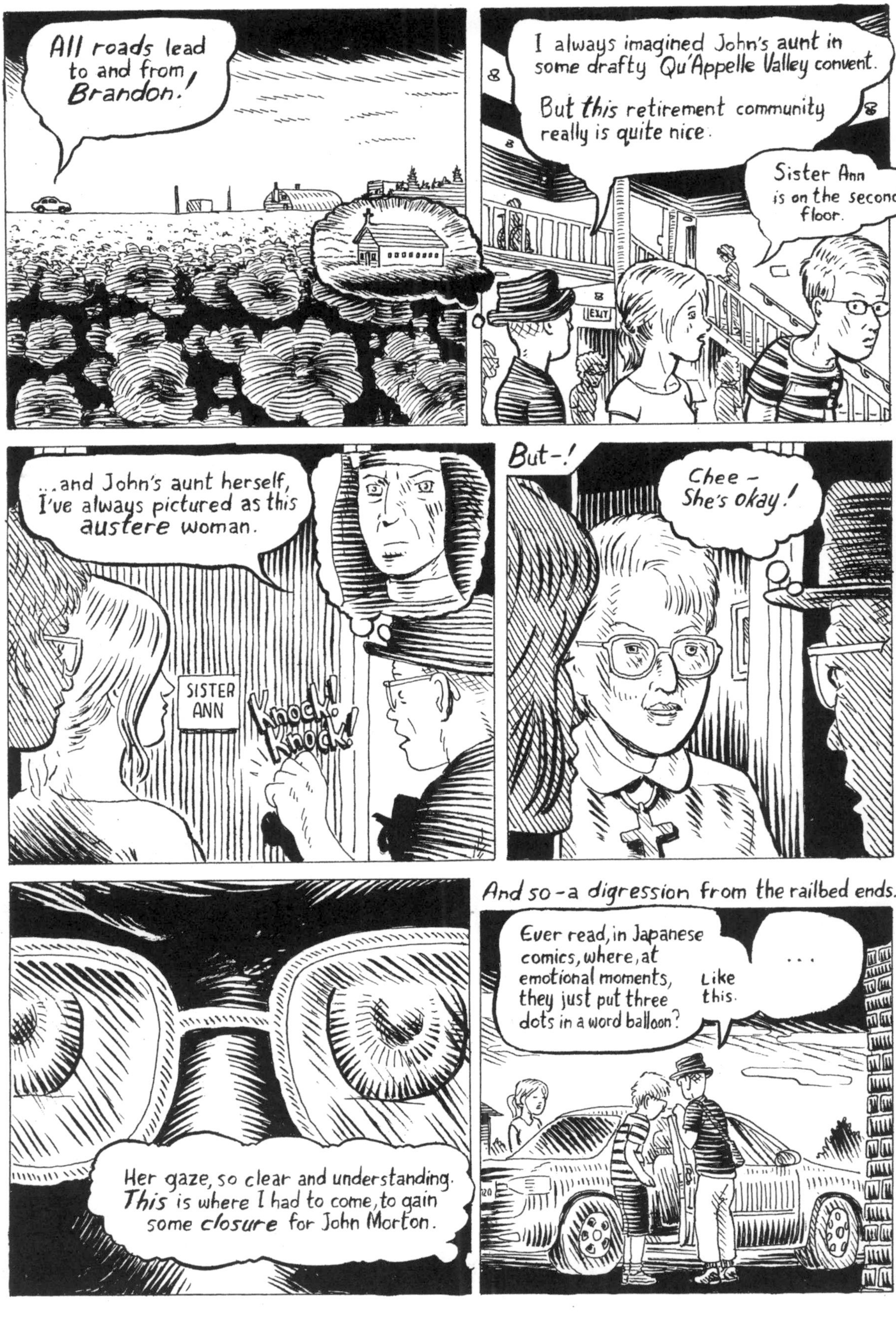
All roads lead to and from, Brandon!
I always imagined John's aunt in some drafty Qu'Appelle Valley convent.
But this retirement community really is quite nice.
Sister Ann is on the second floor.
EXIT
...and John's aunt herself, I've always pictured as this austere woman.
SISTER ANN
Knock! Knock!
But-!
Chee - She's okay!
Her gaze, so clear and understanding. This is where I had to come, to gain some closure for John Morton.
And so - a digression from the railbed ends.
Ever read, in Japanese comics, where, at emotional moments, they just put three dots in a word balloon?
Like this.
. . .

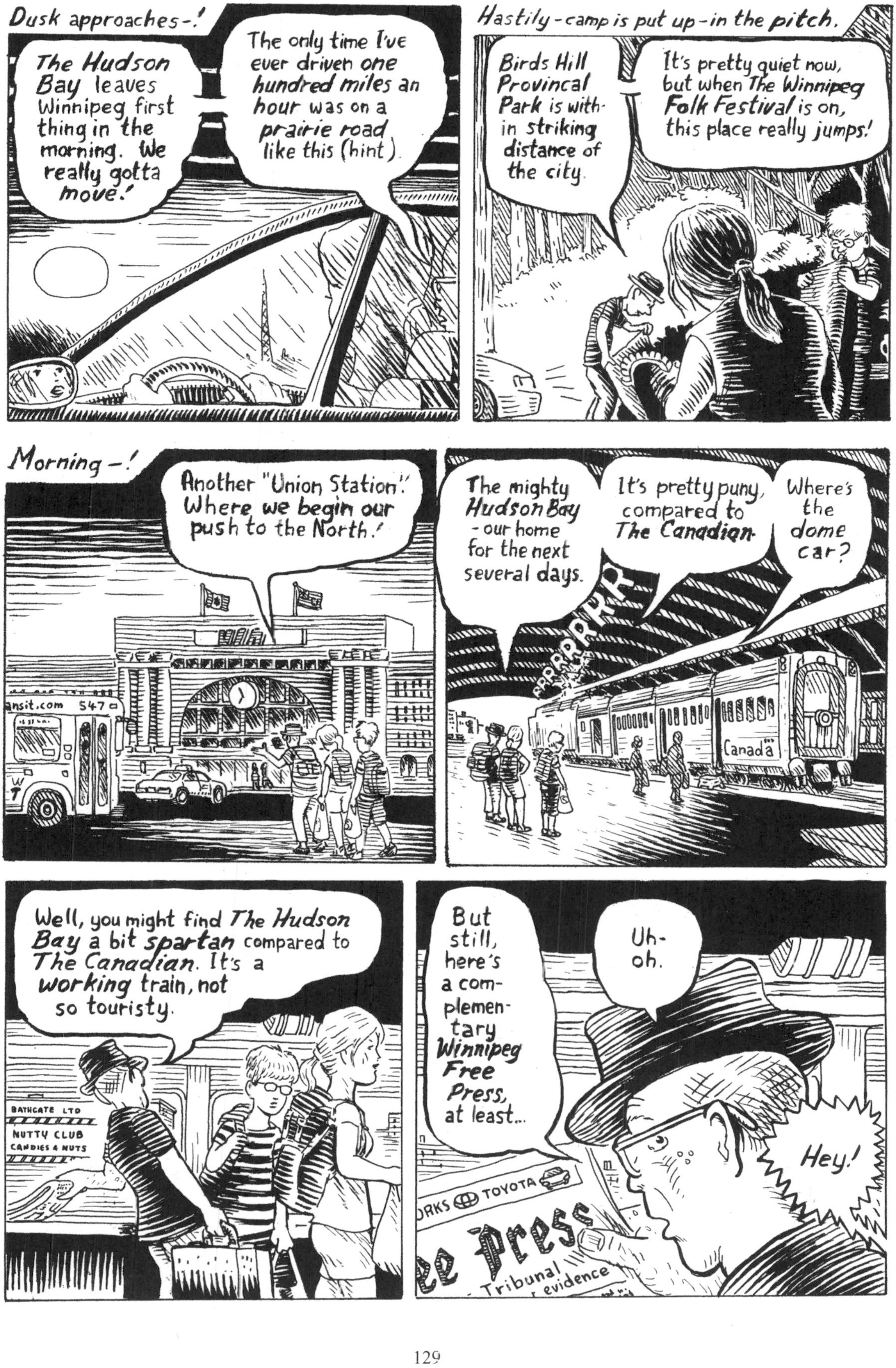

Dusk approaches-!
The Hudson Bay leaves Winnipeg first thing in the morning. We really gotta move!
The only time I've ever driven one hundred miles an hour was on a prairie road like this (hint).
Hastily-camp is put up-in the pitch.
Birds Hill Provincal Park is within striking distance of the city.
It's pretty quiet now, but when The Winnipeg Folk Festival is on, this place really jumps!
Morning-!
Another "Union Station"! Where we begin our push to the North!
ansit.com 547
The mighty Hudson Bay - our home for the next several days.
It's pretty puny, compared to The Canadian.
Where's the dome car?
Canada
Well, you might find The Hudson Bay a bit spartan compared to The Canadian. It's a working train, not so touristy.
BATHGATE LTD
NUTTY CLUB
CANDIES & NUTS
But still, here's a complementary Winnipeg Free Press, at least...
Uh-oh.
Hey!
TOYOTA
Press
Tribunal
evidence

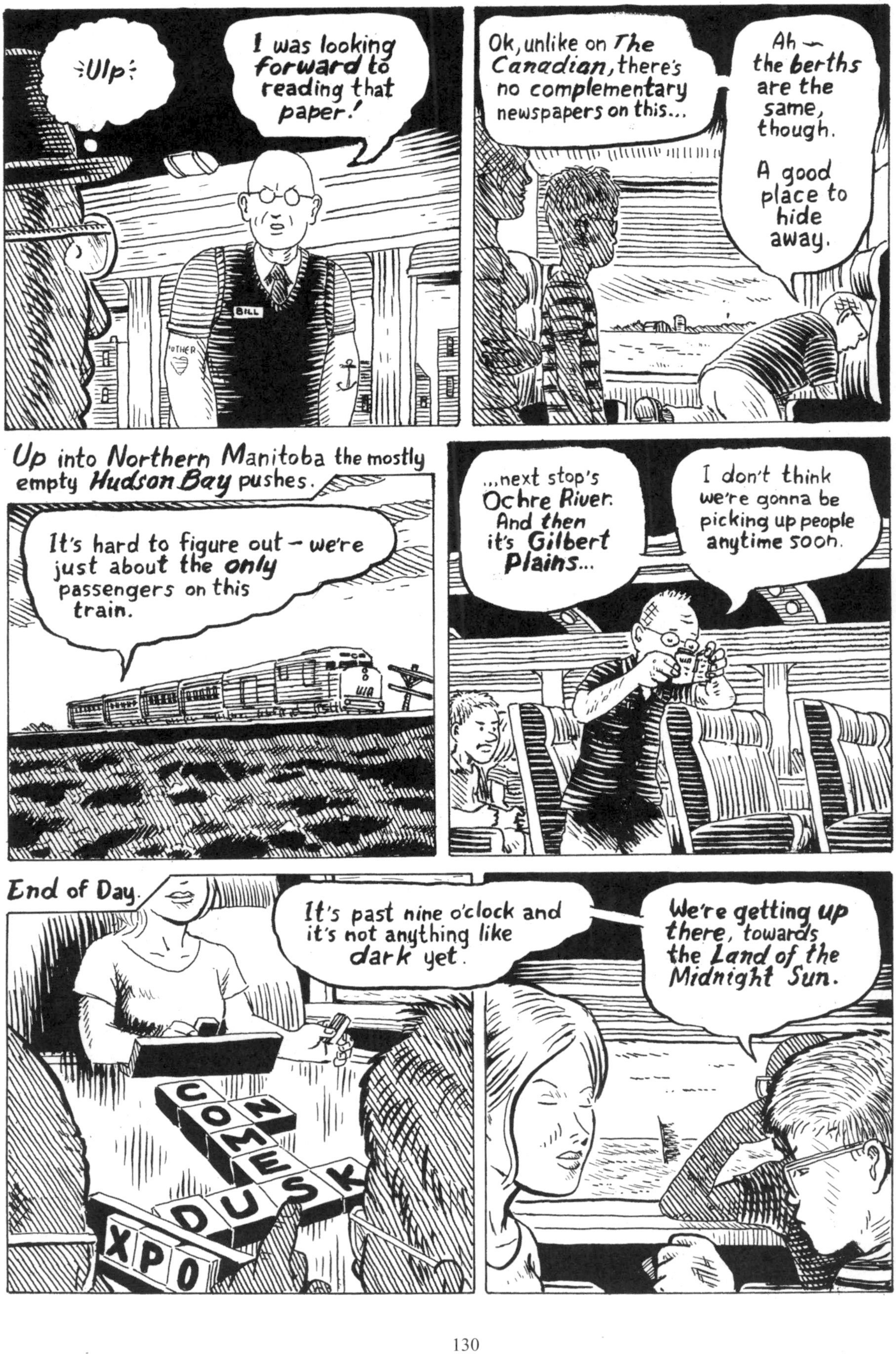
Ulp
I was looking forward to reading that paper!
BILL
MOTHER
Ok, unlike on The Canadian, there's no complementary newspapers on this...
Ah — the berths are the same, though.
A good place to hide away.
Up into Northern Manitoba the mostly empty Hudson Bay pushes.
It's hard to figure out — we're just about the only passengers on this train.
VIA
...next stop's Ochre River. And then it's Gilbert Plains...
I don't think we're gonna be picking up people anytime soon.
End of Day.
It's past nine o'clock and it's not anything like dark yet.
We're getting up there, towards the Land of the Midnight Sun.
CON
COME
DUSK
XPO

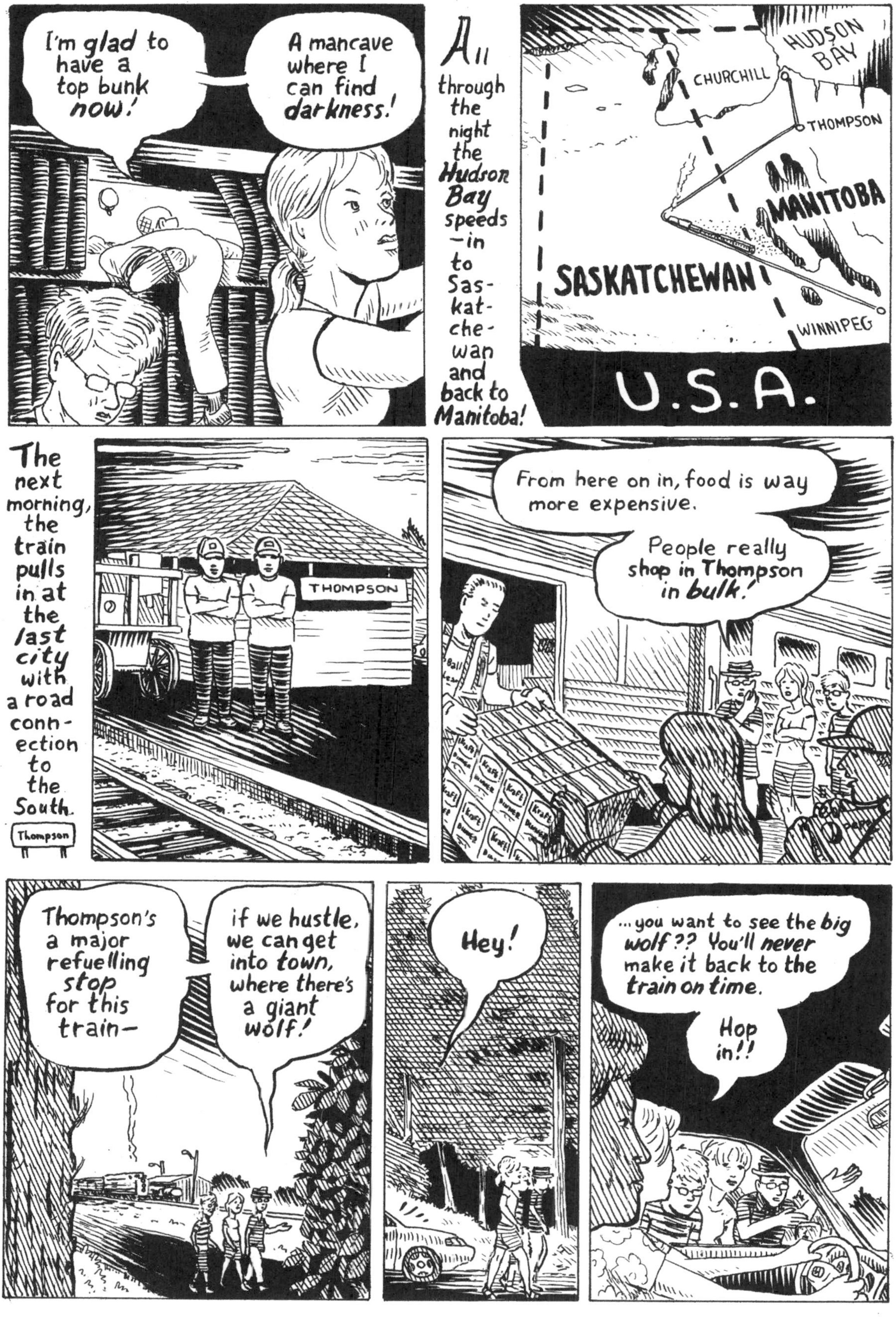
I'm glad to have a top bunk now!
A mancave where I can find darkness!
All through the night the Hudson Bay speeds—in to Saskatchewan and back to Manitoba!
HUDSON BAY
CHURCHILL
THOMPSON
MANITOBA
SASKATCHEWAN
WINNIPEG
U.S.A.
The next morning, the train pulls in at the last city with a road connection to the South.
Thompson
THOMPSON
From here on in, food is way more expensive.
People really shop in Thompson in bulk!
Thompson's a major refuelling stop for this train—
if we hustle, we can get into town, where there's a giant wolf!
Hey!
...you want to see the big wolf?? You'll never make it back to the train on time.
Hop in!!

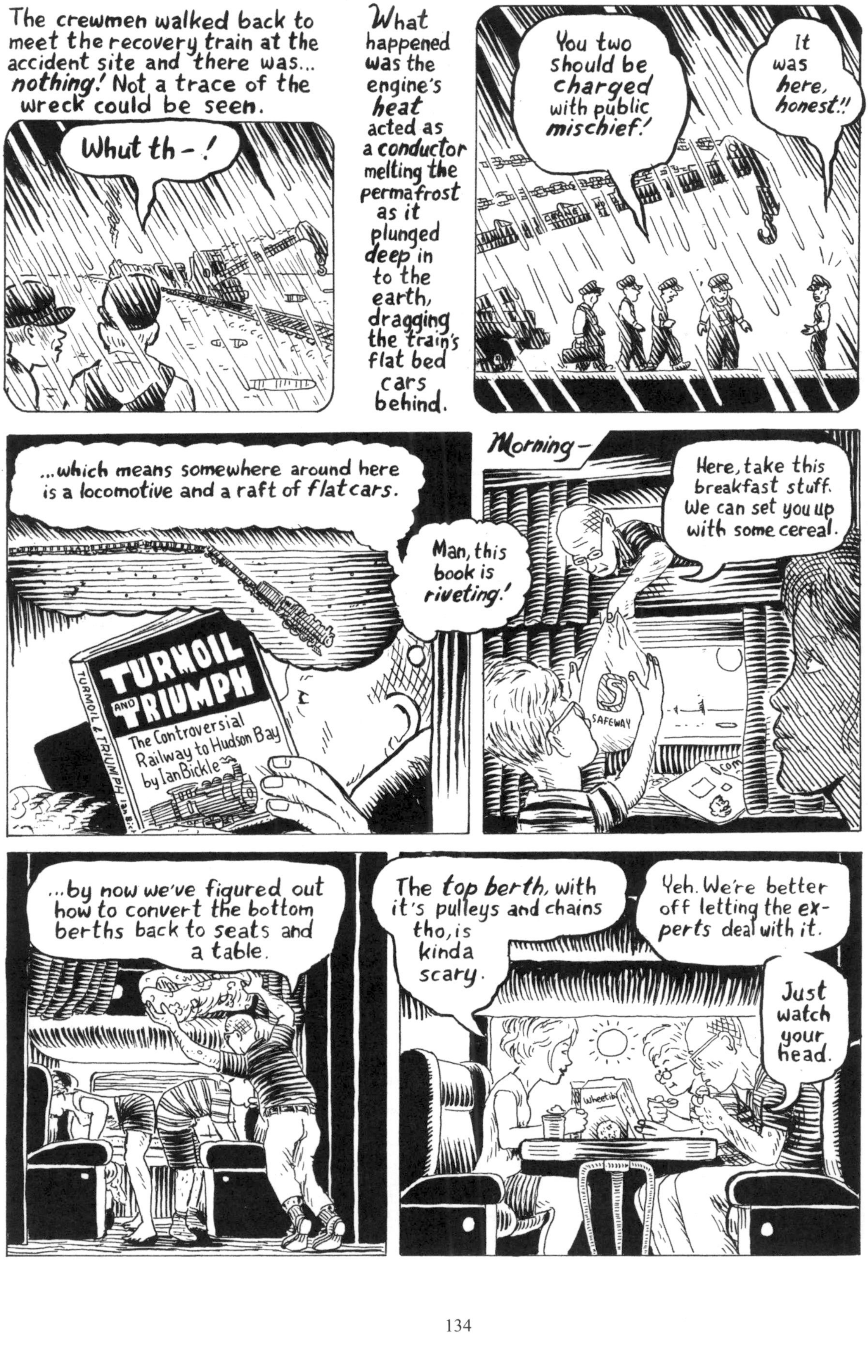
The crewmen walked back to meet the recovery train at the accident site and there was... nothing! Not a trace of the wreck could be seen.
Whut th-!
What happened was the engine's heat acted as a conductor melting the permafrost as it plunged deep in to the earth, dragging the train's flat bed cars behind.
You two should be charged with public mischief!
It was here, honest!!
...which means somewhere around here is a locomotive and a raft of flatcars.
Man, this book is riveting!
TURMOIL AND TRIUMPH
The Controversial Railway to Hudson Bay
by Ian Bickle
TURMOIL & TRIUMPH
Morning-
Here, take this breakfast stuff. We can set you up with some cereal.
SAFEWAY
...by now we've figured out how to convert the bottom berths back to seats and a table.
The top berth, with it's pulleys and chains tho, is kinda scary.
Yeh. We're better off letting the experts deal with it.
Just watch your head.

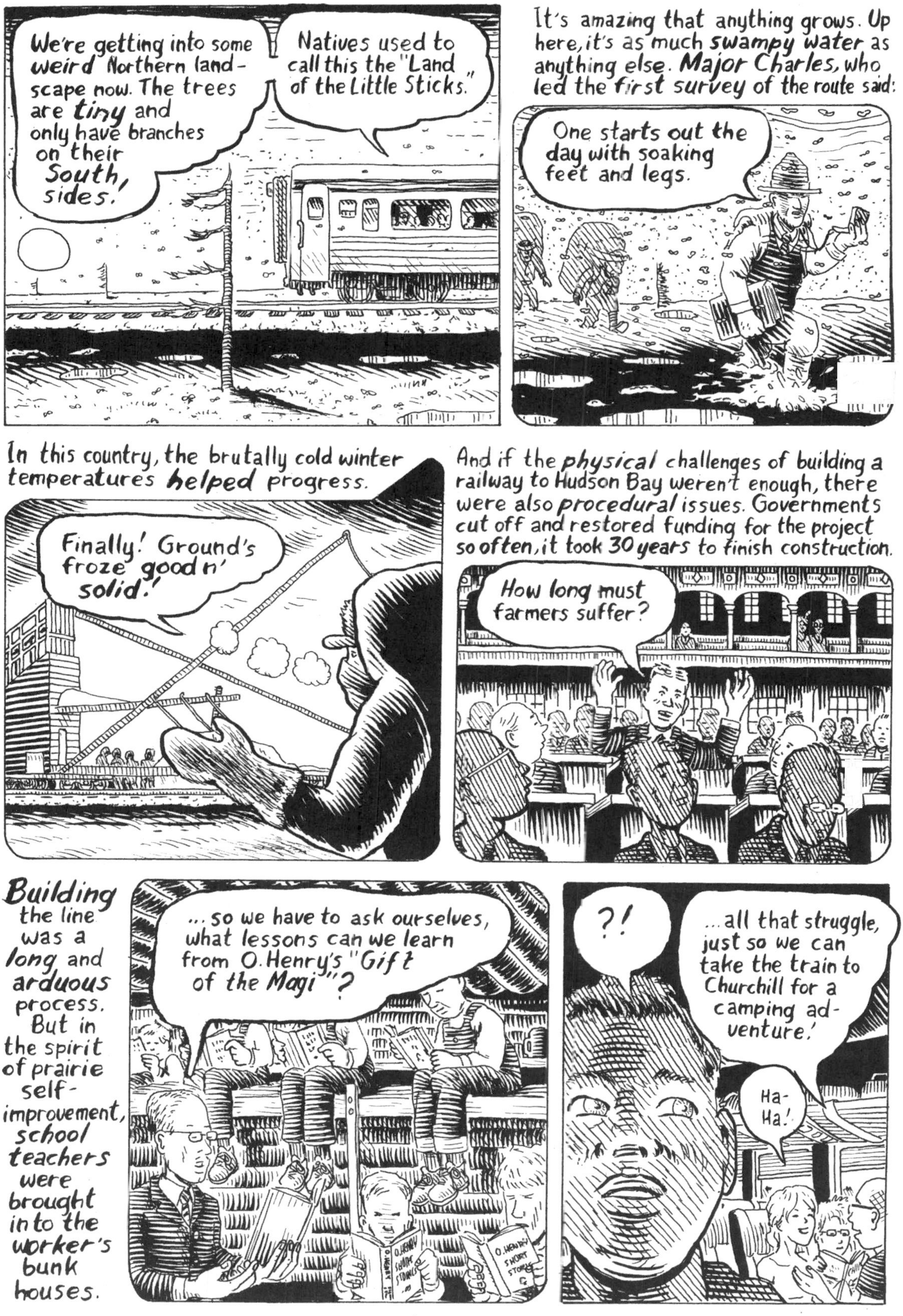
We're getting into some weird Northern landscape now. The trees are tiny and only have branches on their South, sides.
Natives used to call this the "Land of the Little Sticks."
It's amazing that anything grows. Up here, it's as much swampy water as anything else. Major Charles, who led the first survey of the route said:
One starts out the day with soaking feet and legs.
In this country, the brutally cold winter temperatures helped progress.
Finally! Ground's froze good n' solid!
And if the physical challenges of building a railway to Hudson Bay weren't enough, there were also procedural issues. Governments cut off and restored funding for the project so often, it took 30 years to finish construction.
How long must farmers suffer?
Building the line was a long and arduous process. But in the spirit of prairie self-improvement, school teachers were brought into the worker's bunk houses.
...so we have to ask ourselves, what lessons can we learn from O. Henry's "Gift of the Magi"?
O. HENRY SHORT STORIES
?!
...all that struggle, just so we can take the train to Churchill for a camping adventure!
Ha-Ha!

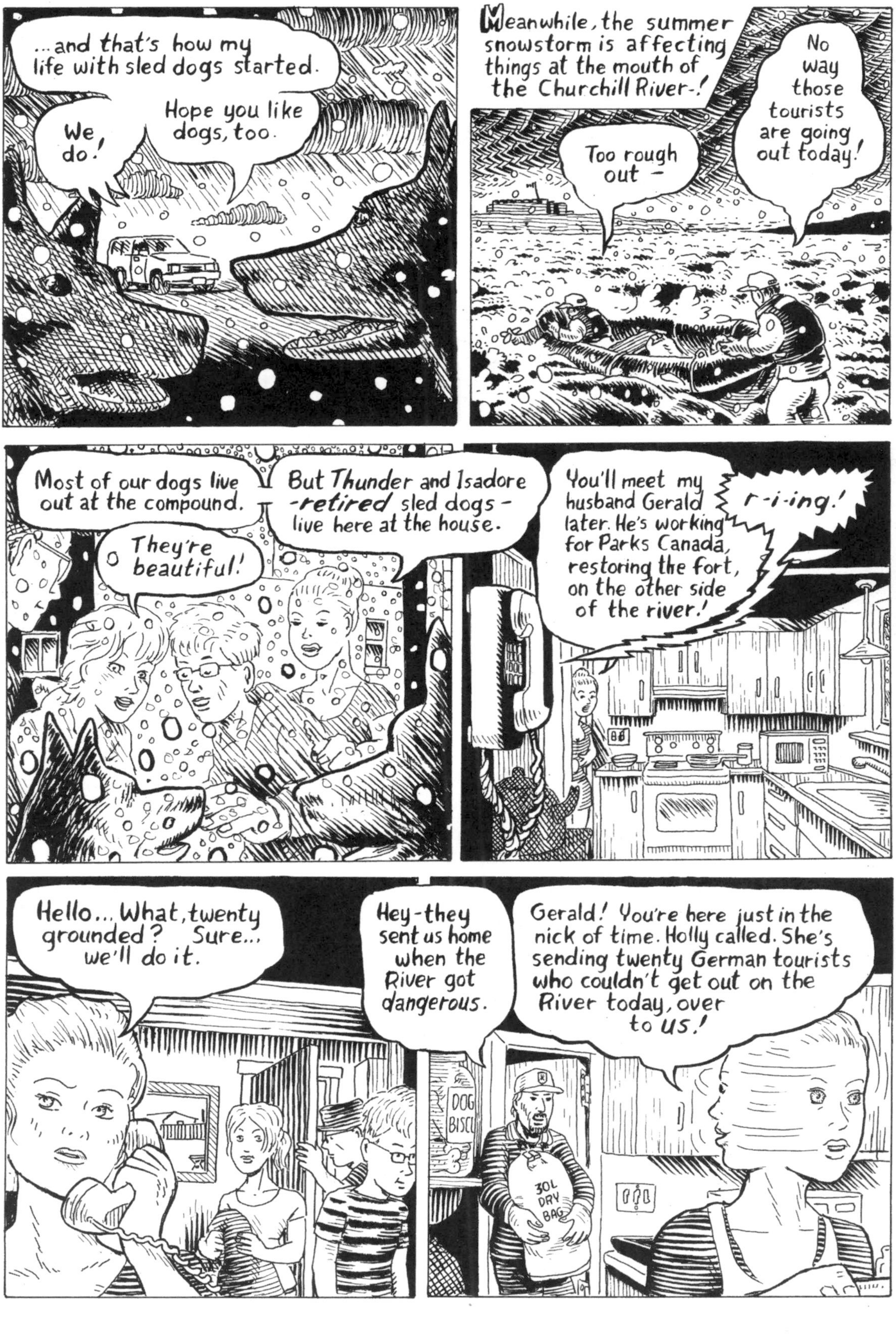
...and that's how my life with sled dogs started.
We do!
Hope you like dogs, too.
Meanwhile, the summer snowstorm is affecting things at the mouth of the Churchill River-!
No way those tourists are going out today!
Too rough out -
Most of our dogs live out at the compound.
But Thunder and Isadore -retired sled dogs - live here at the house.
They're beautiful!
You'll meet my husband Gerald later. He's working for Parks Canada, restoring the fort, on the other side of the river!
r-i-ing!
Hello... What, twenty grounded? Sure... we'll do it.
Hey-they sent us home when the River got dangerous.
Gerald! You're here just in the nick of time. Holly called. She's sending twenty German tourists who couldn't get out on the River today, over to us!
DOG BISC
30L DRY BAG

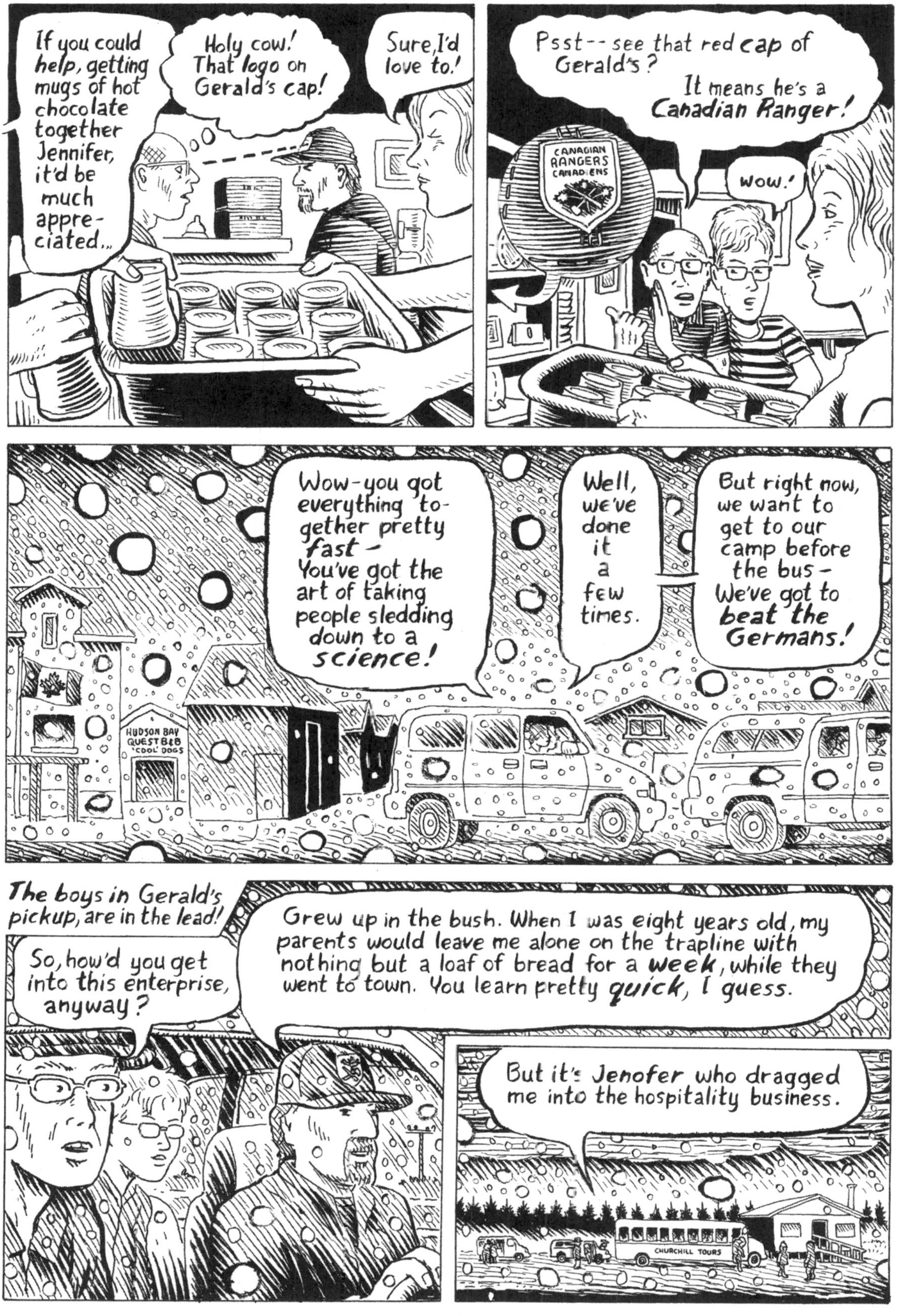
If you could help, getting mugs of hot chocolate together Jennifer, it'd be much appre-ciated...
Holy cow! That logo on Gerald's cap!
Sure, I'd love to!
Psst-- see that red cap of Gerald's?
It means he's a Canadian Ranger!
CANADIAN RANGERS CANADIENS
wow!
Wow-you got everything to-gether pretty fast- You've got the art of taking people sledding down to a science!
Well, we've done it a few times.
But right now, we want to get to our camp before the bus- We've got to beat the Germans!
HUDSON BAY QUEST B&B 'COOL' DOGS
The boys in Gerald's pickup, are in the lead!
So, how'd you get into this enterprise, anyway?
Grew up in the bush. When I was eight years old, my parents would leave me alone on the trapline with nothing but a loaf of bread for a week, while they went to town. You learn pretty quick, I guess.
But it's Jenofer who dragged me into the hospitality business.
CHURCHILL TOURS

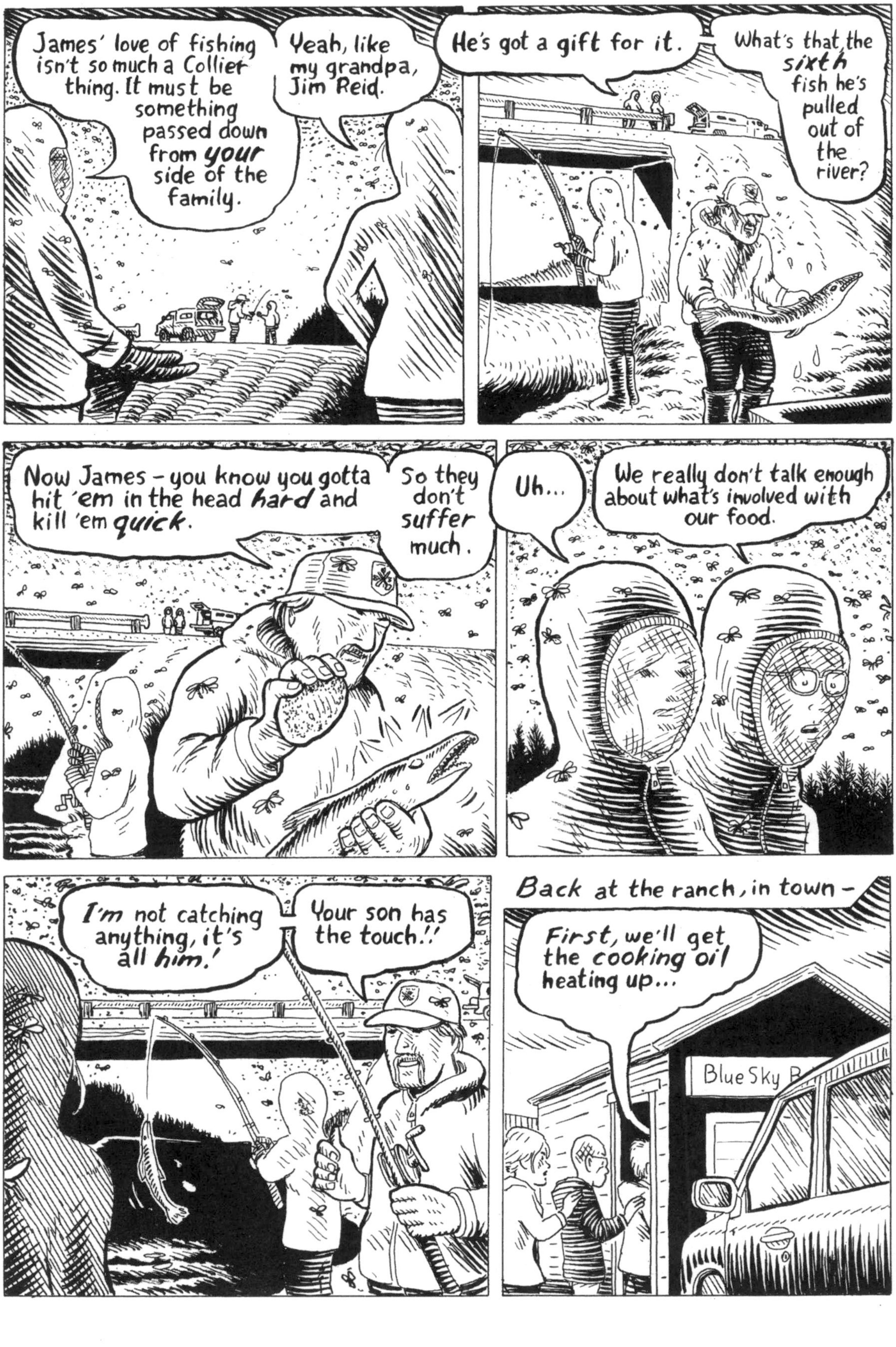
James' love of fishing isn't so much a Collier thing. It must be something passed down from *your* side of the family.
Yeah, like my grandpa, Jim Reid.
He's got a gift for it.
What's that, the *sixth* fish he's pulled out of the river?
Now James - you know you gotta hit 'em in the head *hard* and kill 'em *quick*.
So they don't suffer much.
Uh...
We really don't talk enough about what's involved with our food.
I'm not catching anything, it's all *him*.'
Your son has the touch!!
Back at the ranch, in town -
First, we'll get the *cooking oil* heating up...
Blue Sky R

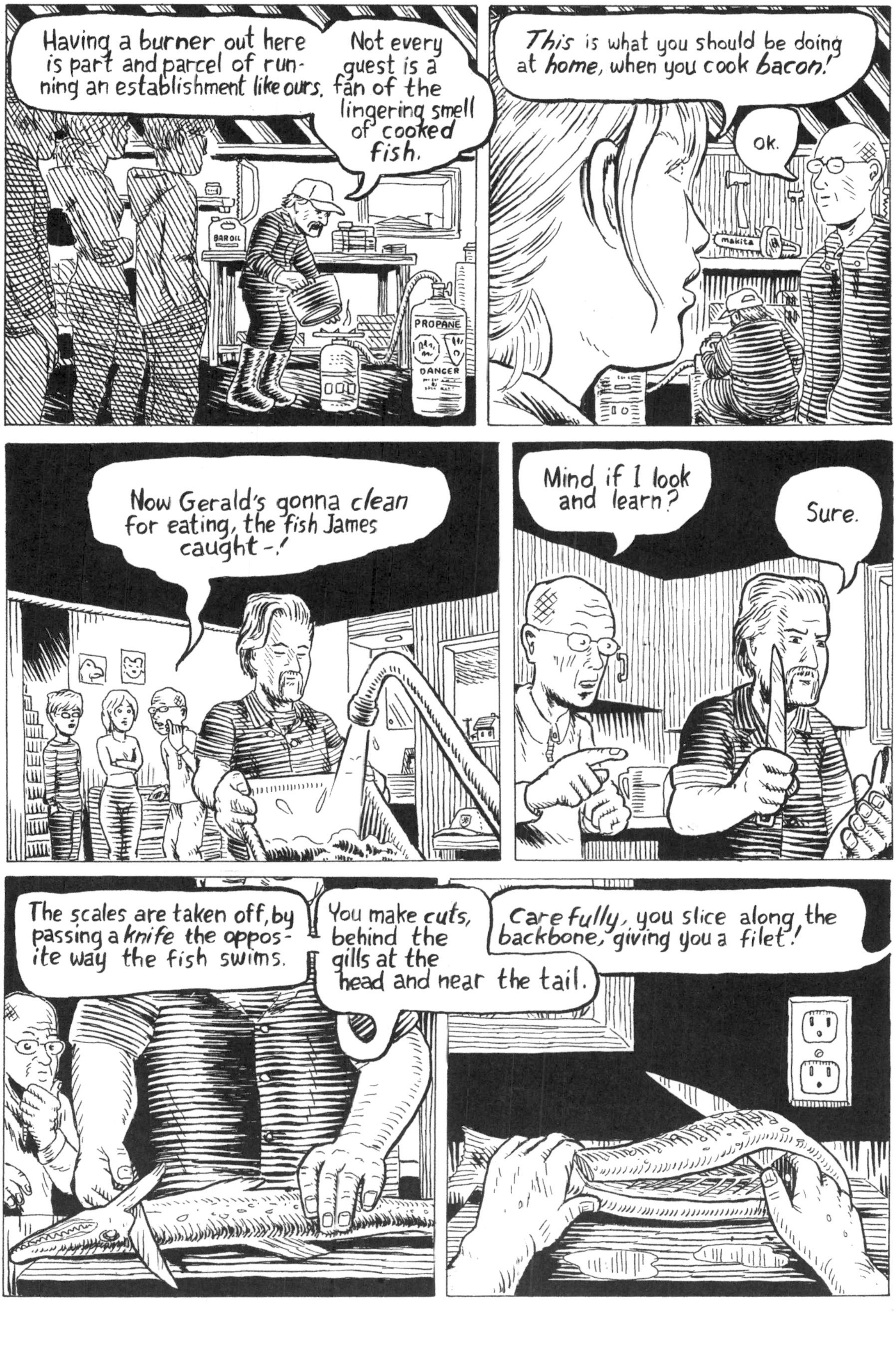
Having a burner out here is part and parcel of running an establishment like ours.
Not every guest is a fan of the lingering smell of cooked fish.
BAROIL
PROPANE
DANGER
This is what you should be doing at home, when you cook bacon!
ok.
makita
Now Gerald's gonna clean for eating, the fish James caught -!
Mind if I look and learn?
Sure.
The scales are taken off, by passing a knife the opposite way the fish swims.
You make cuts, behind the gills at the head and near the tail.
Carefully, you slice along the backbone, giving you a filet!

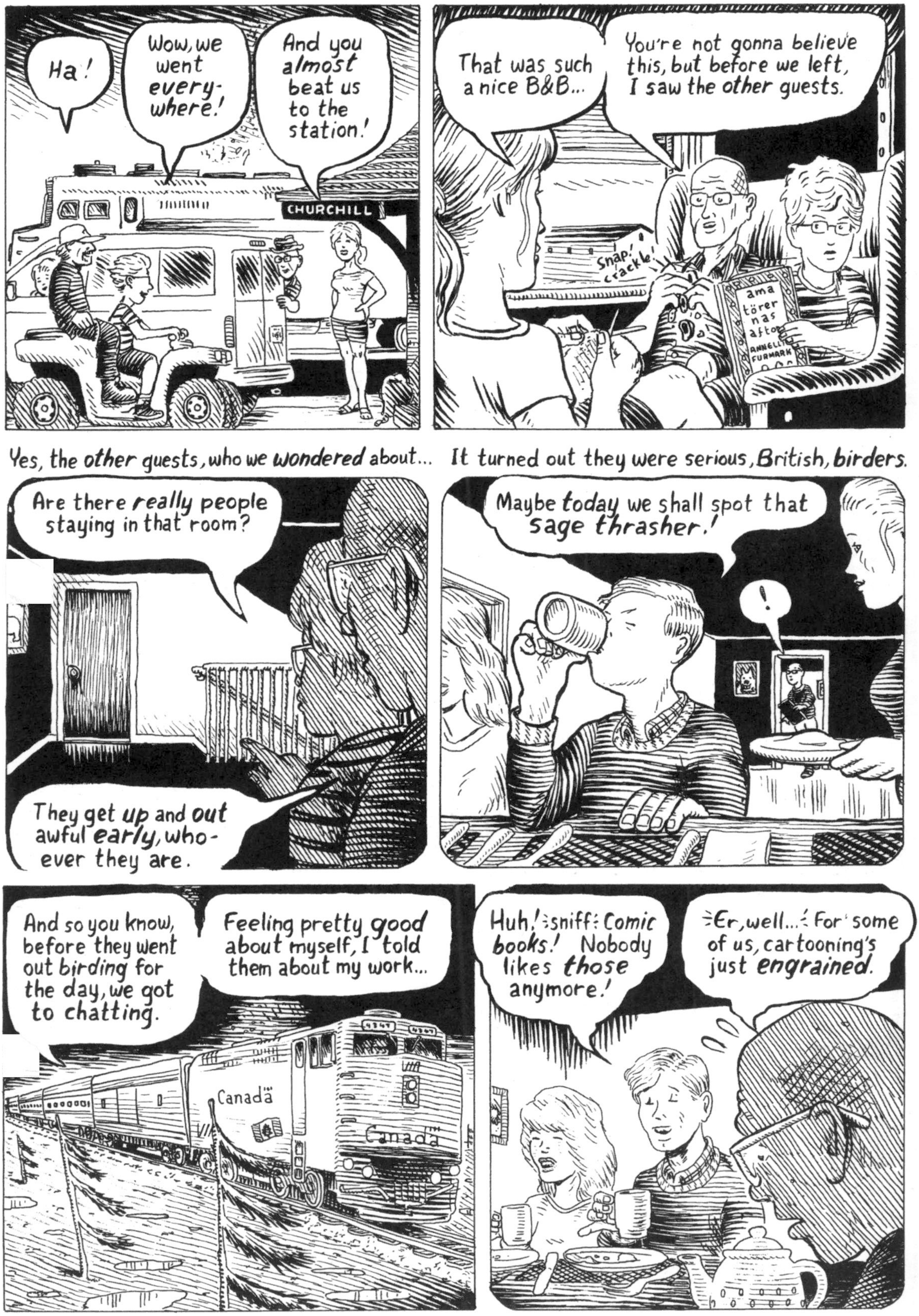
Ha!
Wow, we went every-where!
And you almost beat us to the station!
CHURCHILL
That was such a nice B&B...
You're not gonna believe this, but before we left, I saw the other guests.
Snap! crackle!
Yes, the other guests, who we wondered about...
It turned out they were serious, British, birders.
Are there really people staying in that room?
They get up and out awful early, who-ever they are.
Maybe today we shall spot that sage thrasher!
!
And so you know, before they went out birding for the day, we got to chatting.
Feeling pretty good about myself, I told them about my work...
Canada
Canada
Huh! :sniff: Comic books! Nobody likes those anymore!
Er, well... For some of us, cartooning's just engrained.

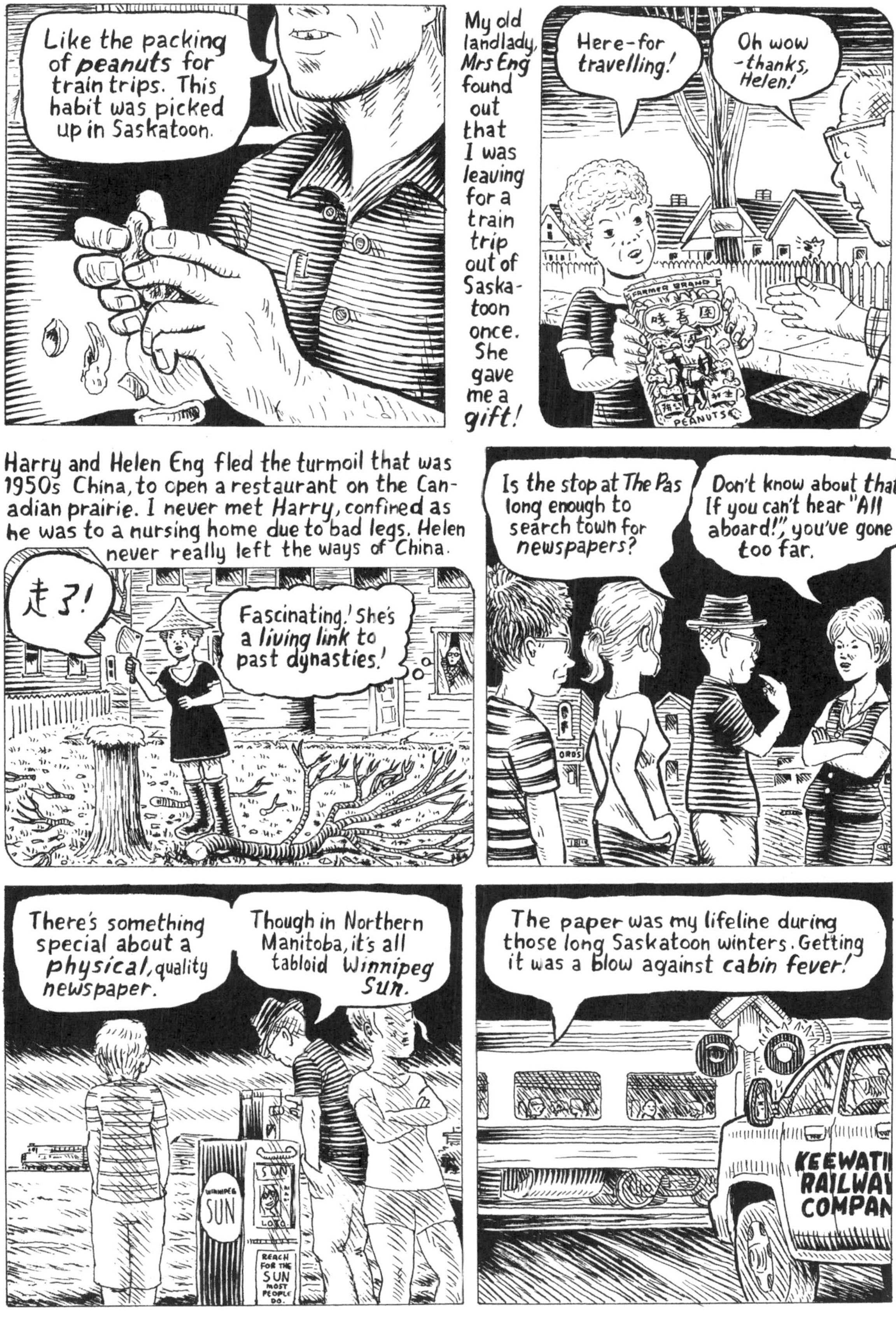
Like the packing of peanuts for train trips. This habit was picked up in Saskatoon.
My old landlady, Mrs Eng found out that I was leaving for a train trip out of Saskatoon once. She gave me a gift!
Here-for travelling!
Oh wow -thanks, Helen!
FARMER BRAND
PEANUTS
Harry and Helen Eng fled the turmoil that was 1950s China, to open a restaurant on the Canadian prairie. I never met Harry, confined as he was to a nursing home due to bad legs. Helen never really left the ways of China.
走了!
Fascinating! She's a living link to past dynasties!
Is the stop at The Pas long enough to search town for newspapers?
Don't know about that. If you can't hear "All aboard!", you've gone too far.
There's something special about a physical, quality newspaper.
Though in Northern Manitoba, it's all tabloid Winnipeg Sun.
WINNIPEG SUN
SUN
REACH FOR THE SUN MOST PEOPLE DO.
The paper was my lifeline during those long Saskatoon winters. Getting it was a blow against cabin fever!
KEEWATI RAILWAY COMPAN

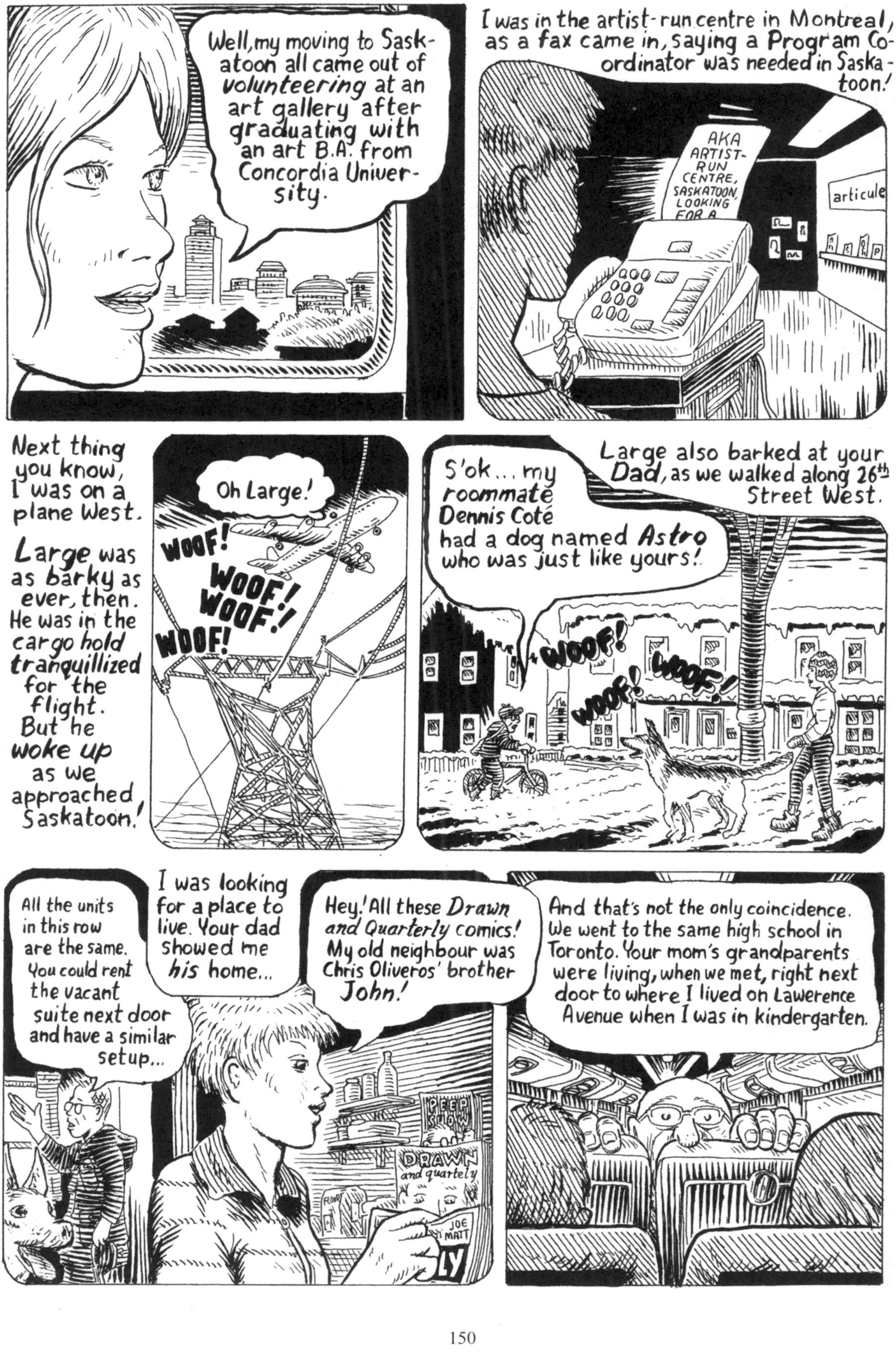
Well, my moving to Saskatoon all came out of *volunteering* at an art gallery after graduating with an art B.A. from Concordia University.
I was in the artist-run centre in Montreal, as a **fax** came in, saying a **Program** Coordinator was needed in Saskatoon!
AKA ARTIST-RUN CENTRE, SASKATOON, LOOKING FOR A
articule
Next thing you know, I was on a plane West.
Large was as **barky** as ever, then. He was in the **cargo hold** **tranquillized** for the **flight**. But he **woke up** as we approached Saskatoon!
Oh Large!
WOOF!
WOOF!
WOOF!
WOOF!
Large also barked at your **Dad**, as we walked along 26th Street West.
S'ok... my **roommate** Dennis Coté had a dog named **Astro** who was just like yours!
WOOF!
WOOF!
WOOF!
All the units in this row are the same. You could rent the vacant suite next door and have a similar setup...
I was looking for a place to live. Your dad showed me **his** home...
Hey! All these *Drawn and Quarterly* comics! My old neighbour was Chris Oliveros' brother **John**!
PEEP SHOW
DRAWN and quartely
JOE MATT
LY
And that's not the only coincidence. We went to the same high school in Toronto. Your mom's grandparents were living, when we met, right next door to where I lived on Lawerence Avenue when I was in kindergarten.

If it's true you gotta suffer for your art, then Saskatoon was perfect. Couldn't afford much heat... My fingers would turn yellow from the cold.

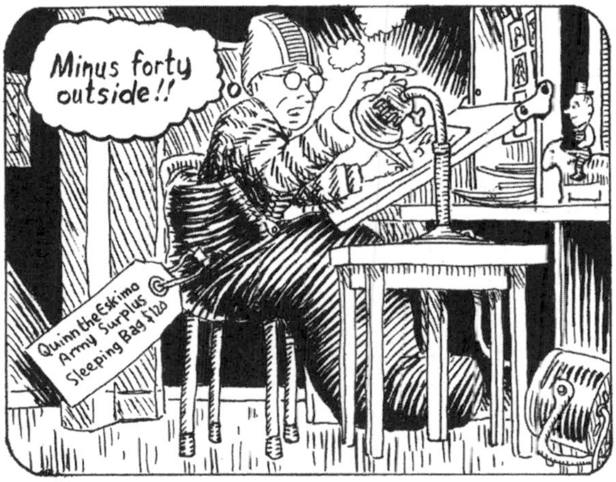
Minus forty outside!!
Quinn the Eskimo Army Surplus Sleeping Bag $120

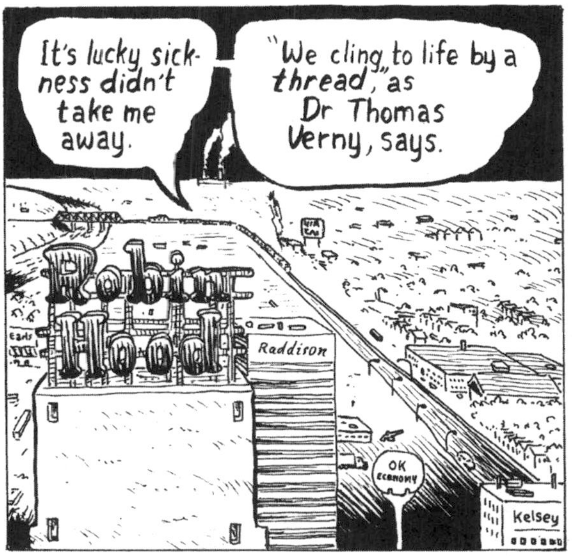
It's lucky sickness didn't take me away.
"We cling to life by a thread," as Dr Thomas Verny, says.
Robin Hood
Raddison
OK Economy
Kelsey

My first trip West on the train, happened in 1984. The idea was to go to Edmonton to see Cousin Ian Gilmour, who was living there.

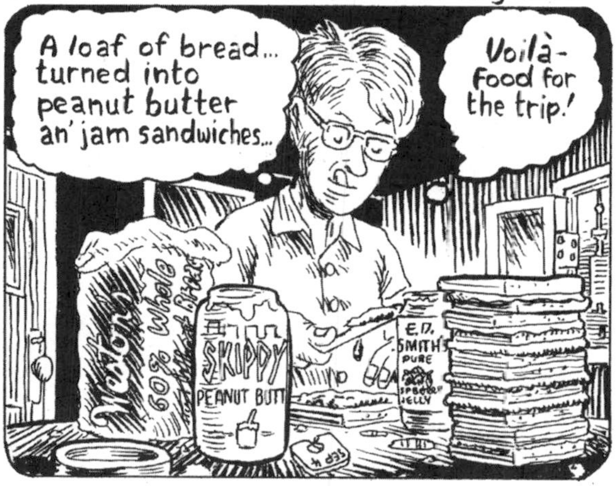
A loaf of bread... turned into peanut butter an' jam sandwiches...
Voilà- Food for the trip!
60% Whole
SKIPPY
PEANUT BUTT
E.D. SMITH'S PURE
JELLY

But instead, out of curiosity, Saskatoon became my Western terminus.

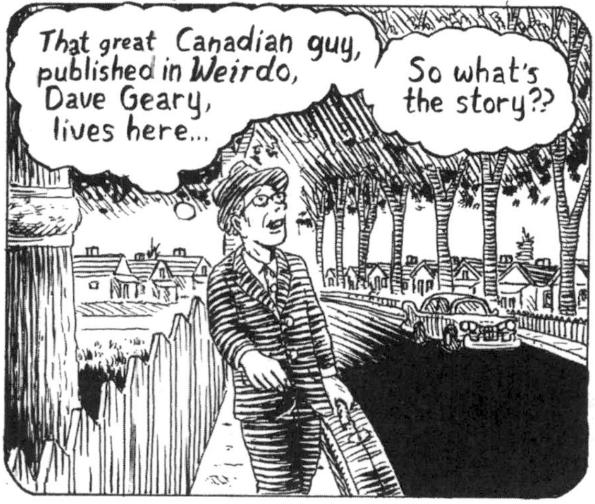
That great Canadian guy, published in Weirdo, Dave Geary, lives here...
So what's the story??

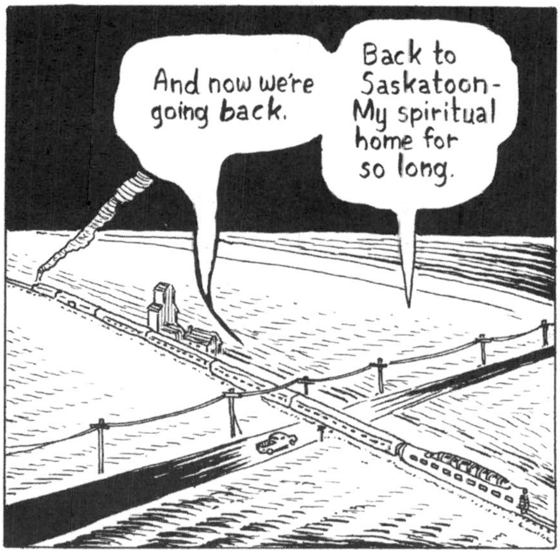
And now we're going back.
Back to Saskatoon- My spiritual home for so long.

The Voyageurs didn't get much further than this. Maybe up to Fort Edmonton or Athabasca Landing. There's only so far you can paddle in a season, from Lake Superior, before freeze up.

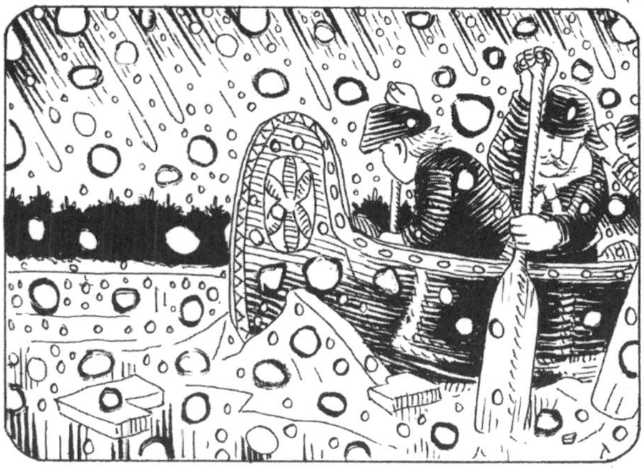

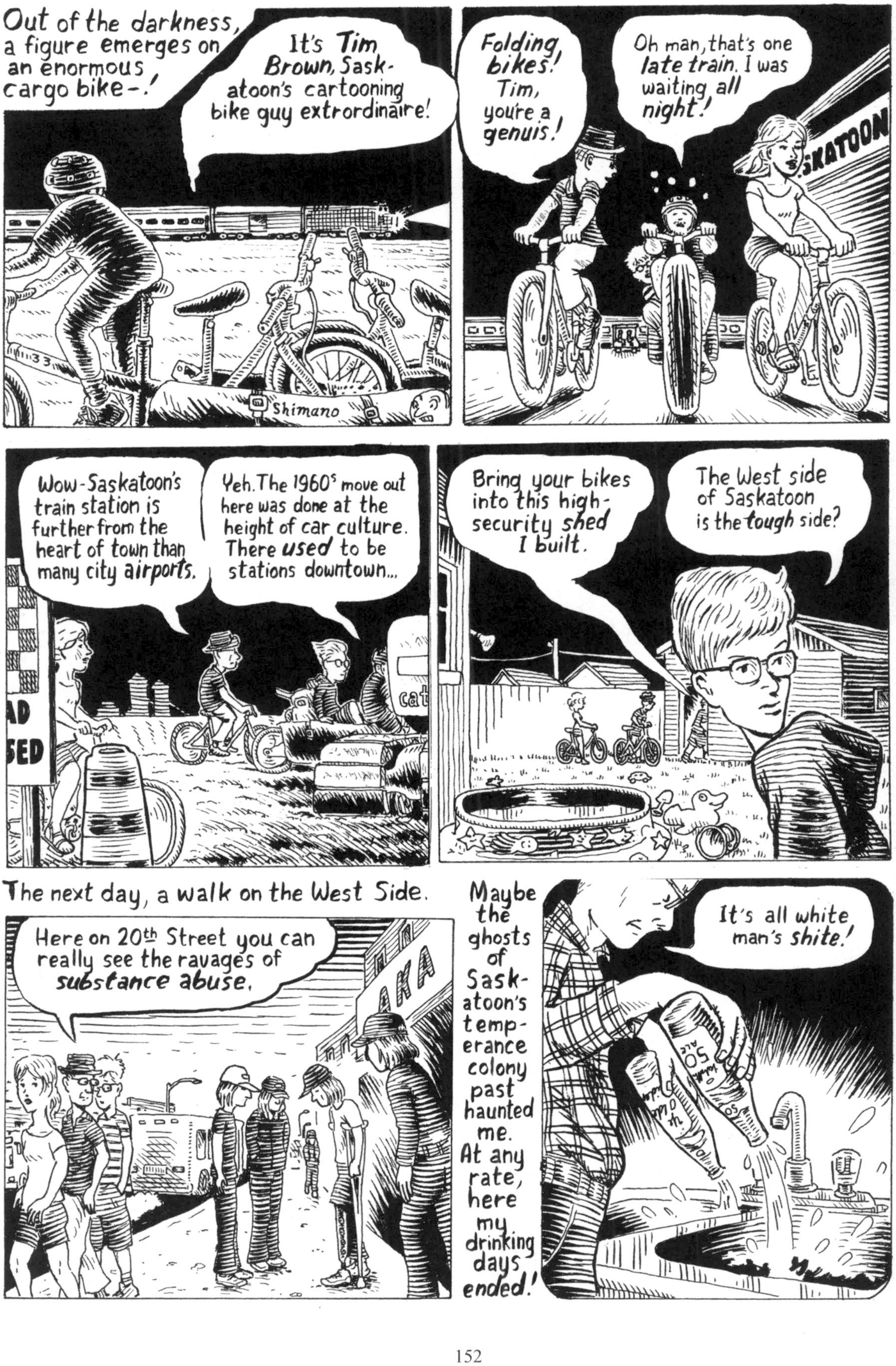
Out of the darkness, a figure emerges on an enormous cargo bike-!
It's Tim Brown, Saskatoon's cartooning bike guy extrordinaire!
33
Shimano
Folding bikes! Tim, you're a genuis!
Oh man, that's one late train. I was waiting all night!
SKATOON
Wow-Saskatoon's train station is further from the heart of town than many city airports.
Yeh. The 1960s move out here was done at the height of car culture. There used to be stations downtown...
Bring your bikes into this high-security shed I built.
The West side of Saskatoon is the tough side?
The next day, a walk on the West Side.
Here on 20th Street you can really see the ravages of substance abuse.
AKA
Maybe the ghosts of Saskatoon's temperance colony past haunted me. At any rate, here my drinking days ended!
It's all white man's shite!

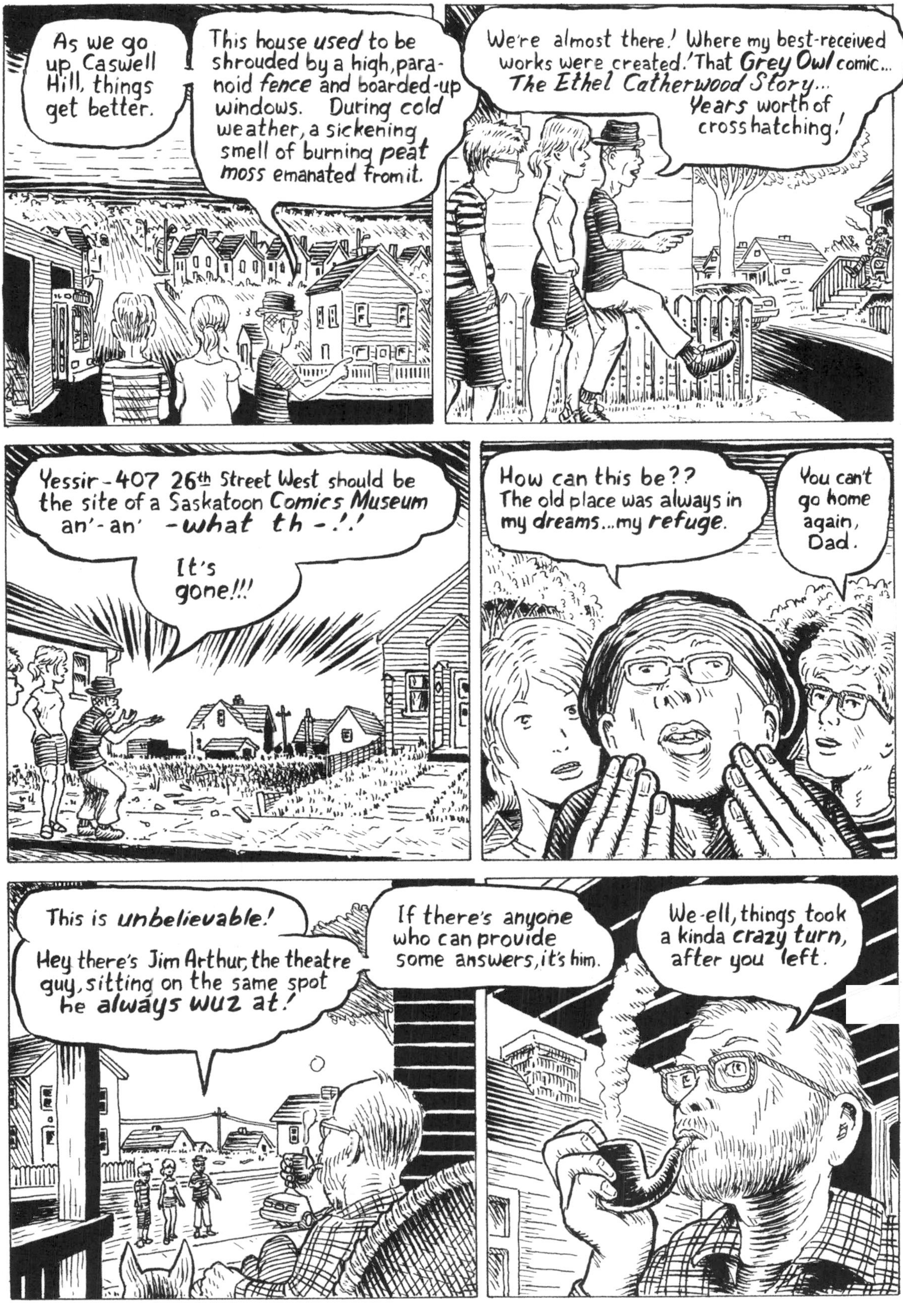

As we go up Caswell Hill, things get better.
This house *used* to be shrouded by a high, paranoid *fence* and boarded-up windows. During cold weather, a sickening smell of burning *peat moss* emanated from it.
We're almost there! Where my best-received works were created! That *Grey Owl* comic... *The Ethel Catherwood Story*... *Years* worth of crosshatching!
Yessir-407 26th Street West should be the site of a Saskatoon *Comics Museum* an'-an' *-what th-!!*
It's gone!!!
How can this be?? The old place was always in my *dreams*...my *refuge*.
You can't go home again, Dad.
This is *unbelievable!*
Hey there's Jim Arthur, the theatre guy, sitting on the same spot he *always wuz at!*
If there's anyone who can provide some answers, it's him.
We-ell, things took a kinda *crazy turn*, after you left.

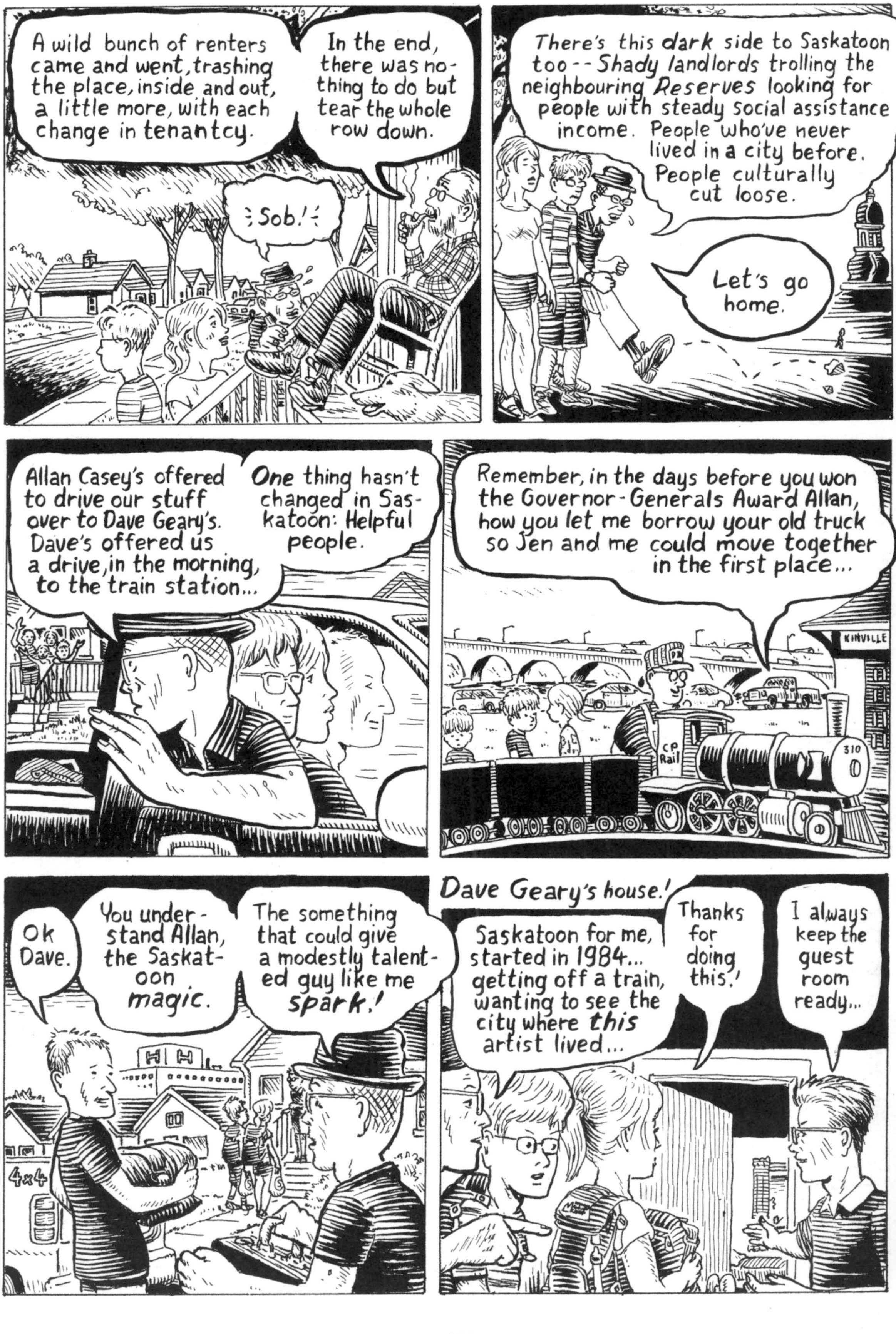
A wild bunch of renters came and went, trashing the place, inside and out, a little more, with each change in tenantcy.
In the end, there was nothing to do but tear the whole row down.
Sob!
There's this dark side to Saskatoon too -- Shady landlords trolling the neighbouring Reserves looking for people with steady social assistance income. People who've never lived in a city before. People culturally cut loose.
Let's go home.
Allan Casey's offered to drive our stuff over to Dave Geary's. Dave's offered us a drive, in the morning, to the train station...
One thing hasn't changed in Saskatoon: Helpful people.
Remember, in the days before you won the Governor-Generals Award Allan, how you let me borrow your old truck so Jen and me could move together in the first place...
CP Rail
310
Ok Dave.
You understand Allan, the Saskatoon magic.
The something that could give a modestly talented guy like me spark!
4x4
Dave Geary's house!
Saskatoon for me, started in 1984... getting off a train, wanting to see the city where this artist lived...
Thanks for doing this!
I always keep the guest room ready...

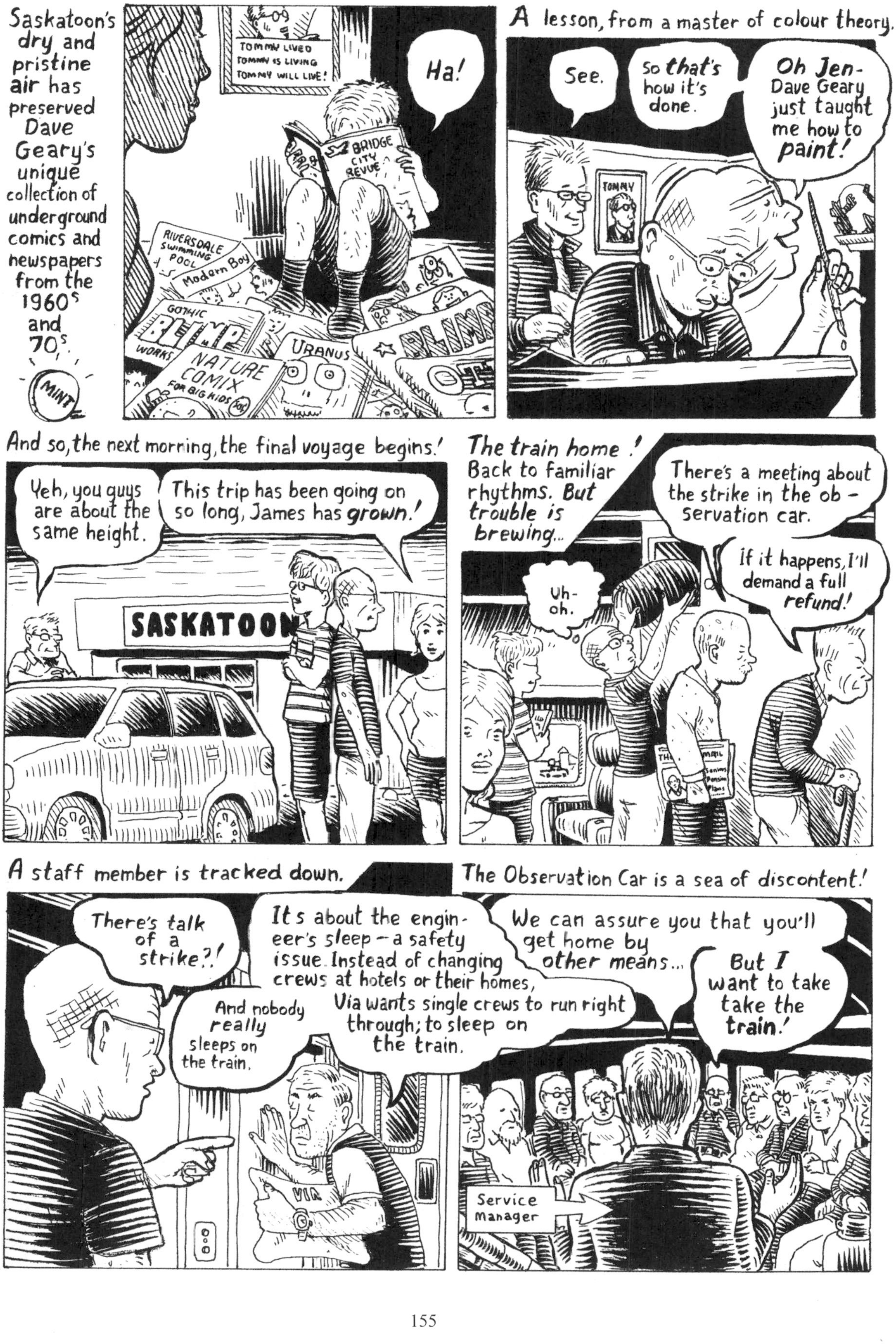
Saskatoon's dry and pristine air has preserved Dave Geary's unique collection of underground comics and newspapers from the 1960s and 70s.
MINT
TOMMY LIVED
TOMMY IS LIVING
TOMMY WILL LIVE!
Ha!
BRIDGE CITY REVUE
RIVERSDALE SWIMMING POOL
Modern Boy
GOTHIC BLIMP WORKS
NATURE COMIX FOR BIG KIDS
URANUS
BLIMP
A lesson, from a master of colour theory.
See.
So that's how it's done.
Oh Jen- Dave Geary just taught me how to paint!
TOMMY
And so, the next morning, the final voyage begins!
Yeh, you guys are about the same height.
This trip has been going on so long, James has grown!
SASKATOON
The train home! Back to familiar rhythms. But trouble is brewing...
There's a meeting about the strike in the observation car.
Uh-oh.
If it happens, I'll demand a full refund!
A staff member is tracked down.
There's talk of a strike?!
It's about the engineer's sleep - a safety issue. Instead of changing crews at hotels or their homes, Via wants single crews to run right through; to sleep on the train.
And nobody really sleeps on the train.
VIA
The Observation Car is a sea of discontent!
We can assure you that you'll get home by other means...
But I want to take take the train!
Service Manager

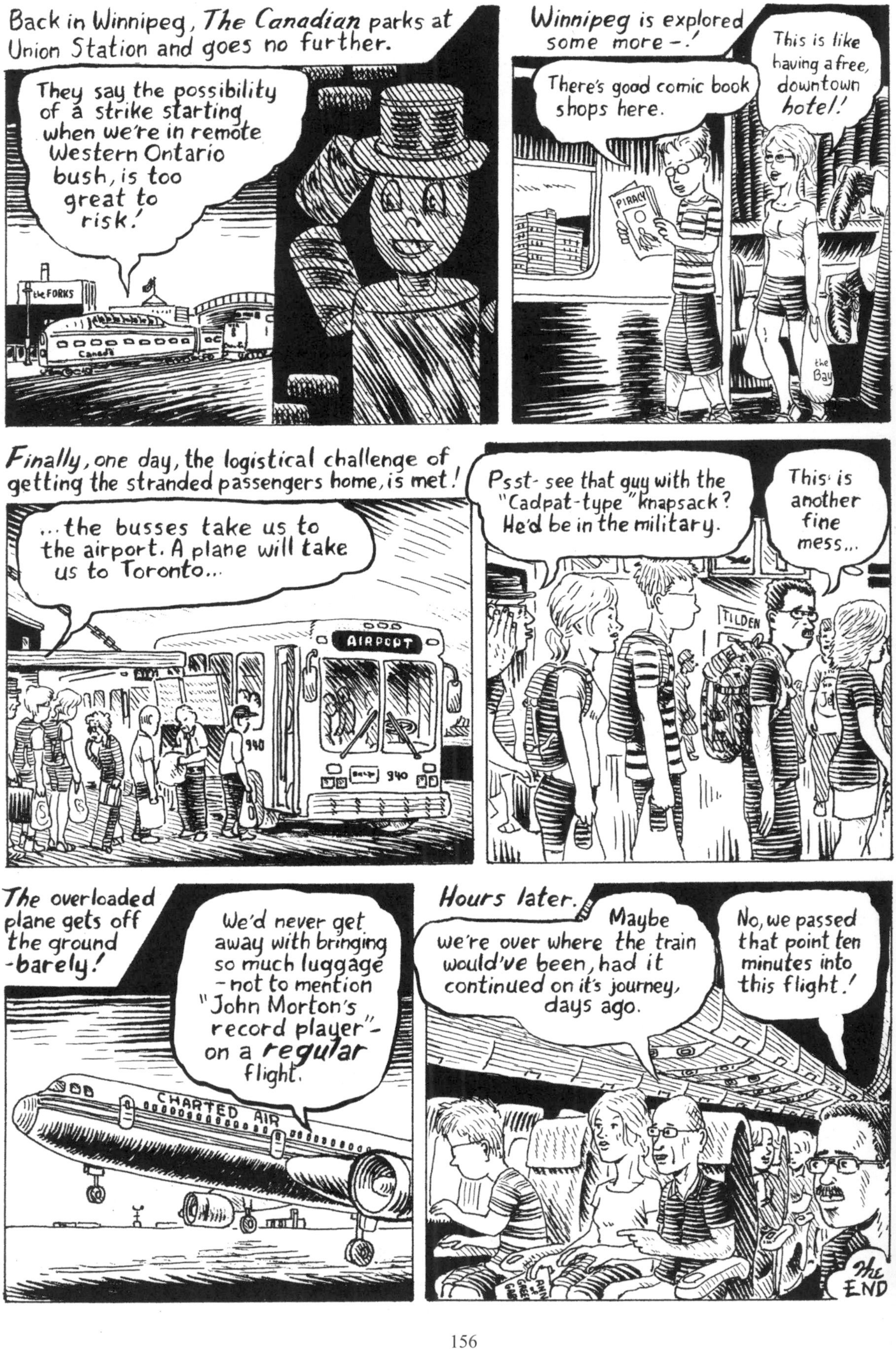
Back in Winnipeg, The Canadian parks at Union Station and goes no further.
They say the possibility of a strike starting when we're in remote Western Ontario bush, is too great to risk!
the FORKS
Canada
Winnipeg is explored some more-!
There's good comic book shops here.
This is like having a free, downtown hotel!
PIRACY
the Bay
Finally, one day, the logistical challenge of getting the stranded passengers home, is met!
...the busses take us to the airport. A plane will take us to Toronto...
AIRPORT
940
Psst- see that guy with the "Cadpat-type" knapsack? He'd be in the military.
This is another fine mess...
TILDEN
The overloaded plane gets off the ground -barely!
We'd never get away with bringing so much luggage -not to mention "John Morton's record player"- on a regular flight.
CHARTED AIR
Hours later.
Maybe we're over where the train would've been, had it continued on it's journey, days ago.
No, we passed that point ten minutes into this flight!
The END